NATIONAL COUNCIL OF NEGRO WOMEN, INC.

NATIONAL HEADQUARTERS:
633 PENNSYLVANIA AVENUE, NW • WASHINGTON, DC 20004
TELEPHONE: (202) 737-0120 FAX: (202) 737-0476

June 1, 2005

Dear Friend of NCNW,

As we celebrate the 70th year of the National Council of Negro Women, we invite you to join us on an extraordinary journey—to empower African American women in their vital, middle years of life and to provide the tools required to make these years truly joyful and fulfilling.

We begin this mission with a national public education campaign to promote sound financial planning and healthy and soulful living for the six million African American women in these key decision making years. The centerpiece of this campaign is the publication of TOMORROW BEGINS TODAY African American Women As We Age. The book will be available for purchase in bookstores this summer.

Since its founding in 1935 by legendary leader Mary McLeod Bethune, the NCNW has always been a place for Black women to turn for guidance, fellowship, and counsel. Thus, it is a natural setting for this important initiative. At the heart of TOMORROW BEGINS TODAY is the "Invest in Yourself Plan," a practical blueprint for identifying and achieving new goals, and turning the vision of improving one's middle years into a reality. To inspire African American women, ages 35-59, to make conscious choices that reflect their values, personal missions, and important new goals, we have tapped outstanding journalists—Sheryl Hilliard Tucker and Kendra Lee, and life coach Valorie Burton to write this inspiring and educational resource.

We have also enlisted the special insights of Mellody Hobson, president of Ariel Capital Management; Vivian Pinn, MD, director of the Office of Research on Women's Health at the National Institutes of Health and Iyanla Vanzant, spiritual counselor and life coach.

This will not always be an easy journey and it will call upon each of us to ask challenging questions about how we manage our finances, how we look after our health, and whether we are living our most satisfying lives. But with TOMORROW BEGINS TODAY as our guide, we will know where we should be headed.

Join us as we begin to invest in ourselves, invest in each other, and lead the way for our sisters because tomorrow truly does begin today.

Sincerely,

Dorothy Height

Dr. Dorothy I. Height
Chair and President Emerita

National Council of Negro Women
633 Pennsylvania Avenue, NW
Washington, DC 20004
202-737-0120
www.ncnw.org
Attn: Tomorrow Begins Today

NCNW gratefully acknowledges permission to reprint previously published material from:
American Obesity Association for the AOA Fact Sheet, Health Effects of Obesity.
Byllye Avery for an excerpt from An Altar of Words.
Renita J. Weems, PhD, William & Camille Cosby Visiting Professor, Spelman College, 2003-05 (Spring 2005) for an excerpt from "Girl, I Know Just What You Mean," www.somethingwithin.com.

Cover photograph and design: Quillard Inc.
Text design by PrintNet, Inc.

ISBN: 0-9765400-0-2

Printed in the United States of America

AFRICAN AMERICAN WOMEN AS WE AGE

EDITED BY CHERYL D. WOODRUFF

NATIONAL COUNCIL OF NEGRO WOMEN

We are now faced with the fact that
tomorrow is today.

We are confronted with the fierce
urgency of now.

In this unfolding conundrum of life and history,
there 'is' such a thing as being too late.

There is no time for
apathy or complacency.

This is a time for
vigorous and positive action.

Martin Luther King, Jr.

The National Council of Negro Women
acknowledges the generous support of RPS
whose grant made this initiative possible.

Tomorrow Begins Today African American Women As We Age

TABLE OF CONTENTS

ACKNOWLEDGEMENTS

No book is ever written alone. The National Council of Negro Women (NCNW) extends its special appreciation to our dedicated team of advisors, consultants, and friends who joined the African American Women as We Age Initiative in a spirit of sisterhood and affirmed that Black women are ready and willing to live longer, better, and happier lives. We thank all those who contributed to the birthing of this book, including:

NCNW Executive Director Cheryl R. Cooper, whose leadership empowered her publishing team to take the road less traveled. Eleanor Hinton Hoytt, the project manager, who took the helm of our virtual publishing company and whose courageous vision for this project has planted seeds for generations to come. Cheryl Woodruff, our editor extraordinaire and MVP, whose brilliance transformed our raw concepts and rich ideas into a meaningful book. Linda Gill of BET Books, whose excellence as a publisher is only surpassed by her generosity of spirit. Thank you for sharing your time, expertise, and resources. Malaika Adero, of Simon and Schuster, who answered our call and helped guide our effort into the mainstream.

Our phenomenal anchor writers, Sheryl Hilliard Tucker, Kendra Lee, and Valorie Burton, who fearlessly embraced our mission, gave powerful voice to our vision. Mellody Hobson, Vivian Pinn, and Iyanla Vanzant, who wrote our special section introductions and gave generously of their minds and hearts. Byllye Avery, Joanne Banks-Wallace, Linda Bradley, Kimberly Garrison, Hilda Hutcherson, Shiriki Kumanyika, Marilyn Martin, Annelle Primm, Brenda Rhodes Miller, and Renita J. Weems, who through interviews and special contributions gave our book a richness that we treasure.

Our PrintNet family: the master printer, Jeff Shaw; our exceptional text designer Cindy Shaw; and Kathy Vigland, who as colleagues always delivered excellence and unfailing support. The talented creative design and photographic team, Tamika and Robert Quillard, who created our outstanding book cover.

Ronald Manuel of Howard University, for his research design and analysis of national secondary datasets. Roderick Harrison of the Joint Center for Political and Economic Studies, our book statistician, who developed our demographic portrait of African American women. Ajeenah Haynes, our research assistant, who contributed to the research design and put the "self" in life satisfaction. Ogilvy Public Relations who conducted the focus groups in the five cities and the African American women, ages 35-59, who gave their time and voice by participating in the ten focus groups and four pilot studies.

Valerie L. Rochester, who offered invaluable manuscript feedback and incredible support. The meticulous Nicole Crawford-Tichawonna, our angelic copy editor, whose craft is unparalleled. Tiana Allen and Jaynelle St. Jean, who helped prepare the manuscript for press. Paul Coates and Roland Bland, who offered us sound publishing and printing advice. Simone Cooper and Beverly Robinson for their support of our message.

A special thanks to the African American Women as We Age National Advisory Committee, whose initial support and encouragement helped shape this initiative.

FOREWORD

By

Dr. Dorothy Irene Height

Chair and President Emerita

The National Council of Negro Women

If Black women are to make the rest of life the best of life, then middle life is the place to begin.

In 1983, on his one hundredth birthday, the renowned composer, musician, and performer Eubie Blake quipped, "If I'd known I was gonna live this long, I'd have taken better care of myself." Although spoken in jest, his comment strikes a serious chord that is echoed in *Tomorrow Begins Today: African American Women as We Age.*

The National Council of Negro Women (NCNW) has a long history of examining issues affecting women throughout the life span. That is why I am so pleased that *Tomorrow Begins Today* provides optimistic counsel for a rapidly growing segment of the population: the six million African American women in middle life.

Middle life is a very powerful place for women. It's a time when we begin to question our life's purpose and when we take the time to re-examine who we are and where we are going. African American women now live longer. If Black women are to make the rest of life the best of life, then middle life is the place to begin. Middle life is when you must seriously begin to face the old habits that have not served you well in the past. I encourage you to take this time for self-reflection, redefinition, and renewal.

Tomorrow Begins Today is the first book of its kind to consider what African American women ages 35-59 want out of life. It applies much-needed research, focus group findings, expert opinions, and personal observations to the concerns of African American women. It is a manual for improving your physical and mental health, increasing your financial stability, and maintaining an overall sense of well-being as you live and age.

Candid and compassionate, this fascinating book is full of invaluable lessons for women experiencing this new phase of life. As I read, I was struck by the fact that regardless of how African American women in middle life may be portrayed in the media or perceived by others, in our own eyes we are resourceful, hopeful, and eager to live life fully and see what the future holds for us.

In a world that often focuses on what's wrong with Black women, NCNW dares to explore what's right with Black women. Many in the NCNW study defy pervasive stereotypes, report high levels of optimism and confidence, and claim the right to be "happy."

Usually, I don't talk about being "happy" because it sounds so trivial. But being happy with yourself, with who you are and what you do, with the way you live your life and share your gifts is tremendously important. Happiness comes from living intentionally.

For those who might question the relevance of happiness to the lives of Black women in middle life, consider the implications of positive psychology research studies which suggest, "that happy people often contribute more to their communities, have better relationships with others, and are more creative..."

Although written specifically for African American women in middle life, *Tomorrow Begins Today* covers topics and provides useful information for women of all ages. Women under thirty-five years old who read the book will learn strategies that will allow them to help their mothers, aunts, and older friends and relatives. Women over fifty-nine years old can also benefit from much of the advice because it inspires and motivates all women to take charge of their lives.

My experience has been that many Black women struggle with the idea of self-love. We often feel that taking care of self first is somehow selfish or insensitive. We've been taught that value and self-worth stem from nurturing the emotional and physical needs of others. Yet, I've discovered during my ninety-three years of living that taking care of *self* is at the core of a meaningful life.

What also has come through for me is how important it is for women to recognize their ongoing need for personal support and encouragement. *Tomorrow Begins Today* reminds African American women—who may have spent their entire lives being "Superwomen" for everyone else—that they must and can allow themselves the freedom to pay attention to their own lives and concerns.

Mary McLeod Bethune, the founder of NCNW, was a strong proponent of self-help as the best help. It guided her work and it remains a cornerstone philosophy of NCNW today. The very clear emphasis on self-care, self-love, and self-help encourages you to trust your own abilities, experiences, and knowledge. This combination is exactly what African American women need and what NCNW has long advocated.

***By living intentionally, with a clear purpose,
a workable plan and uncompromised attention to our health,
our resources, and our own well-being
we can take real control of our lives.***

Time and again, I've found myself nodding in agreement where the book stresses the importance of having a sense of purpose in life. I am grateful that life gifted me with a sense of purpose from an early age. My family, my church, my school, and my community nurtured a sense of purpose in me as I grew up in Rankin, Pennsylvania. I understood that what I did and how I treated others really did matter. It was not enough for me to simply learn because I loved learning; I felt compelled to put what I learned into practice.

No matter where I have gone or what I have done I have always reflected on the purpose of my actions. And I still do. I have found new meaning and purpose in the African American Women As We Age Initiative through the insights it has discovered about an often forgotten group of women. This initiative demonstrates that even in middle life, one can still make "course corrections" or positive changes that will bear fruit as one lives and ages. Rather than viewing middle life as the start of a downward spiral, see it as a new beginning. It's never too early!

As Eubie Blake reminds us, a vital part of that new beginning is to take better care of ourselves as we age. *Tomorrow Begins Today* will help African American women at the crossroads of middle life to do just that by learning to plan ahead. For if we expect to live long and live well, we must take the necessary steps today to make that expectation a reality.

But living a long time is really not the point. Longevity can be a terrible thing if there is no substance to it.

By living intentionally, with a clear purpose, a workable plan and uncompromised attention to our health, our resources, and our own well-being we can take real control of our lives. Now is the time for African American women in middle life to open the window wide and to discover new meaning and new ways of reclaiming joy. We must break free of the stigma associated with middle life and celebrate our arrival at this threshold of opportunity as we pause to embrace unimagined possibilities. NCNW has created an amazing compass that will help Black women chart a new course for tomorrow—beginning today.

FINANCE

Mellody Hobson

SLOW AND STEADY WINS THE RACE

Sheryl Hilliard Tucker

INVEST IN YOURSELF

YOU GOTTA HAVE A PLAN

EARN MORE, DIAL DOWN DEBT AND PROTECT EVERYTHING

SAVE MORE, INVEST WISELY, AND RETIRE IN STYLE

Introduction

Slow and Steady Wins the Race

By Mellody Hobson

For richer or for poorer? No, it's not a wedding vow—it's a choice. Your choice. As women, we need to decide how we want to live our lives; and each of us will have our own answer. I am not suggesting that money can buy happiness, but I know for sure that financial independence is liberating. Investing changes lives. It is transformative—because money creates freedom by expanding choices and opportunities. When women stop living for the next paycheck, worrying about each and every bill or how to put food on the table—we become free to focus on how we can lead more fulfilling lives and how we can make a difference in the world.

Like so many people, the lack of money in my own family had a tremendous impact on me. My mother was a traditional housewife and because of divorce, things changed. To raise her family, she became an entrepreneur. But no matter how hard she worked, money was always an issue, which she spoke of often. Being the youngest child by many years, I grew up observing everyone else in my family. And as a student of my environment, I vowed as a little girl that I would never live with the kind of financial pressure my mom felt.

In 1991, when I was twenty, I worked as an intern at Ariel Capital Management, the investment firm I lead today with

John Rogers. That summer, I discovered a world I had known nothing about—investing. I learned it is, without a doubt, the key to real wealth in this country. America's wealthiest families did not become rich on a paycheck. They outpaced everyone else through their investments and knowledge of the stock market.

Almost fifteen years later, I still find the work of advising people about their financial future incredibly rewarding. Helping individuals, particularly women and minorities, and most notably, African American women, is my calling.

For the past eight years, Ariel has partnered with Charles Schwab on our annual *Black Investor Survey*. Our goals are to better understand the investing patterns of our community, shine a light on the economic disparity between Black and white America, and make the stock market a subject of dinner conversation. Last year, data showed that 80 percent of white Americans invest in the stock market, whereas only 68 percent of African Americans were invested. The statistic is even lower for African American women. If we really want to share in the full benefits of American society, we need to participate in the production and management of its wealth.

Too Many Women Are Unprepared

It is essential that every woman becomes financially savvy, because it is almost guaranteed that at some point, you will become responsible for your household's finances. The list of reasons is long—outliving a spouse, divorce, or taking care of an aging parent. Whatever the cause, every woman should have a plan so she is not caught off guard.

Unfortunately, too many of us are in financial jeopardy. Take, for example, the shocking statistic that three out of every four poor, elderly Americans are women. This alone should be a wake-up call for those women who *can save and don't, who can invest but won't.*

I am not discounting that inequality and discrimination still exist. The glass ceiling is very real in the workplace and boardroom; and there is a dramatic wage gap between men and women in our country. On average women earn 76 cents for every dollar their male counterparts take home. Additionally, many women are uncomfortable negotiating salaries and promotions, which puts them at an even greater disadvantage. But too many women in higher-paying jobs still face a fiscal fiasco. These women are at risk simply because they are unprepared.

THE MATH MYTH

What is holding us back? In my view, too many women are hiding behind what I call the "math myth." The perception that women are not good at numbers is unfounded. Female entrepreneurs represent the fastest-growing segment of business owners in the U.S. Last year, nearly half of all privately held firms were owned by women—adding up to about 10.6 million businesses. Moreover, one in five of these companies is owned by a woman of color. Women-owned companies employ 19.1 million people and generate almost $2.5 trillion in sales. To sum it up, we are critical to the U.S. economy in terms of influence and economic impact. Even beyond business, women have significant influence. On a day-to-day basis, women are in charge of 85 percent of all consumer spending decisions in the U.S. This gives an entirely new meaning to the power of the purse.

Another investing roadblock for women is that many choose to leave investment decisions to their spouses or want to believe that someone will take care of them. It is important to determine if you have become one of these women—and if so, how you might become more self-sufficient.

One of my favorite sayings is by singer/songwriter Judy Collins. She said, "As women, we're raised to have rescue fantasies. I'm here to tell you no one is coming." I reiterate this not to make anyone feel lonely, but simply to emphasize that planning on someone else taking care of you is not a financial plan.

Planning on someone else taking care of you is not a financial plan.

According to the 2002 Census, 25 percent of the female population have never married. Within this demographic, 21 percent of white women are still single, and the figure is double for Black women. Even if you live with a wonderful husband or significant other, as we say in the financial world, "Past performance does not guarantee future results." People leave, they get sick, they die. And yet, most women—single, married, divorced, whatever their status—are left to make their most important financial decisions during times of great emotional duress. The only way to avoid this scenario is to plan ahead.

Invest in Yourself

I'm going to share a few of my tips—some of the basic rules I follow. Think of them as choices that can help you master your money. These are followed by Sheryl Hilliard Tucker's expert guidance that is rich in detail on how you can become even more financially savvy.

To get started—it is essential to create your own financial identity. This is important for establishing good credit. My recommendations include having a bank account as well as a credit card in your name. Regarding credit cards, I recommend having one and only one, because it makes it easier to resist the urge to splurge.

Most importantly, saving for retirement is a must. On average, women outlive men by five to seven years, which means we require even more resources for retirement. The earlier you can begin saving, the more you can benefit from the power of compounding. Many people do not realize the stock market has outperformed all other investments for almost eighty years, including real estate.

Enrolling in your company's 401(k) plan is a great way to enter the market—and, if possible, maximize your contributions. If you are not with a company that contributes to your retirement plan, as most Black women aren't, you should open an individual retirement account (IRA). Even if you are sixty-five, your life expectancy is still another twenty years which gives your investments ample time to keep growing.

Unfortunately, there are no scholarships available for retirement.

I think it is particularly important for women to prioritize savings, because by nature we are nurturers. We want to take care of others. Often, women consider themselves better mothers if they focus on their children instead of themselves. I like the analogy of an oxygen mask on an airplane to illustrate this point. You are always told to put your oxygen mask on first before helping your child. The same can be said for retirement. Unfortunately, there are no scholarships available for retirement. You need to prepare for your future first, and then focus on your children's education.

I find it is important to approach savings as a daily or monthly goal. For example, make an effort to save $5 a day for the next three months. Three months later, increase this amount to $10 a day. Every three months, increase your commitment by $5, from $10 to $15 to $20. By the end of the year, you will have saved $4,500 for emergency needs and established a long-term savings strategy that will benefit you the rest of your life.

It sounds hard, but you are worth it. Think about all the non-essentials you might buy and take a look at what you can cut out or cut back. Take, for example, drinking bottled water, which is a very expensive habit. The average price is ninety cents a gallon, and the average consumer drinks almost forty gallons of bottled water in two months. That is $216 each year. Switching to tap water or even a filtering system would dramatically cut costs. These are little things, but they really add up.

Investing is a habit. I like to think of saving as I would any long-term goal, like staying in shape. A new runner would not set out to run a marathon, but instead would begin with shorter distances like one mile, three miles, and even a half marathon. It's about patience and sticking with it. As my company's motto goes, "Slow and steady wins the race." It has changed my life and it can change yours too.

Mellody Hobson is president of Ariel Capital Management, LLC—a Chicago-based investment management firm founded in 1983 with more than $21 billion in assets. A graduate of Princeton University, Hobson is actively involved with a variety of civic and professional institutions, and serves as a board member of the Chicago Public Library, The Field Museum, The Chicago Public Education Fund, and the Sundance Institute. Additionally, she serves as a trustee of Princeton University and is a term member of the New York Council on Foreign Relations.

Hobson's extensive media experience includes her role as a regular financial contributor on ABC's *Good Morning America*. In 2004, *The Wall Street Journal* profiled Hobson as one of fifty "Women to Watch" in the corporate world. In 2004, *Time* magazine identified her as one of twenty-five influential businesspersons setting the global standards for management, ethics, marketing, and innovation.

Chapter 1

Invest In Yourself

Money means different things to different people. But the most important factor in achieving your financial goals is defining what money means to you. When you think about money, what comes to mind? Do you dream of fun vacations and shopping sprees? Or have nightmares of bills with high late fees? Does talking money make you anxious? Does having money make you proud? Are you always wishing for more? Or is it enough to be financially secure?

Despite racism and sexism, we middle aged and older African American women think of ourselves as survivors. No matter how dire our situation is, we believe that God will help us find a way. Although no one really talks about it, Black women are the ultimate optimists—we root for the underdog and celebrate when those close to us do well. "Good for you!" is what we say when friends get promoted, children get accepted to college, or sorority sisters and churchwomen raise lots of money at fund-raising events. We stress the importance of positive role models in our community, especially self-made brothers and sisters. These leaders don't have to be rich, because the currency for our role models is achievement, not money. But why is that? What's wrong with talking about financial success?

Although African Americans say financial stability is key to living the American Dream, reports a 2004 study by the League of Cities, Black folks aren't all that comfortable talking about money. And when we do, the conversation often turns negative. Doesn't the Bible warn us that "money is the root of all evil?" Well, no. If you read your verses carefully, II Corinthians 6:10 declares that "the *love* of money is the root of all evil." Nevertheless, African Americans often associate money with greed, power, and livin' large—as we struggle to understand the role that money plays in our lives.

Like most Americans, we're reluctant or too embarrassed to say flat out that money makes us happy or feel important—African American women often look upward for a more spiritual foundation for our joy and sense of worth. Money buys the things we want, pays for the trips we love to take, allows us to be generous to our friends, our church, and our favorite causes. It pays for child care, our weekly hairdo, and a night on the town. It helps us sleep at night knowing that we can provide for our families and save to build a retirement nest egg.

But what about middle aged Black women? Overall, the participants in the National Council of Negro Women (NCNW) focus groups have felt good about their finances and have reported that they are making strides in securing their financial futures. The younger women ages 35 to 49 are clearly more comfortable about their financial status and are slightly more positive about their prospects for the future. Most of the younger women, (two-thirds are single or divorced) describe themselves as the financial decision-maker in their home. A good majority already track their spending and have started building a retirement savings plan. The older women in the group are more likely to be married, with more debt and credit card woes, and less in savings. The good news is that more than half the women are already investing in stocks, bonds, and mutual funds.

The NCNW focus groups represent a breakthrough generation of Black women—they've busted through the shackles of poverty and have financial resources that past generations of Black folks couldn't even dream of. But the optimism and financial satisfaction expressed by the women in the NCNW study may not reflect their true financial status.

Our uneasiness when it comes to discussing all things financial often reveals a disconnect between what we say and what we do. Though very few women in the groups feel knowledgeable or comfortable with financial planning, and admit they got a late start, most believe they will meet their financial goals. We say we're committed to achieving our financial objectives, yet we don't define them in a way that can be measured by our personal bottom lines. When asked about their life ambitions, for instance, most of the women in the NCNW study have expressed broad dreams and aspirations. Few women have well-defined plans matched with the goals and strategies necessary to turn their dreams into reality.

On a closer look at our attitudes about money, it's clear that money means different things to different Black women.

Livin' Large and Losin' Money

For many of us, celebrities, the media, and pop culture influence how we define our lifestyle, and therefore, how we spend our money. Who doesn't crave a bit of the diva life with the funds and finesse to dress to impress at any occasion? But smart divas know their limits, as even the most style-conscious celebrities brag about mixing Gucci with Gap. Unfortunately, not all of us got *that* message.

We all know Sisters who are livin' so large that we had to coin a name for it: *Ghetto fabulous*. Ever check out the lineup of Black actresses starring in the shows on the UPN network? From *Girlfriends* to *The Parkers*, from plus sizes to the smallest petites, the stars are stunning, the clothes are humming, and the apartments are divine. Trying to live up to these glamorous lifestyles can put you on the fast track to financial ruin.

Have you ever heard of the term "affluenza?" Several years ago PBS Television did a special on the epidemic of affluenza in America. Here are two definitions of this very telling word.

> ***Af-flu-en-za*** *n. 1: the bloated, sluggish, and unfulfilled feeling that results from efforts to keep up with the Joneses. 2: an epidemic of stress, overwork, waste, and indebtedness caused by dogged pursuit of the American Dream.* *–affluenza.org*
>
> ***affluenza*** *(AF.loo.en.zuh) n.: an extreme form of materialism in which consumers overwork and accumulate high levels of debt to purchase more goods (affluence + influenza).*
> *–Wordspy.com*

Now you get it? Life for many of us is a struggle to keep up with the Ms. Joneses. Who hasn't bought an expensive outfit that completely shot the budget just to look good at a party or impress a man? Have you ever gone to a trendy restaurant or booked a pricey vacation that you couldn't afford just to prove you can keep up with your friends? When was the last time you purchased a to-die-for sofa, purse, or pair of shoes, even though it meant not paying a few bills? Enough said.

Money Can't Buy Me Love?

For many Black women, when it comes to frittering away our money, it's *not* all about me. Do you find yourself doling out presents and cash to your children, your siblings, your friends, or your man, trying to please them or win their affection? Weighing your needs against those of your loved ones is complicated. Maybe you want to save and your spouse or partner likes to spend, spend, spend—and you're not comfortable talking about your clashing values. Although you're kicking hard to keep your head above water, you suffer in silence as your family slowly starts drowning in debt. And we all know about juggling priorities, like saving for retirement or paying for college, can be gut-wrenching. Even when our children are grown, we seem always to be helping them out. You love your kids, but....

The Imposter Syndrome

New York psychologist Linda Anderson, PhD sees many African American women who are successful in their careers or other aspects of their lives, but are totally at odds with their own financial realities. "These women often feel like imposters," explains Anderson. "They've worked hard to achieve success, but they don't feel like they deserve to be comfortable. Having money isn't consistent with their self-image. They tend to describe themselves as struggling, even when they have more resources than their mothers or grandmothers ever imagined."

Why is this? Why do some of us keep seeing ourselves in the same financial straits we experienced in childhood even though we've managed to move beyond? Another New York psychoanalyst, Kathleen White, PhD, refers to this quandary as "social class change anxiety." In *Shifting*, a recent study on the double lives of Black women in America by Charisse Jones and Kumea Shorter-Gooden reveals that a large number of Black women feel pressure to compromise their true selves in order to fit into American society.

Feeling uncertain about their future and unable to leverage their resources, "these women tend not to enjoy their money, are not comfortable focusing on their finances, and don't feel empowered to plan for the years ahead," explains Dr. Anderson.

What About Financial Peace of Mind?

Don't get me wrong. Not all Black women are pretending they're in the money, trying to buy love, or ambivalent about their accomplishments. About 27 percent of African American women live below the poverty level, in a battle for survival as they struggle to make ends meet. And, believe it or not, a growing number of Black women are creating real wealth for themselves—moving up the corporate ladder and building prosperous enterprises.

So what do we all have in common? We, African American women, want to make smart decisions about our money so we can achieve some level of financial security, financial happiness, financial serenity, financial dignity and financial peace of mind. But the vast majority of us aren't sure how to make these desires come true.

Over the next few chapters, I'm going to use what we've learned from the NCNW research and my twenty-five years as a financial journalist to explore what money means to you, who or what influences how you spend your money, and how you can take control of your finances to afford the life you've always wanted. Whether you are single or married, whether you make financial decisions together or let the other person take the lead, every adult woman has to come to terms with her relationship with money and what she wants her money to do for her.

If you are married or in a partnership, you face additional challenges. "Too often we give up our power when it comes to men and money," says certified financial planner Gwendolyn Kirkland of Kirkland, Turnbo & Associates in Matteson, Illinois. "Many women are afraid to assert themselves and get comfortable with investing. I have clients who are reluctant to meet with me unless their husband or another male member of their family comes with them. Then, if they do come alone, they realize just how much they really know and they feel more free to ask questions."

The information, advice, insights, and tools in these chapters will help you develop a healthier relationship with money so you can create your very own "Invest in Yourself Plan." I know, you think managing your money—even the little you have—is too hard. You're not interested in stocks, bonds, and mutual funds. And who has the time to decipher credit card terms, unravel the mysteries of retirement savings plans, or stick to a budget?

Despite our time-pressed schedules—when was the last time you enjoyed a full night's sleep?—more women than ever are managing their families' finances. As executive editor of *MONEY* magazine, I've spent the past five years researching how Americans deal with their money.

In the past few years, we've experienced a huge drop in confidence when it comes to managing our money. The stock market crash, 9/11, and the economic free fall that followed left everyone feeling a little shaky in the money department. Nevertheless, NCNW's research has confirmed that African American women remain confident. But for our confidence to be realized, we need a kick-butt plan.

Developing a Winning Money Mind-set

Shaky? Yes. Defeated? Absolutely not. Savvy money managers realize you don't have to be rich to be debt-free, an accountant to pay your bills on time, or an investment pro to build a nest egg for your retirement. But you do need to think like these experts to achieve financial stability or security. Yes, your kids must be fed. Your house must be cleaned. Work is work, church is more than one day a week, and hair appointments can't be missed. There are a thousand and one reasons why now is *not* the time for you to get your financial life in gear—but there are probably a few more important reasons to make the time.

- You want to give your family the best things in life.
- You want to be the proud owner of your own home.
- You want to help care for your parents if necessary.
- You want to feel the joy of living without debt.
- You want a job that pays you what you're worth.
- You want to enjoy a vacation without having to worry about paying for it.
- You want to sleep peacefully knowing you have money in the bank.
- You want to take control of your money.
- You crave financial peace of mind.

With a new attitude, determination, information, ideas, insight, and, of course, a plan, you can do all of this and more. But you'll need to cultivate a "millionaire's mind-set" to get started. Does that make sense to you? Probably not. But in the real world, millionaires do not live large twenty-four hours, seven days a week. In fact, the typical American millionaire can be rather tight with her money.

First and foremost, report Thomas Stanley, PhD, and William Danko, PhD, authors of *The Millionaire Next Door*, millionaires tend to be self-made people who live well below their means and lived that way long before their net worth hit seven figures. They are compulsive savers who believe that financial independence is very important to their well-being.

Why should you really care what millionaires think when you're just trying to pay your bills on time? Because the NCNW research and other studies confirm that 86 percent of middle aged Black women have problems paying their bills. Thinking like a millionaire is the best way to take charge of your financial life.

African American women—even those with very little money to spare—who are serious about achieving financial serenity must first strive for financial independence. How do we get there? We must work *hard* to earn as much money as we can and we must work *smart* to make the most of the money we have.

"Everybody has to start somewhere," says Deborah Owens, Baltimore's host of *Real Money*, a personal finance radio show on WEAA, an affiliate of National Public Radio. "Our first step is to *learn how to live within our means.*"

What comes to mind when you read this statement?
If I'm in control of my money, I'm in control of my life.

Does being in control of your money or your life seem like a fantasy only the very rich enjoy? Let's get real. It's very difficult to have peace of mind, let alone a healthy financial life, when you live paycheck to paycheck, robbing Peter to pay Paul and never seeing your savings grow. A study conducted by Automatic Data Processing, a payroll-processing service, revealed that forty-two million Americans live paycheck to paycheck. Financial hassles caused by mismanaging money triggers way too much stress for Black women—stress that contributes to high blood pressure, depression, anxiety, and overeating,—Drs. Marilyn Gaston and Gayle Porter report in *Prime Time: The African American Woman's Complete Guide to Midlife Health and Wellness.*

Some women compound their financial woes by shopping to alleviate stress. They call it "retail therapy." I've been guilty of that. How many times have you convinced yourself that the best stress-buster is a sparkling little pick-me-up present after a tough day at work? But when the splurging gets out of control, more serious issues may be at hand, explains Dr. Anderson. "Depressed Black women, for instance, may overspend as a way to fill up the void resulting from loneliness or an unhappy relationship."

The reality is that money can be your master. Money can be your slave. Whether money rules you or you rule your money is up to you. Stupid money mishaps, too much debt, and too little savings happen when you don't have a plan for your money. And it doesn't matter how much money you have. Money is a daily event. You have to make money decisions every time you reach into your wallet, every time you pick up a checkbook or dip into your savings. Every time you do this you have two choices: You can build debt or build wealth. And remember, warns Gwendolyn Kirkland: "Debt is a four-letter word."

The Roles of Money

For many of us, the role money plays in our lives started back in our childhood—even if we barely had enough money to survive. So think back to how money was used in your home.

- Were you given money as a payment for something that you did, such as chores?
- Did your mother or grandmother use money to bribe you or encourage you to do something like get better grades or stop picking on your younger brother?
- Was money used as a reward for achieving a goal, like being asked to sing a solo at church?
- Or, was money withheld from you as a punishment when you did not follow the rules?

Keep these four roles of money in mind—*payment, bribe, reward, and punishment*—every time you dole out your own cash to lovers, friends, and family. If you find yourself playing the role of a human ATM, you may want to evaluate why you're so willing to give up your cash.

- Do you like *paying* family or friends to do things for you?
- Do you *bribe* or lure friends or lovers with money to be with you?
- Do you want to *reward* folks who helped you reach your goals?
- Do you enjoy the power of withholding money as *punishment* when your children do something you don't like?

All very heavy stuff...but money is serious business. Just think about that famous quote from that infamous 1980s Academy Award-winning movie *Wall Street*: "The main thing about money is that it makes you do things you don't want to do."

But it shouldn't be that way. What you do with your money should reflect your priorities and what makes you happy—not how it makes you look in the eyes of others. Plus, even the sweetest love affairs and friendships often go sour when *your money's* the glue that's holding you together.

A few years ago, MTV presented a special program featuring superstars in the music industry discussing how they manage their money. I'll never forget Missy Elliott's take on the perils of living large with your friends when you have to pay the tab. To paraphrase, the rap diva asked: "Who wants to be the one always paying for everyone else to have a good time?" Financing everyone's fun may signal to others that you are in the money, but what happens when you can no longer foot those hefty bar bills?

Researchers throughout the ages have been exploring the connection between money and happiness. I must say that the topic has intrigued me quite a bit. Since I conduct lots of research on how Americans feel about their money, I was thrilled when Jean Chatzky, my colleague at *MONEY* magazine, asked me to help her launch a major study on money and happiness that was the basis of her book, *You Don't Have to Be Rich: Comfort, Happiness and Financial Security on Your Own Terms.*

Believe it or not, although money plays a role in your happiness, experts say that it is not as important as you may think. Studies show that people who, say, win the lottery, aren't much happier than they were when they were just average Janes.

What's more important to your happiness than making money?

- Developing healthy, meaningful relationships
- Having the freedom to choose what you want to do
- Feeling good about yourself
- Being good at doing what you choose to do with your life

Although money may not play the primary role in what makes you happy, being in control of how you spend your money is key. Remember: You can control your money or your money can control you. That's probably why people who say they are financially happy, according to the Chatzky study, are good money managers who are organized, pay their bills on time, save, and believe in setting goals.

So how do we stop this vicious cycle of never having enough money to save, pay our debts, and live the way we want? How can we reduce the guilt, anxiety, frustration, and anger from always having to juggle to make ends meet?

"You will never reap your full financial blessings, until your financial life aligns with the values that guide you," explains financial consultant Mary Grate-Pyos, author of *Wealthy Woman—Wise Choices*. In other words, you must strive for financial integrity. The Syracuse University M.B.A. explains:

> "You lack financial integrity when you consistently pay bills late; incur bills that you have no intention of paying; charge expenses that you know you cannot pay at the end of the month; engage in financial agreements you know you cannot honor; write checks against accounts where there are insufficient funds; own expensive cars parked in your parents' driveway while you live in their home where you do not pay rent; consistently arrive late for work and leave early; never repay the money you borrowed from your sister-in-law; or hide purchases in your trunk or other places so that your spouse will not know what you bought."

The Six Pillars of Sound Money Management

Our financial foundation for achieving financial integrity, taking charge of—and ultimately enjoying—our money depends on how well we do six basic things: *Earn, plan, protect, save, invest,* and *spend.*

This is your chance to look deep into your life's crystal ball to think about what you want out of these six areas, and what you'll need to achieve your goals. The worksheets in each section will keep you focused on your needs and challenges.

Have you ever set goals and had them fall through? The NCNW research reveals that African American women need help clarifying their goals and developing plans to make them happen. The Goals Institute (www.goalsinstitute.com)—now you've heard of everything, right?—offers the following five tips as key to making your goals or resolutions stick:

1. Write your goals down—and break big and long-term resolutions into smaller goals with shorter time horizons.
2. Make your goals laser-clear. Vague ideas won't help you visualize what you want to accomplish.
3. Create new habits and rituals to replace your old ones. Adopting new behaviors will be necessary to end destructive ones, like nonstop shopping or giving money to people for the wrong reasons.
4. Measure and monitor your progress. Constantly evaluate how you are doing and write down your progress.
5. Stay focused.

So no more excuses that goals, like rules, are made to be broken. In the chapters that follow, you'll learn easy-to-implement money strategies and tools to fix your money mishaps and put you on the road to financial wellness. So sharpen your pencil and clear your mind. It's time to develop your very own "Invest in Yourself Plan."

What goes in your "Invest in Yourself Plan?" When asked about the top money mistakes they have made over the years, most Americans find two areas that dominate the list: Not saving enough and getting into debt. Financial planning can help you deal with both of these, as well as help you focus on some of the biggest money decisions you must come to terms with. Let's look at your specific challenges within the six pillars of money management: *Earn, plan, protect, save, invest,* and *spend.*

Earn

- Look at your career prospects and develop a plan to boost your earnings.

Plan

- Determine your net worth right now (that's your starting point on this adventure to financial wellness), assess your cash flow (money coming and money going), and develop a budget or spending plan and learn to live within your means.
- Drastically reduce your debt—especially credit card debt.
- Make smart choices when it comes to home ownership. Remember that for most Americans, their home is their biggest financial asset.
- Resolve family conflicts around money so that you can make intelligent decisions about your family's finances.

Protect

- Cover your family in case of illness, disability, accidents, or death with adequate insurance.

Save and Invest

- Dedicate yourself to saving more and learning the fundamentals of investing to help build wealth.
- Steadily build your nest egg to save for a comfortable retirement.

Spend

- Commit yourself to making smarter decisions about spending money.

Earn more. It should be no surprise that the first entry in our financial to-do list is *EARN MORE.* Earning more and spending less is the most effective way to climb out of financial quicksand. As one woman from the Los Angeles NCNW focus group put it: "My idea of financial security is to make enough money so I don't have to worry."

Very few of us are in the position to enjoy the fruits of our money working for us in the form of stock dividends or income from profitable investments like real estate. (That can happen, but first things first.) So for now, think of your income as the working capital for your life. In other words, what you have to live on. The more you earn, the more you need help in getting your financial life on track.

As a whole, Black women still lag behind the earning power compared to white or Asian women, and all men. According to 2003 Census Income Tables, compared to white men, white women earn seventy-three cents on the dollar; Black women, sixty-one cents; Hispanic women forty-eight cents; and Asian/Pacific American women, seventy-four cents. Unfortunately, racism and sexism still are ongoing factors in this unbalanced equation.

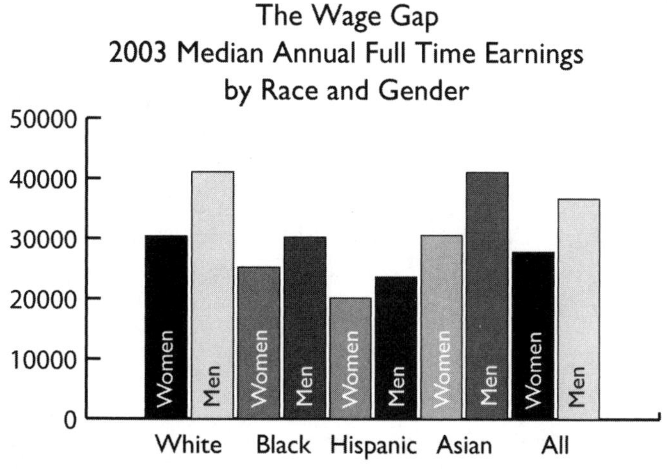

Source: Census Historical Income Tables P-41

Education is also a major determinant. The lifetime impact of these wage differences is enormous, warns a Women's Institute for a Secure Retirement (WISER) 2002 report, "Minority Women and Retirement Income: Your Future Paycheck." The average Black woman will earn approximately $464,000 less than the average white man over a thirty-five-year career.

The Wage Gap By Education

(2001 median earnings for full-time, year-round workers, 25 years and older)

	High School Graduate+	Bachelor's Degree	Master's Degree	Doctorate Degree
All Men	**$33,037**	**53,108**	**66,934**	**81,077**
White	$34,792	53,307	67,425	81,773
Black	$27,422	42,999	51,336	51,263
Hispanic	$26,944	44,778	60,661	70,933
All Women	**$24,217**	**39,818**	**48,276**	**60,425**
White	$24,676	40,172	48,552	60,431
Black	$22,355	36,259	43,870	61,101
Hispanic	$21,614	34,110	46,169	42,302

Source: U.S. Census Bureau, 2002

As you can see, African American women have a ways to go before we are on par with the earnings of all men. The numbers don't lie. Black women with Bachelor's degrees earn 80 percent more than those with high school diplomas. Master's degree holder: 96 percent more, PhDs: 174 percent more. Employers must make pay equity a priority. More of us must embrace the wealth-building power of education.

Being out of work—whether you quit, get fired, or are downsized—can wreak havoc with your financial life. Not only do you lose a paycheck, your health and life insurance and opportunities to fatten your retirement savings disappear as well. That's why negotiating a solid severance package is essential and we'll tell you how in chapter three. We'll also touch on some of the advantages and concerns about taking the entrepreneurial path to build your wealth in that chapter.

So now it's time to get to work. What are the best ways to boost your income in the next few years? Vague goals are hard to achieve, so be as specific as possible. Focus on concrete resources like education, skills training, developing a stronger, more connected network of colleagues and friends, as well as changing your attitude and behavior at work. I'll ask you to revisit these goals after the section "How to Boost Your Income," which provides specific strategies, tools, and resources to help you.

How can I earn more?

My primary short-term goal: ______________________________

____

My primary long-term goal: ______________________________

____

Major obstacles to achieving these goals: __________________

____

What I need to do to achieve these goals: _________________

____

Plan well. Your willingness to develop and follow a financial plan that guides your money decisions is the second step to affording the life you really want to live. Did you know that people with written financial plans are more likely to have twice the savings of those without? But creating a plan doesn't mean that you have to pay a financial adviser to draft one or use financial software like Quicken or Microsoft Money to generate it. At this stage, you can do a lot with just a pen, a notebook, and a positive attitude. As you travel further along on this trek to financial independence, you may need to use a computer or calculator to crunch some numbers or you may require the guidance of an experienced financial adviser to map out a realistic game plan for your money.

So it's time to sharpen that pencil again. Identify your primary money-management goals for the next few years. Are getting your financial papers organized, developing a bill payment system, and becoming more disciplined among your top priorities? Chapter two, "You Gotta Have a Plan," is packed with strategies, tools, and resources to help you.

What will help me manage my money better?

My primary short-term goal: ______________________________

____

My primary long-term goal: ______________________________

____

Major obstacles to achieving these goals: __________________

____

What I need to do to achieve these goals: __________________

____

Protect everything. What do I mean by everything? You and your family's health, your home, your car, your family's future if you get injured, disabled, or die. Sounds expensive? It can be. But think about this: According to the American Bankruptcy Institute, about 51 percent of personal bankruptcies are due to overwhelming medical expenses.

Nobody likes to deal with insurance. Thinking about illness, death, car crashes and house fires isn't easy. But the liability you face without the proper insurance coverage can be devastating to your family's well-being as well as your financial stability. That doesn't mean paying a fortune for the best insurance policies from reputable companies.

There's a slew of different types of insurance—many you will never need—so focus on the five biggies: Health, life, home, auto, and disability. Do you have coverage on all five fronts? Use the form below to think about where you stand and what you need.

Does my insurance adequately cover my family's needs?

My primary short-term goal: ______________________________

____

My primary long-term goal: ______________________________

____

Major obstacles to achieving these goals: ____________________

____

What I need to do to achieve these goals: ____________________

____

Save more. Putting away at least 10 percent of your paycheck every cycle is what experts encourage to achieve short-and long-term savings goals—like a down payment for a home or to start paying cash for things we want and need. We all have good intentions to save—it may have been on your list of New Year's resolutions—but then life (and perhaps a sale at Macy's) gets in the way. Your son can't live without those new sneakers, and your daughter wants to go to camp. Your mother needs a few dollars to tide her over until her pension check comes in. Your best friend talks you into taking a quick vacation that's not in your budget. And baam! You're digging yourself out of that money pit once again.

What's the solution to this crisis? "Carve out a set amount, even as little as $10 to $20 a week, and put your long-and short-term savings on automatic pilot," advises Houston certified financial planner Cheryl Creuzot, CEO of Wealth Management Strategies.

"If you don't see the money in your checking account, you won't spend it. Decide where you want to park your money—say a money market account or mutual fund—and have your bank transfer over some money every month or every time you get paid. This is the absolute best way to get on track."

This won't be easy to hear. So toughen up. *You will* jeopardize your future happiness and security if you don't get serious about saving today. You need an emergency rainy-day savings pot in case you lose your job, the roof on your house starts leaking, or your health insurance doesn't fully cover a necessary procedure. Some experts say a three-to six-month financial cushion is enough. If your job is in a dying industry or your company's in trouble, err on the high side. Buying things on credit is not the only way to purchase the things you want and need. Cash is still king. Savings is the only way to build your stash.

What do you want to save for? This is the time to commit your goals to writing. Are you nervous about your retirement? How to fund the children's college education? Do you want to buy a house? Are you covered if you get pink-slipped next week?

What will help me save more?

My primary short-term goal: ______________________________

____

My primary long-term goal: ______________________________

____

Major obstacles to achieving these goals: ____________________

____

Resources to help me achieve these goals: ___________________

____

Invest wisely. What's the ticket to your fortune? Stocks, bonds, mutual funds, annuities, real estate, collectibles. I know you're laughing now. But you have to park your long-term savings somewhere—and your money must make a whole lot more than the 1 or 2 percent of a bank or credit union savings account if you want to beat inflation. It's the old risk versus reward dynamic that's in play here. If you're not willing to take some risks, you won't enjoy the rewards of having your money work harder for you. Don't fool yourself: Money pros aren't the only ones who can deftly navigate the investment world. If you're reading this book, you can master the basics of investing. I guarantee that. But I'll warn you now. I don't believe that there's any way to get rich quick. Investments that sound too good to be true probably are.

Like most Americans, African Americans must become more knowledgeable about investing. It's hard to be confident in our investment decisions when we aren't sure how the game is played. The Seventh Annual Ariel/Schwab Black Investors Survey (2004) found that 69 percent of African American investors polled, compared with 48 percent of white investors, could not correctly answer six of the ten multiple-choice questions concerning basic investing facts and terminology.

What would you like to learn about investing? What do you want your investments to fund? Understanding your goals and time horizon to meet them will determine how you build your investment portfolio. Does that sound too grand for your wallet? Well, hold on. Do you have an employee retirement 401(k) or 403(b) savings plan at work? That's an investment portfolio. Do you have an IRA (individual retirement account)? That's an investment portfolio.

How can I learn to invest wisely?

My primary short-term goal: ______________________

____

My primary long-term goal: ______________________

____

Major obstacles to achieving these goals: ____________

____

Resources to help me achieve these goals: ____________

____

Spend smartly. Did you ever hear the phrase, "If it's on your a_ _, it's not an asset?" It's one my friend Michelle Singletary, the financial columnist at the *Washington Post* and author of *How to Get What You Want with the Money You Have,* often uses. And this Sister knows what she's talking about when she writes her columns and lectures on the value of investing and the perils of spending more than you can afford. Although we may find ourselves in the unfortunate situation of relying on credit cards to pay for everyday expenses that challenge our budgets, most of us get into credit card hell by simply spending too much money shopping! We see, we want, we gotta have it. And we sure know how to justify our spending, don't we?

I once bought a good friend of mine a pair of earrings for her birthday from her favorite boutique. I asked the owner what color stones would work best with some of the outfits that she had bought in the past year. We agreed that a blue-green combo would be great. My friend was delighted. A few months later she wore the earrings when we went out. I laughed, saying that I hadn't seen that outfit before. Looking sheepish, but smiling, she admitted that the earrings spurred her to spend $400, buying a pair of shoes, slacks, a blouse, and a sweater to complete the look. All that to coordinate with a pair of earrings.

Fortunately, my friend can afford those splurges because she has a financial plan that will adequately fund her future. She knows that indulgences like that are a once-in-a-while treat, not an everyday way of life.

So your mission here is simple. Think about ways to stop spending. What will it take for you to commit to this goal? Where can you go to learn how to be a value shopper and get the best deals when you shop?

How can I commit myself not to shop til' I drop?

My primary short-term goal: ______________________

____

My primary long-term goal: ______________________

____

Major obstacles to achieving these goals: ______________

____

What I need to do to achieve these goals: ______________

____

Putting It All Together

How are you doing? I know this has not been easy. It's both exhilarating and frightening to dream about the goals that we want to achieve. Aim too low and you won't find yourself in a much better place a few years down the road. Aim too high and you may be overwhelmed by the possibilities and the work it will take to succeed. This book is designed to help you work through your issues and face your realities and possibilities.

Read the money chapters straight through or use this section like a Chinese menu, mixing and matching the sections that are most appealing or relevant to you. Above all, personal finance must be, well, personally relevant to you. So I'm giving you permission to focus on you now. Because no matter how we try, getting anyone else in our family and household—our partner, our children, or our parents—to be real about their money is almost impossible, unless we're comfortable and confident about our own relationship with money.

What Does Money Mean to You?
There are no right or wrong answers to the following questions. The answers are how you feel about the areas covered in the questions. Be honest. No one needs to see how you respond.

If you're married or in a committed relationship, it may be a good idea to record your answers on a separate piece of paper if you want your spouse or partner to take the test so you can share your responses. Getting a better handle on how you both think about money could be the breakthrough you need to learn how to manage your money together like a winning team.

1. **Money means different things to different people. Complete this sentence: To me, having lots of money means that I am:**
   - ❑ Successful
   - ❑ Secure
   - ❑ In control of my life
   - ❑ Happy
   - ❑ Independent
   - ❑ Powerful
   - ❑ Important

2. **How confident are you in your ability to make smart money-management decisions when it comes to everyday events like paying bills or choosing a credit card?**

   ❑ Very confident
   ❑ Somewhat confident
   ❑ Not very confident
   ❑ Not at all confident

3. **How confident are you in your ability to make smart decisions about your investments and long-term savings?**

   ❑ Very confident
   ❑ Somewhat confident
   ❑ Not very confident
   ❑ Not at all confident

4. **Do you earn enough money to support your lifestyle and still have enough to save for the future?**

   ❑ Yes
   ❑ No

5. **If you had a windfall of $5,000 and could only do one thing with the money, what would you do?**

   ❑ Buy presents for your kids, spouse, friends, or relatives
   ❑ Pay off your debts
   ❑ Save or invest the money
   ❑ Give it to your church or a charity

6. **What's the least amount of money that you would need to feel rich?**

   ❑ $50,000
   ❑ $100,000
   ❑ $250,000
   ❑ $500,000
   ❑ $1 million
   ❑ $5 million or more

7. Of the following things you can buy, have, or do, what symbolizes the good life to you? (Choose two.)

- ❑ Owning a nice home
- ❑ Taking nice vacations
- ❑ Owning your dream car
- ❑ Having a good-paying job
- ❑ Having fine things (clothes, furnishings, etc.)
- ❑ Living in a prestigious neighborhood

8. What on this list would make you the happiest? (Choose two.)

- ❑ Owning a nice home
- ❑ Taking dream vacations
- ❑ Having a good-paying job
- ❑ Having fine things (clothes, furnishings, etc.)
- ❑ Living in a prestigious neighborhood

9. Money is important to my happiness.

- ❑ Agree
- ❑ Disagree

10. If I am in control of how I spend my money, I am in control of my life.

- ❑ Agree
- ❑ Disagree

11. I try to have as much fun now as I can and let the future take care of itself.

- ❑ Agree
- ❑ Disagree

12. Different people have different ways of coping with stress. Choose the two activities that help you relax the most.

- ❑ Smoke or drink alcohol
- ❑ Eat
- ❑ Exercise
- ❑ Shop
- ❑ Listen to/play music
- ❑ Have sex
- ❑ Sleep
- ❑ Pray or meditate
- ❑ Watch TV/go to movies

13. Managing money is hard and time-consuming.

- ❑ Agree
- ❑ Disagree

14. In your opinion, how good are your chances of retiring comfortably?

- ❑ Very good
- ❑ Fairly good
- ❑ Not very good
- ❑ Not good at all

15. I'm willing to learn how to manage my money so that I can live a financially stress-free life and retire comfortably.

- ❑ Agree
- ❑ Disagree

Chapter 2

YOU GOTTA HAVE A PLAN

Now that you've identified your goals for the six pillars of financial planning—earn, plan, protect, save, invest, and spend—are you ready to start building your very own "Invest in Yourself Plan?"

This chapter will help you lay the groundwork to become the chief financial officer of your life. That sounds cool, but scary, right? Trust me, it's not as hard as you think. It will take discipline, some sacrifice, lots of patience, and dedicating a few hours a week over the next several months to get your financial act together. Is it worth it? Indulge me just a few minutes and then you can answer that question for yourself.

Close your eyes. Imagine that it's the end of the month. All of your bills are paid—and were paid on time. Your financial records are in order—you even know where your car insurance policy is. You have set aside some money in your retirement account, you're on track to reduce your debt, you bought your daughter a new bike with cash, you've enjoyed a few nights out with your friends, and you're steadily building up your vacation savings account to take a cruise in a few months. Best of all, your financial stress is at a manageable level and you're starting to feel confident and in control of your life. So I'll ask you again: Is it worth it?

How can you achieve this state of financial nirvana? To get where you want to go, you must first know where you are. Start by giving yourself a financial checkup using the questionnaire ("Are You a Savvy Money Manager?") and two worksheets on the following pages ("How Much Am I Worth?" and "Where Did All My Money Go?"). If you opt to use a financial adviser, he or she will have you do these same types of exercises, so even paying for help won't let you slide through this process.

The figures you collect will provide the insight—as well as the information—you'll need to create a budget tailored to your specific needs. But a budget alone is not enough. The lynchpin to becoming a better money manager is having an easy-to-use system based on some of the most successful tricks of the trade. I call it the **K.I.S.S.** approach to personal finance—**Keep It Simple, Sister.**

The goal? Put the bulk of your personal finance duties on automatic. Let's get started. I'll walk you through every step.

HANG ON—WE ARE IN THIS TOGETHER

I know, I know. We all have our money demons. But you have to start somewhere and no self-improvement plan can be successful without a foundation based in reality. As you start to wallow in self-doubt, fighting that funny feeling in your stomach when dealing with all things financial, keep this in mind. This time you are not alone. Every woman reading this book will be experiencing the same type of anxiety as you are battling, trying to determine what it will take to achieve financial peace of mind. So, as the old saying goes—when the going gets tough, the tough get going. As a Black woman, you know when it's time to get tough. Well, girlfriend, this is one of them.

The questionnaire below will help you assess where you stand in terms of basic money-management practices. There are no trick questions or score sheet involved. The results will tell you what you need to do: Transform every "NO" answer into a "YES." Don't be too discouraged if you have lots of checks in the NO column. The "Invest in Yourself Plan" is designed to help turn that situation around.

Are You A Savvy Money Manager?

	Yes	No
Do you save part of your income every month?	❑	❑
Do you pay all of your bills on time each month?	❑	❑
Do you know how much you spend each month?	❑	❑
Do you seek out financial advice and services from reliable sources?	❑	❑
Do you know your credit score or credit rating?	❑	❑
Do you have adequate health and disability insurance?	❑	❑
Do you have home or rental insurance?	❑	❑

	Yes	No
Do you have enough life insurance?	❑	❑
Do you file your taxes (federal, property, etc.) on time?	❑	❑
Do you keep your important financial papers in a fireproof file or a safe deposit box?	❑	❑
Do contribute the maximum amount to a retirement savings account, such as a 401(k), 403(b), 457, IRA, Keogh, etc.?	❑	❑
Have you calculated how much you will need to retire comfortably?	❑	❑
If you have children, have you started thinking about paying for college?	❑	❑
Do you have a health care proxy or living will?	❑	❑
Do you have a will?	❑	❑
Do you have an easy, streamlined system for paying your bills?	❑	❑
Do you know how much debt you have?	❑	❑

Take a Financial Snapshot

Now it's time to take a financial snapshot of your life. The two easy-to-use, straightforward financial management tools below are designed to clarify your current financial standing. "What Are You Worth?" is a *net worth statement* that provides a clear financial picture of your life. "Where Does My Money Go?" is a *cash flow statement* that captures what happens to your money once it leaves your bank account and your wallet. If working on financial forms manually turns you off, check out two solid money-management software programs that offer similar documents: Quicken and Microsoft Money. You can also find similar net worth, cash flow, and budget forms in software programs like Microsoft Word or Microsoft Excel, which may already be loaded on your computer.

If you were dismayed by the wage gap discussed in chapter one, the net worth gap between Black Americans and others is alarming. In

2001, the median net worth (defined as assets minus liabilities) of African Americans fell by 16.1 percent between 1996 and 2002, from $7,135 to $5,988. The median net worth of whites, on the other hand, grew 17.4 percent, from $75,482 to $88,651. (Pew Hispanic Center.)

What Am I Worth?

(Net Worth Statement)

As a strong Black woman, you're truly worth your weight in gold. But how do you stack up on a financial statement? Here's your chance to find out. Pull out your latest bank and investment statements, bills, and any other relevant financial records. You'll need these to fill in the exact amount of each of your assets and liabilities (how much you owe) in the spaces provided on the worksheet. Complete this exercise at least once a year to track how much your wealth is growing—and it will grow with your **"Invest in Yourself Plan."**

ASSETS	Amount
Cash and savings (savings accounts, money-market funds, Treasury bills)	1. $
Taxable investments (exclude retirement accounts)	
Stocks and stock mutual funds	
Bonds and bond mutual funds	
Stock options (if exercised today)	
Value of privately owned business	
Investment real estate	
Cash value of life insurance policies	
Other investments	
Total taxable investments	2.
RETIREMENT ACCOUNTS	
IRAs	
Employer savings plans: 401(k), 403(b)	

ASSETS	Amount
Self-employed plans: Keogh, for example	
Annuities	
Estimated value of company pension	
Total retirement accounts	3.
COLLEGE SAVINGS ACCOUNTS (529, COVERDELL, ETC.)	
HOME AND PERSONAL PROPERTY	
Home	
Car(s)	
Art, collectibles, jewelry, and furnishings	
Other personal assets	
Total home and personal property	4.
TOTAL ASSETS (Add lines 1, 2, 3, and 4.)	5.
LIABILITIES	
Mortgage debt (balance of mortgages and home-equity loans or used lines of credit)	
Car loans/leases	
Student loans	
Credit card balances	
Other loans (401(k), installment, personal lines of credit, etc.)	
Other debt	
TOTAL LIABILITIES	6.
NET WORTH (Subtract line 6 from line 5.)	7.

Where Does All My Money Go?

Don't you sometimes wish there were such a thing as the spending police? That way we'd have a squad of tough cops looking over our shoulders every time we opened our wallets or checkbooks. Members of the squad certainly would have stopped me from buying those beautiful black Ralph Lauren pants last winter. Sure they were on sale, but did I really need more black trousers? What was I thinking? Well, I remember being grumpy and feeling like I deserved something special. So I went to one of my favorite stores—this time it was Bloomingdale's—and bought the pants. I didn't even try them on. They sat in the shopping bag for weeks before I tried them on. (You see, I really didn't need the slacks.) A month later, the thrill was gone—besides they were a size too large. Fortunately, I kept the receipt and so I took them back.

Instead of giving in to my urge to blurt out, "I'll take that," I probably should have walked out of the mall, headed home, and checked my latest bank or credit card statement for a jolt into reality. A hot bubble bath could have been the perfect antidote to my frazzled nerves. But like many women, when I feel stressed I honestly believe that the only two things that can make me feel better are shopping and chocolate. Does that work for you?

Every year Americans across the country make New Year's resolutions, to curb our spending, lose weight, pay bills on time, lose weight—oh, did I mention that already?—and finally get control of our financial lives. But when you have a shopping jones, somehow your resolve just seems to melt away.

Perhaps over indulgence isn't your vice. Your money dilemmas may be based on more sobering concerns—unemployment, a job that doesn't really pay a living wage, ongoing medical bills not covered by your health insurance, necessary repairs on your aging home, a relative who needs money to make ends meet.

No matter what's causing you to have a shortfall each month, you can't lose track of your financial reality. "More money will never solve your problem if you're not managing the money you have," says Deborah Owens of the NPR radio show *Real Money.* "So take small steps to cut corners and tap all of the resources you have available to you."

The first step to getting a handle on your spending is to take a hard look at where your money went over the last two months. Start by pulling out your bills, bank and credit card statements, and other vital financial documents to fill in the "Where Does My Money Go?" worksheet (see page 40).

Write down your after-tax income for the month. Next, list your monthly expenses by type, including any money you saved or funneled into your 401(k), 403(b), IRA, or other retirement plan. Fill in housing, food, car payments, credit cards, personal or student loans, utilities—every single bill you have paid. If you don't think that the last two months represent what you typically spend on a particular category (say, clothes or entertainment), in a given 30 days use the last four months as a guide and divide that amount by four. Don't forget any non-monthly bills, like your kids' athletic fees for basketball in the winter months and your quarterly insurance payments. Just divide the annual fees by twelve to see what you need to set aside each month.

Be realistic—estimate the little stuff you pay for with the cash from your way-too-often trips to the ATM. This includes the coffee and muffin you buy every morning, your manicures, and the movies. If you're not sure about your daily out-of-pocket expenses, keep a spending journal for up to a week, jotting down everything you buy.

Marilyn was certainly not a happy camper when her financial planner asked her to write down every single purchase over the next seven days. "Who wants to be bothered tracking every single cent?" she asked. "How can that help me get rid of this $10,000 in credit card debt?" What she discovered amazed her. After adding up just her daily lattes ($3 a day x 5 = $15 a week; $60 a month; $720 a year), her weekly manicures ($20 a week x 4 = $80 a month; $960 a year), her daily cigarettes ($4.25 x 7 = $29.75 a week = $119 a month; $1,428 a year) and her dinners out twice a week ($25 x 2 = $50 a week; $200 a month; $2,400 a year),she realized that the little things add up fast. To find out what it would take to pay off her $10,000, Marilyn used the credit card calculator on the American Savings Education Council Web site (www.asec.org). She discovered that by increasing her monthly payments to $338, she would be debt-free in three years if she stopped using the card. Marilyn was thrilled: "I know I can do that!"

WHERE DOES MY MONEY GO?

(Cash Flow Statement)

	Month 1	Month 2
MONTHLY NET INCOME (from all sources) after taxes and other withholdings		
INVESTMENTS/SAVINGS		
Contributions to 401(k), 403(b), 457 or other employee savings accounts		
IRA or other type of retirement account		
Savings account		
Investment account		
College savings		
HOUSING		
Rent or mortgage		
Second mortgage (i.e., home equity loan or line of credit)		
Homeowner's/Renter's insurance (divide annual cost by 12)		
Utilities (gas and electric)		
Telephone/Mobile phone		
Water/Sewer/Trash		
Home maintenance		

	Month 1	Month 2
TRANSPORTATION		
Car payment 1		
Car payment 2		
Car insurance (divide annual cost by 12)		
Gas		
Car repair		
HOUSEHOLD EXPENSES (Food and other family/personal expenses)		
Groceries		
Dining out (breakfasts, lunches, snacks, and dinners)		
Tuition/Day care/Child support		
Dry cleaning		
Clothing		
Personal care (hair, nails, etc.)		
Recreation/Entertainment		
Vacations (take an approximate annual figure, perhaps what you spent last year, and divide by 12)		
Gifts		
MEDICAL		
Health insurance		
Doctor and dental visits (out-of-pocket costs)		
Medications		

	Month 1	Month 2
INSURANCE (divide annual cost by 12)		
Life insurance		
Disability insurance		
DEBT		
Credit card payments		
Student loans		
Personal loans		
MISCELLANEOUS EXPENSES		
Church offerings:		
Expense 2:		
Expense 3:		
TOTAL EXPENSES		
INCOME minus TOTAL EXPENSES		

Are you coming up with a positive, negative, or break-even bottom line? Unless you're ready to downsize your major living expenses (like your mortgage or rent) or bring in more income, paring back those everyday goodies and weekly splurges is unavoidable. Let's do a little math. Are you paying more than 20 percent of your income on debt, not including your mortgage? The money to pay down your debt and increase your savings has to come from somewhere. Remember, everyday cash expenses shouldn't make up more than 5 percent of your monthly expenses.

The Ultimate Invest in Yourself Budget

Now we're ready to take on the first *big* challenge in the "Invest in Yourself Plan:" Develop a get-real spending plan—better known as that pain-in-the-neck, six-letter word, b-u-d-g-e-t. Just saying the "b" word is enough to bring on a migraine headache. Still, planning how you spend your money is a necessary evil—so get over your reluctance. The more you warm up to developing a budget, the closer you'll be to getting your financial house in order.

But drafting up a document that outlines your income and expenses is not enough to make a budget a living reality. In lieu of the spending police, you and only you can put the necessary controls in place to stay on track. Remember in the first chapter when I outlined the five-point plan on how to achieve goals? Replacing destructive habits with positive new behaviors is paramount to making changes in your financial life.

Using the information in your "Where Does My Money Go?" worksheet, fill in all of your fixed costs in the "Invest in Yourself Budget," then complete the budget form found on www.money.com. Look for Money 101 on the side menu and go to Lesson 2: Making a Budget. Or try the online tools and software listed earlier in this chapter.

Ever hear of the concept "pay yourself first?" asks Houston financial planner Cheryl Creuzot. Even if you're not saving a dime now, think about how much you can save or invest (including money that goes into your retirement account at work) and fill this amount in first. Your savings target should be at least 10 percent of your take-home pay (15 percent would be ideal.) If you come up with extra money after you put aside the 10 percent (okay, this may be a stretch), funnel that money into your savings, not into extra nights on the town or new clothes. If you're coming up short in the savings arena, identify what expenses you can eliminate. Brainstorm what it will take to pay your bills in full and on time every month—while reducing your revolving credit card balances. The K.I.S.S. money-management plan on page 44 will help.

Your Budget Targets	
Taxes:	25 percent of gross income (federal, state, FICA withholding, local and property)
Housing and Total Debt:	35 percent of gross income
Insurance:	4 percent of gross income (health, home, life, auto, disability)
Living Expenses:	26 percent of gross income
Savings and Investments:	10 percent of gross income*

Your Budget Targets

**Note: 15 percent is the ultimate target, but 10 percent is the first target you'll try to reach. This may seem high, but think about your future. Your pension (if you have one) and Social Security will not cover your living expenses in retirement.*

Source: www.money.com

The "Keep It Simple, Sister" Money Management System

Simple has become the buzzword of the new century as overworked, overwhelmed, overstressed women strive to bring some order and calm to their lives. A whole line of books and magazines like *Real Simple* offer ample ideas on how to streamline clutter, get organized, and stop doing things that make you crazy.

A major component of the simple life is having a streamlined financial system that will help you do everything from paying your bills on time to finding your important papers. Why is this so important? For one, paying your bills late triggers a host of major problems. It ruins your credit rating. It forces you to pay huge late fees. It can increase your interest rates on your credit cards, even if you're paying that bill on time. That's why it is so important to read the fine print in credit card offers and steer clear of a card that is subject to what's called "universal default." According to www.bankrate.com "a record number of credit card companies have built 'universal default' clauses into their agreements, which allow them to raise your interest rate if you're late making a payment—even to someone else!"

Are you motivated to simplify your financial life? Let's get started with six easy solutions to take the hassles out of managing your money.

1. **Consider the convenience of online bill paying.** This process has certainly saved my life. Most banks and many credit unions offer this feature and it's usually free. Check out your bank or credit union Web site to review the terms. You can also use sites like Yahoo! or Quicken, but some of these charge a fee. A third alternative is to pay billers at their site. However, I'd recommend starting with your bank's Web site, so that you can consolidate all of your online bill paying.

   Getting started is easy. You go to your bank's Web site online bill-payment center, enter your account, Social Security number, and choose a password. Then enter the contact information and account numbers for all of the companies that bill you every month, quarter, or year. This system can be used for occasional bills, as well. You can do this at one sitting, or when each bill arrives. Each entry only takes about three minutes to complete.

   Some bills like mortgage or rent can be set up to be paid automatically on the same date every month; insurance policies can be paid on a quarterly cycle. Just be sure you have money in the account when the bill is due to be paid. See if your bank will send alert e-mails if your funds are low.

   Studies show that people who pay their bills as they receive them are happier than people who pay all their bills once a month. So for accounts that fluctuate each month, schedule the payment amount and due date when the bill arrives in your mail or e-mail. Some billers offer electronic bill presentment for those trying to live the paperless lifestyle. Give the bank enough time to process the bills so that they arrive on time. Some of your bills may go to companies that are not set up to take electronic transfers. In that case, many banks will simply mail out a paper check on your behalf.

2. **Use the telephone.** If you're still skittish about having too much of your financial life floating out in the World Wide Web—understandable, but not practical these days since there's probably more about you on the Internet than you'll

ever know or be able to control—think about using the phone as a bill-paying tool. Many companies let you draw the money from your checking account, or credit or debit card to make payment. Some charge a fee, some do not. The payments are usually credited to your account right away and withdrawn from your checking account or billed to your card within a day or so.

3. **Use one credit card.** Or better yet, a debit card to track all your expenses, from your cigarettes to major purchases. That's the easiest way to track your expenses to fill in your "Where Does My Money Go?" worksheet, discussed earlier in the chapter.

4. **Set up an automated savings plan.** Listen to financial pro Cheryl Creuzot: Have money from your checking account automatically transferred into a savings or investment account every week or month so you won't be tempted to spend it. Although many people think luck and timing are the best ways to grow your nest egg, experts insist that saving money on a regular basis is really the tried-and-true way to build wealth.

5. **Organize your financial papers.** A chief component of the Keep It Simple, Sister, money-management system is to easily be able to find important documents and records, and know how long you must keep them. Fortunately many Sisters say they're already on top of this one, according to a 2001 Fannie Mae study on African American women and their finances. As for the rest of us: Most of your basic documents can be kept in a file cabinet, alphabetized by category. For example, a file labeled "Telephone" should include your contract for your home phone and cell phone.

   A sturdy, fireproof, waterproof small home safe is perfect for important items you need on hand. These should be easily replaceable in case your home is completely destroyed by fire or floods: Emergency cash (after 9/11, planners suggest keeping a few hundred dollars at home under lock and key), insurance policies, and a copy of your will.

   Safe-deposit boxes (which your bank may let you use free of charge or rent for a small fee) are safe havens for records you really need such as deeds, titles, birth, death, and divorce certificates, as well as some of the items suggested below. Keep a list of all of your financial accounts, and an inventory of your valuable possessions in the box.

Bank Checking and Savings Account Statements
Since more banks are no longer mailing canceled checks, keep your bank statements for three years if you think you'll need them for proof of purchase. Hold on to any statements that show how much money you paid for home improvements until you've filed a tax return after you've sold your home.

Credit Card Statements
Save these for a year—and be sure to check them every month to make sure all of the charges are yours. With the increase in identity theft, staying on top of your expenditures is very important. Also make sure that a purchase doesn't appear on your bill more than once. Keeping your statements will help you remember where you bought something if it breaks and must be returned. You also may need to refer to these statements when you prepare your taxes.

Debts
In addition to your mortgage contract, save records for your student loans, home equity loans, car loans, bank loans, and other large debts. Then, when they're paid off, keep the final statement that says so. This is important if you need to dispute an item on your credit report.

Insurance Policies
Keep your insurance policies—auto, disability, health, home, and life—at home. And stash a list of all your policies (with policy numbers, customer service phone numbers and your agents' contact information) in your safe-deposit box.

Investment Records
Whether you receive hard copies or print online versions, save monthly statements from your mutual fund companies and your brokerage firm. Once you receive your year-end statement, toss the monthly statements—as long as the annual statement shows all transactions for the past twelve months. Save your annual statements indefinitely. If you have certificates of ownership for stocks, bonds, or other investments, keep them in a safe-deposit box at the bank.

Legal Documents

Make sure you have the most updated copy of your will at home and a copy in your safety deposit. Your lawyers should retain the original. Get rid of your old will to eliminate confusion after you die.

Real Estate Documents

The title to your home, the deed of purchase, your mortgage contract, and your sales contract should be kept in a bank safe-deposit box. Save any receipts for capital improvements or property repairs you have made, such as putting on a new roof or finishing your basement. You'll need these records to minimize the taxes you might owe someday if the profits from the sale of your home exceeds $250,000 for singles, $500,000 for couples.

Receipts for Valuable Items Such as Furniture, Silverware, Furs, and Jewelry

Insurance companies will want to see receipts if you report any of these items as lost or stolen.

Retirement Accounts

Hold on to all annual statements from your retirement accounts. The statements will document your contributions and your earnings.

Tax Returns

Keep copies of your income tax returns for the past three years. The three-year holding period also applies to documents that substantiate claims you made on these returns. You'll need them if you are audited by the Internal Revenue Service. For more information about the IRS and record keeping, get IRS Publication No. 552, *Record Keeping for Individuals* (www.irs.gov; 800-829-3676).

Warranty Statements

Keep all major appliances or electronics warranties, along with a receipt proving the date of purchase. Write down the make, model, and serial number for all items, if applicable.

Records You Can Toss:

- Old, expired insurance policies
- Receipts for cars you don't own anymore
- Pay stubs from earlier years
- Expired product warranties
- Old annual reports and proxy statements

Choosing A Financial Planner, Adviser, Broker, or Insurance Agent

Do you need professional financial advice? A talented pro can serve as your financial coach to help put and keep your financial house in order. She can give you a soup-to-nuts, full-service financial plan, or she can advise you on specific concerns such as the best way to pay down your debt, develop a budget, or build an investment portfolio. Surveys have found many women feel that financial professionals don't treat them with the same level of respect as men. That's why you should find an adviser or agent through a referral from a trusted friend, colleague, or relative who has his or her financial life together. Even with this tip, it's good to do your own assessment. Here are some questions to ask:

"What are your qualifications?" Make sure she has the right credentials to be an adviser. Find out how long she has been in the field. Although a financial pro may sport a virtual alphabet soup of certifications after his or her name, for full-service financial planning consider these types of pros:

- Certified Financial Planner (CFP)
- Chartered Financial Consultant (ChFC)
- Certified Public Accountant (CPA)
- Personal Financial Specialist (PFS)
- Charter Financial Analyst (CFA)

To find out which type of financial pro would best serve your needs, go to www.fpanet.org for a complete list.

"How much personalized attention will I get?" Ask how many clients he or she has and who your primary contact will be—the pro or an assistant.

"Who's your typical client?" Ask if he or she specializes in serving any particular types of clients: Young professionals, retirees, divorced women, or widows, for instance.

"How will you be paid?" My first choice to develop a financial plan that goes from budgets to investments is what's called a "fee-only" planner. These professionals charge anywhere from $100 to $300 an hour to $1,500 to $3,000 for a full-fledged financial plan, depending on how complicated your finances are. Although insurance agents and stockbrokers also develop these plans, many experts recommend going for a fee-only planner since she won't be compensated through commissions on expensive financial services like load mutual funds, insurance products or annuities.

That doesn't mean you need to run from planners who get paid through commissions. If the financial adviser represents sound products, she can put together a great plan and portfolio of financial products that suit your needs. Again this is where your trusted network of friends, etc., can help check out what's for sale. More and more financial pros offer a sort of combo plan. They'll receive a commission, if you buy any products. If not, they'll charge you a fee for their service. Or, they will get paid through a combination of commission and fees. Either way, the compensation package shouldn't exceed the fees quoted above.

"Do you have any questions for me?" You don't want cookie-cutter financial plans, so make sure she is interested in your concerns, goals, and financial challenges.

Stay away from anyone who offers unrealistic promises. You've heard it before: If it sounds too good to be true, it is. Also steer clear of any financial pro who discourages you from doing a background check or pushes you to make decisions without clearly explaining everything to you and encouraging you to read on your own.

What to Expect From Your Financial Professional

In addition to developing a solid financial plan or advising you about specific concerns, your planner should:

- Answer all of your financial questions and explain in plain English anything he wants you to do or buy.
- Clarify how your decisions will impact your goals.
- Make sure that your decisions incorporate your values, interests, and dreams.
- Help put your choices into action in a timely and efficient manner.
- Monitor your progress against your financial plan.

What Can't Your Adviser Do?

- Predict the future.
- Guess what you are thinking.
- Guarantee the performance of investments.
- Protect you from destructive financial habits.
- Take on the role of a therapist or marriage counselor.

Your Responsibilities As a Client:

- Be honest and open about what you want to achieve.
- Provide the necessary financial and other information to develop a plan.
- Be willing to ask questions when you don't understand something.
- Stick to your plan.

Chapter 3

Earn More, Dial Down Debt and Protect Everything

What do you need to do to give yourself some financial peace—and afford the life you want to live? Addressing your biggest money challenges associated with earning, planning, protecting, saving, investing, and spending is a great way to get started. This chapter offers advice, information, insights, and worksheets on each one of these challenges except for spending. I've sprinkled smart spending tricks throughout the four chapters of this section. So, do you have your notebook out, a highlighter, and lots of pencils? You'll need them to develop your "Invest in Yourself Plan."

Earn More: How to Boost Your Income

Remember that ol' school rap song that went something like, "It's like a jungle out there. Sometimes I wonder how I keep from going under?" I find myself mumbling these words when nothing at the office seems to be going just right.

How is the daily grind of the workaday life treating you? With a tight job market, continued downsizing, and the threat of more jobs being outsourced and sent to lower-paid workers in other countries, many women of color are concerned about their future. Are you feeling overworked and underpaid, with prospects for a better job looking rather slim? Maybe it's time for a career check-up—and perhaps a serious career makeover.

But looking for a better job, higher pay, or better benefits when you're over forty is not easy. Age discrimination continues to be alive and well throughout the workplace.

A 2004 study by Catalyst, a leading authority on women in the business world, explored the challenges Black professional women continue to face at work. "Advancing African American Women in the Workplace: What Managers Need to Know" found that although three-quarters of the largest five-hundred U.S. companies have formal diversity programs, 37 percent of African American women see their opportunities for advancement to senior management positions in their companies declining over time. Latina and Asian women are slightly more optimistic about their prospects.

If you're not feeling the love like these women, there are two things you must do: First, advocate in your organization for stronger, more meaningful programs to level the playing field for people of color. Second, do a career audit on yourself. The women surveyed in the Catalyst study agreed that success in business for Black women means: Exceeding expectations, communicating effectively, connecting with mentors, building positive relationships with managers and colleagues, and using their cultural backgrounds to enhance performance.

Successful makeovers—in the name of beauty, fashion, or careers—start with a comprehensive audit of your current situation. But you have to be honest. Be brutal if necessary. You can't move forward if you don't know where you're starting from. Answer the questions below and use the final column to map out your next steps—even when you answered YES. There's always room for improvement.

Boost Your Income Worksheet

	Yes	No	Action Plan For Change *(set a deadline)*
Are you employed?	❑	❑	
If not, do you have a job-search plan? *(If you're not employed, answer the questions based on your last job.)*	❑	❑	
Do you earn what you think you are worth?	❑	❑	

	Yes	No	Action Plan For Change *(set a deadline)*
Have you recently reviewed your employee benefits package?	❑	❑	
Do you use all or most of your benefits?	❑	❑	
Do you enjoy what you do?	❑	❑	
Do you like your work environment, your colleagues, your boss?	❑	❑	
Do you get credit for your work?	❑	❑	
Do you have a good reputation at work?	❑	❑	
Are you part of the network of key players in your department, company, or industry? *(In other words, are you in the loop?)*	❑	❑	
Are you on a career track for advancement?	❑	❑	
Do you have a supportive boss?	❑	❑	

	Yes	No	Action Plan For Change *(set a deadline)*
Are you considered a top performer or a go-to person on your job?	❑	❑	
Do you need additional training/education to move ahead in your field?	❑	❑	
Do you take advantage of on-the-job or job-sponsored training programs?	❑	❑	
Are your computer skills up to date?	❑	❑	
Do you have a job description?	❑	❑	
Does your boss know what you do and is he or she aware of your recent accomplishments?	❑	❑	
Do you have a mentor?	❑	❑	
Do you use performance evaluations as a time to discuss your career goals and steps for advancement?	❑	❑	
Is it time to look for a new job?	❑	❑	

Now that you have a better idea of where you stand in your career and an assessment of your skills, are you ready to do some fine-tuning? Or is it time for a career overhaul? Whether you're unemployed or have a job you love, these pointers will help boost your earning power:

Go back to school. Yes, education does count, as evidenced by the "The Wage Gap Factor" table in chapter one. But degrees aren't the only thing to consider. Job training programs, management courses, and computer classes can help you build a portfolio of valuable and transferable skills. Check out your human resources department for classes offered at work. Community colleges and professional or trade associations are also good places to look for low-cost classes. The Internet offers a variety of online degree, certification, and training programs. Many employers provide tuition reimbursement or education subsidies, especially if you're taking courses directly related to your job or industry.

Consider lateral moves to round out your work experience. Very few people boast about a new job that doesn't involve a promotion or a bump up in pay. But sometimes you must go sideways to get ahead. Maybe you haven't had enough budget management experience or perhaps your presentation style isn't commanding lots of respect. A zigzag move in and out of different departments might just polish up your resume and position you for a better-paying position. It could also widen your network.

Job-hop with a plan. Jumping in and out of jobs is a ploy that many twenty-somethings use to establish their careers. That may work when you're starting out, but by the time you're forty, your moves should be much more strategic. Too much job hopscotching on your resume may signal that you aren't focused on your career or that you have problems getting along with others. If you're not itching to leave your current gig because it's a dead-end job with few prospects, ask yourself these two questions before you move on:

- Will the new position advance my career, even if it's a lateral move?
- Am I moving on just because I can't stand my boss or coworkers? (Keep this in mind: People join companies, but leave bosses.)

Consider a career switch. If you're contemplating a new field or industry, see a career counselor for advice. She can retool both your resume and how you present your skills to help make the transition. A one-on-one session will cost upwards of about $100, so check out community colleges and universities in your area for low-cost alternatives. Many career counselors offer night courses at local colleges, so this is an excellent place to find leads. You can also locate a counselor through the National Career Development Association (www.ncda.org; 866-367-6232). To investigate fast-growth fields that need your talents, go to the U.S. Bureau of Labor statistics Web site (www.bls.gov). Libraries usually stock the bureau's *Occupational Outlook Handbook*, which forecasts hot job fields. What's on the fast track over the next decade? Education, travel, advertising, and management consulting, to name a few.

Polish your interviewing skills. It may have been a while since you last pounded the pavement looking for a job. Or perhaps financial difficulties forced you to latch on to the first employer who offered a paycheck. But finding a job that will put you on the path to building wealth requires work. If you're over forty, check out an organization called Forty-Plus. This nonprofit organization offers job search services, training programs, and support groups for experienced managers and professionals. To find a chapter in your area call 202-387-1582 or log on to www.40plus.org. AARP is an excellent resource for job hunters over fifty as well as victims of age discrimination (888-687-2277; www.aarp.org).

Tap into the power of your network. Clearly explain your career objectives to everyone who will listen. Career counselors say that 70 percent of all managerial or white-collar jobs are filled through the corporate grapevine. Tap sorority sisters, church members, professional colleagues, and high school and college alumni groups. Don't be shy. Inquire about possible openings at the companies where your friends, relatives, and former colleagues work. Ask them about career advancement opportunities and training programs, and whether their employers' compensation packages (including salary and benefits) are competitive for the industry or in that region of the country.

Do your homework. Use Internet search engines like Google to find stories about companies you are interested in. Go to the companies'

Web site and click on the media or pressroom buttons to find out how the company is doing. Read about the company in past issues of business magazines and the business section of your local newspapers that you can find in the library. A librarian can be a great source for this type of research.

Polish off your resume or write one from scratch. Job-hunting Web sites like Monster.com have resume centers with forms to fill in and samples of good resumes tailored for specific industries. Do not include your salary history on your resume. You may over-or underprice yourself before getting a foot in the door.

Be prepared for unusual, and sometimes intrusive, questions during interviews. If you haven't been on a job interview in a while, you may be surprised by the questions being asked these days. No matter what you are asked, keep your cool. Remain positive and enthusiastic. This is not the time to sound off. If you're uncomfortable discussing something, say so and move on—perhaps with a question of your own.

If you're asked why you left your last job, for instance, think twice before you say you were fired. Instead focus on why the fit may not have been right for you and your last company or industry. "Say something like, 'As you see from my resume, I have extensive sales experience. While I was able to transfer my skills to the technology industry, it was a long sales cycle and I realized I prefer the immediate impact I achieved when I sold pharmaceuticals'," explains Denise Hockaday of DBM, a career transitions firm.

You may have to write an essay on the spot about your past successes and failures. You could be asked to solve a real business problem that is taxing the interviewer. You might be required to take a psychological test to see if you have the right mental stuff. Many employers are doing legal and credit checks on prospects. I know I have stressed this before, but it's worth repeating: Some employers view bad credit as a character flaw, and this blemish can prevent you from getting a job.

To market yourself properly, prove that you have what it takes to get the job done. The more you know about the company, the better you can position yourself as a valuable player. But don't overplay your cards, or wax on about what a great person you are. Focus on how your qualities and skills will benefit the firm. Provide concrete examples of your major accomplishments at past jobs that are relevant to this position. And be sure to ask well-thought-out questions about workplace challenges.

Hold off discussing your personal challenges regarding the job until you have an offer, advises Charlene Hayes, vice president of human resources for Johns Hopkins University in Baltimore. "Bringing up demands like leaving work by 5:00 p.m. every day to pick up your child could knock you out of the running early in the game. Let the interviewer process the value you bring to the position. There's plenty of time to negotiate the details once she wants you aboard."

Having the Big Talk: Salary Negotiations

Whether you're looking for a job or want more money for the one you have, arm yourself—with facts, that is—before going into a salary negotiation. Know the going rate for people in your industry with your experience and education. Salary.com, HotJobs.com, and Monster.com are all great sites to find out this information. Plus, check out your professional or trade association sites for salary survey reports.

During a Job Interview

Let the interviewer start the salary discussion. If asked what you're looking for, make sure you know all the details of the postion before you spurt out a number. Then cite a figure at the high end of the range based on your homework—"but be reasonable given your skills, experience, and education," says Hayes. You may need to negotiate, so here are a few options:

- Tell your prospective employer that you are weighing other options if you receive a lowball offer.
- See if you could raise your overall pay by combining a salary with a bonus.
- Ask if the company would review your pay within six months.
- Be willing to walk away if the salary is way too low. This may prompt a better offer or leave you without a job. Use your network to determine whether the job is worth taking a cut-rate salary.

Same Job, New Pay Level?

You want to stay, but you sure need more money. What about a raise? (I know you're laughing now!) Yes, even in this tightwad corporate environment, someone's getting paid, so why not you? If you're a top performer, go for it.

Most salary reviews occur after annual performance meetings, but that doesn't mean you have to wait to ask for a raise. The best time to request a pay hike is after you've accomplished a major goal or achieved some impressive success. Explain that you want to earn a reasonable salary that reflects your skills and achievements, but don't get into specifics. Don't accept just any deal. If you've been a star at work, you'll have a lot more leverage. If your boss lowballs the first offer, ask why you're getting such a skimpy raise. If she won't or can't budge, ask for a salary review in a few months when budgets are reset or business improves. Inquire about performance pay—either a spot bonus for the next time you exceed expectations or a year-end bonus based on how well you've done in the past twelve months.

Above all, don't be confrontational. Salary negations should be a cooperative dialogue. Be confident and polite. Don't threaten to quit, even if your next step is to look for a job. Threats can backfire if the boss calls your bluff.

Employee Benefits That Boost Your Pay

Steady employment has benefits far greater than a paycheck. Corporate, academic, and government jobs come with financial perks that often are grossly undervalued in our community. In fact, benefit packages can represent up to 35 percent of an employee's salary. Consider the cost of benefits that are important to you when you're weighing a new job offer. A bump up in salary is always great, but if you have to pay the full freight for your health insurance premiums, you may not come out ahead.

You're probably familiar with typical employee benefits such as subsidized health-care coverage, pensions, employee retirement savings accounts (401(k)s, 403(b)s or 457s), and life insurance.

But what about some of the buried bennies that some employers offer, but many employees never bother to investigate?

A 2004 MetLife survey found that 59 percent of African American employees surveyed worried about having sufficient health insurance and 49 percent worried about their retirement savings running out. But here's where things get crazy: 64 percent of full-time employees placed a higher value on vacation days than employer-funded pension plans, disability insurance, life insurance, and long-term-care insurance. Let's get real!

Employers offer reduced rates for everything from additional life and long-term-care insurance to closing costs when you buy a new home or refinance your mortgage. Other goodies include subsidized child-care services, free admission or discount tickets to cultural attractions such as museums, concerts, and live theatrical productions. My employer has built relationships with many major retailers, which allow me to download 15-percent-off coupons from the Internet to some of my favorite stores.

One specific benefit that too few people take advantage of is flexible spending accounts (FSA). These accounts let you pay medical expenses not covered by your health plans, as well as dependent-care costs and transportation costs with pretax dollars from your paycheck. Your employer has a list of qualified expenses—from co-pays for doctor visits to monthly bus passes. You determine how much you want to set aside each year. Trust me. This is one benefit you don't want to pass up. Say you pay $5,000 a year for childcare. Depending on your tax bracket, you can recoup hundreds of dollars in tax savings. Not bad!

You must use up the money in your account(s) before December 31 or lose your balance. Talk to your benefits department to find out how your plan works and the dollar limits.

Other perks that pay:

- Tuition and health club reimbursement plans
- Weight Watchers at work (lower weekly fees)
- Free checking
- Mortgage programs (lower rates with selected lenders)
- Credit unions (credit unions offer great rates on car loans,

mortgages, credit cards, CDs, and savings accounts.
- Discount coupons to local restaurants
- Access to corporate travel deals for personal travel
- Low-cost vacation packages and cruises
- Discount prices for computers and electronics

You're Fired: Walk out the Door With Everything You're Due

Have you been downsized, rightsized, laid off, or part of a reduction in force? Perhaps you've been pink-slipped, let go, asked to resign, or simply shown the way to the door? Although no one seems to get fired or quit their jobs anymore, more than 4.9 percent of African American women 35 to 59 years old were unemployed in 2004. That number jumps to 9 percent when you factor in all Black women over twenty years old.

So if you find yourself out of work or the status of your job is getting shakier every day, here's how to exit the company on your own terms. Remember, this is not the time to get emotional. So here are some tips for getting some of the things you deserve.

You're offered a buyout package or you're about to be downsized

Many companies looking to reduce costs by shedding workers sometimes dangle buyout offers before choosing which employees to let go. Before taking the offer, be realistic and consider your chances of surviving a downsizing. Seriously eye a buyout if your company is in dire financial straits, your job isn't critical to the primary function of your department, or you can easily be replaced by a cheaper worker. Another reason for accepting a buyout: You expect to be downsized if enough people don't take the buyout. Keep in mind that buyouts for volunteers who opt to leave are sometimes more generous than severance packages for those who are asked to go.

Size up the offer. Whether you take a buyout or a severance package, make sure it includes at least one to two weeks' pay for every year you worked, health insurance for the length of time of the payouts, and perhaps career counseling and tuition reimbursement for retraining. Then think about whether this is enough to tide you over until you get a job or your other retirement benefits kick in.

Negotiate for more. "First of all, ask for career transition services to help you assess your skills, write a powerful resume and learn networking, interviewing and negotiating skills." explains Denise Hockaday of DBM. "Also, if you've been a valued employee and can make a case for why your job search may take an extended length of time (e.g. specialized area or troubled industry), ask for a bigger payout. Explore the opportunity to extend your end of service date by working part-time or as a consultant or contractor, and see if your health care benefits can be extended as well. Be sure to have a conversation with your human resource department before you sign any paperwork."

If you are close to retirement the company may also be willing to "bridge" your years of service to retire with a full pension or retiree health-care coverage. Keeping your e-mail address and phone number so you will still seem employed can be a very smart move when you start job hunting.

You've been fired

As a matter of courtesy, you may give your employer two or more weeks' notice when you plan to leave, but that doesn't mean you're owed the financial version of that when you're asked to go. You may walk away with almost nothing if your work has been below par, your attitude was bad, or you're considered hard to get along with. In this case, find out what your employer plans to say when called for a reference check. If you've worked with a supervisor or manager who appreciated your talents, ask to use her as a reference.

The whole game changes if you feel that you were unjustly fired due to racism, sexism, ageism, or the political nonsense that goes on in many workplaces. Your first step is to confront your supervisor or human resource officer with your concern, and perhaps an attorney. Present a tight case with documentation, if at all possible.

Package or not, identify ways you can downsize your finances until you get another job. Three months used to be the norm; now even highly qualified individuals are taking six months to a year to find employment. Plus you may be offered less money than your past job if you're over fifty years old. Use the negotiating tips you learned earlier to get the salary you deserve.

What Is COBRA and Why Do I Need It?

Losing your medical coverage when you leave your job can be devastating to your health and your finances. The Consolidated Omnibus Budget Reconciliation Act (COBRA) gives workers and their families who lose their health benefits (under certain circumstances) the chance to continue group health benefits provided by their group health plan for limited periods of time. The premiums could run you anywhere from $500 to $1,000 a month. On the other hand, an extended illness, a severe injury, or surgery could wipe out your savings and put your entire finances in jeopardy.

Doing Your Own Thing: Entrepreneurship

Ever dream about being your own boss? Setting your own hours. Dealing with clients on your own terms. Making the money you've always dreamed about. We all romanticize about having our name on the door. And for many Americans, entrepreneurship has been the path to independence and great wealth.

Before I joined *MONEY* magazine, I was the editor in chief of *Black Enterprise*, the nation's leading authority on African American-owned businesses. I've interviewed the owners of some of the largest, most successful Black firms in the world as well as small, profitable boutique operations. And I'm happy to report that over my years at *Black Enterprise*, more and more of them were women. In the beginning, most of the women owners at the top firms inherited their businesses from their fathers or husbands. By the mid-1990s more of these multimillion-dollar enterprises were founded by the woman in charge.

The Center for Women's Business Research in Washington, D.C., estimated there were 414,472 privately held firms owned by African American women, employing nearly 254,000 people and generating $19.5 billion in 2004. Over three-quarters of these are service businesses, 6.3 percent are in retail trade, and another 2.3 percent are in finance, insurance, and real estate.

Citing these statistics thrills me and reinforces the current trend of more Black women starting their own ventures. But let's be straight.

Starting a business is hard work and takes way more money and time than entrepreneurs ever anticipate. There are very few sources for start-up capital. Most lenders and investors want to see a major return on their investment and that means supporting businesses that already have a track record. Using credit cards, raiding your savings, and tapping the equity in your house to start and feed a venture is risky business, which is why so many start-up small business owners have major debt problems and low credit scores.

The vast majority (89 percent) of African American businesses don't have employees. Being self-employed can be a much easier route to take than starting a business with employees and lots of overhead. No matter how large or small your entrepreneurial dreams may be, I suggest taking a class at your local college on starting a small business to learn how to develop a solid business plan and identify the resources you need to get started. Interview every single business owner who will tell you his or her story. Try to find someone with deep knowledge about the financial aspects of business ownership to help you run the numbers. And then run the numbers again. Then take stock of your financial condition. It takes time to start earning money from a new business, typically eighteen months. Can you survive without a paycheck for that long? Make sure you've gotten enough dough to support yourself and your family for a while before plunging into entrepreneurship.

If you're serious about creating wealth through a personal enterprise, I applaud you. Go for it! But do your homework before you take the plunge.

Here are eight sources that can help:

- *Black Enterprise* magazine and Web site (www.blackenterprise.com)
- International Franchising Association (www.franchise.org; 800-543-1038)
- National Association for the Self-Employed (www.nase.org; 800-232-6273)
- National Association of Female Executives (www.nafe.com; 800-927-NAFE)
- National Association of Women Business Owners (www.nawbo.org; 800-55-NAWBO)

- Center for Women's Business Research (www.nfwbo.org; 202-638-3060)
- Small Business Administration (www.sba.gov; 202-606-4000)

Boost My Income Plan

After reading this section, think about your career priorities and what you need to do to boost your earnings—whether it's finding a new job or making some strategic moves at your current workplace, getting more out of your employee benefits, or perhaps starting your own venture.

Boost My Income Goal: ______________________________

Major obstacles to achieving this goal: ____________________

____

What I need to do to achieve this goal: ___________________

____

Resources: ______________________________________

Timetable: ______________________________________

Step 1: ____

Step 2: ____

Step 3: ____

Dial Down Your Debt

There's no doubt about it. The American Dream doesn't come cheap, and it's sure a lot more fun shopping than paying bills. Although about 48% of credit card holders carry a balance of less than $1,000, reports Fair Isaac, 10% are far less conservative in their use of credit cards and have total card balances in excess of $10,000. According to the NCNW, Black women weigh in with $2,000 on average in credit-card debt. And though that may not seem like much, poor credit ratings and paying bills late plague many Black women these days.

A 2003 Consumer Federation of America study reported that 76 percent of the African Americans surveyed expressed concern about meeting their monthly payments on all types of debt other than their mortgage. When asked, "What would you do with a $5,000 windfall?" three-fourths of African American women said their main priority would be to pay down debt.

Regularly spending more than you can afford may be a sign of a more serious problem. Shopping, for instance, can be as addictive as gambling, drugs, or alcohol. Some people rely on credit to cover cash flow shortages for a variety of reasons, like losing their jobs or playing large medical bills.

Unfortunately, the impact of too much debt and late payments can be devastating, no matter what causes the problem. Since many companies and employers equate big debt loads, late payments, and bad credit ratings with poor character, these problems may cause you to pay more for your utility services, car insurance, and mortgages, and even worse, keep you from getting your dream job.

But dwelling on how much money you owe isn't going to fix the problem. You need a debt-reduction plan. Start by answering these ten questions to see where you stand. Unfortunately, even a few checks in the YES column are a sign of trouble.

Are You Head Over Heels in Debt?

	Yes	No
Do you have more than four credit, debit, or charge cards (include everything from bank and gas cards to department store cards)?	❏	❏
Do you only make minimum payments on your credit cards?	❏	❏
Does more than 20 percent of your paycheck (after taxes) cover your monthly credit card and loan notes (excluding mortgage and car)?	❏	❏

	Yes	No
Have you ever borrowed money or used cash advances from a credit card to pay down your debt?	❑	❑
If you were to go purchase a car today, would you need a friend or relative to cosign the car loan before you'd be approved?	❑	❑
Have you maxed out on all or most of your credit cards?	❑	❑
Have you lost track on how much you owe?	❑	❑
Are you using your credit cards to pay everyday bills like gasoline or food because you don't have any money?	❑	❑
Are bill collectors hounding you for late or back payments?	❑	❑
Are you dipping into your savings to pay off your bills?	❑	❑

If your debt problems are severe, consult a nonprofit or not-for-profit consumer credit counseling group. For a certified professional credit counselor, contact the National Foundation of Credit Counselors (www.nfcc.org; 800-388-2227) or the Association of Independent Credit Counseling Agencies (www.aicca.com). Myvesta, (www.myvesta.com; formerly Debt Counselors of America) is a widely trusted nonprofit financial crisis center that offers personal counseling, debt management help, and advice on avoiding bankruptcy and foreclosure.

Be careful, fraud is rampant in the credit and debt repair industry. And the nonprofit or not-for-profit status of these services does not mean that they are free. You or your creditors will pay for the service. The fees collected from creditors are based on a percentage of the amount you pay on the plan. If you pay, make sure that the initial fee is no more than $75; monthly fees should be about $35.

How does debt counseling and management work? For a small fee, these firms will negotiate a payment plan (including reduced fees or interest rates) with your creditors. Some services require you to pay them one monthly sum and they pay your creditors. Others allow you to pay your creditors according to the payment plan that was worked out. Please note that your relationship with the credit repair service will appear on your credit report.

When is filing for bankruptcy necessary? According to the American Bankruptcy Institute, bankruptcy has two main purposes: First, bankruptcy gives the people who are owed money—the creditors—a share of the money that the debtors can afford to pay back. Second, bankruptcy gives debtors a fresh start, by canceling many of their debts, through an order of the court called a "discharge." Although this may seem easier than going through the credit repair steps outlined in this chapter, don't be fooled. Since bankruptcy stays on your credit report for seven to ten years, this isn't something that you want to jump right into to ease the pressure of creditors calling.

Good Debt, Bad Debt

No matter whether you use a pro or develop your own get-out-of-debt plan, you must come to grips with the role of debt in your life. For instance, despite widespread concerns, some debt is good. This includes anything that you really need (a new home, a car, or education, for instance) but can't afford without wiping out cash reserves or liquidating investments.

Improvements that add value to your home—remodeling your kitchen or bathroom, for example—may be worth refinancing your mortgage or taking out a home equity loan or line of credit. Many home-remodeling projects, like a paint job, don't add value to the home. In this case, pay cash or borrow and pay off the loan in five years or less. Never borrow more than you can afford to pay back. If you can't cover the monthly payments, you can ruin your credit ratings even if you plan to recoup the money when you sell the house.

When is it downright dumb to borrow? The fastest way to debt hell is to spend on things that are consumed quickly like a vacation, clothes, restaurant meals, gambling, and regular monthly expenses such as insurance or utility bills. If carrying cash makes you uncomfortable, use one credit card and pay off the balance each month.

Another alternative: Use a check, debit, or ATM card that draws funds directly from your checking account to pay for your purchase.

That way you only can spend money that is already in your account. Debit cards are ATM cards that carry a MasterCard or Visa logo and allow you to charge purchases. Choose the credit option and sign for your purchases rather than punching in your PIN to save on fees.

According to the National Consumers League, debit card issuers usually have a maximum liability of $50 if the card is reported lost or stolen within two days of discovery. Liability increases to $500 if reported within sixty days. If you neglect to notify the bank within sixty days after a bank statement is sent, you could lose everything in your checking and overdraft accounts.

Check your financial institutions for its specific policy. Also, debit cards don't always come with the warrantees that some traditional credit cards offer.

What about big-ticket expenses like furniture or appliances? If you can't afford to pay cash for necessary items like a stove or washing machine, your best bet is to use your lowest-interest credit card and commit to paying off the balance as soon as possible. If you extend the payments, you could wind up paying for that refrigerator five times over. Think twice before opening up credit lines just to buy one item—even if the store promises no interest or payments for six months. If you don't pay the balance in full, you may owe six months of high-rate interest, plus the remaining balance. When it comes to furnishings, a little delayed gratification can do you some good. Find ways to save the money to buy the item with cash. Work a few extra hours or take on a freelance project to temporarily boost your income. Always look for sales. What is the point of paying retail, when in a few more weeks most items you yearn for will be on sale, somewhere?

How Credit Cards Work

We all know the thrill of slapping down that plastic and getting something that we crave but can't afford. It's one of life's most wonderful guilty pleasures. We all remember times when we couldn't believe that the store was actually letting us take home that fabulous leather coat or designer handbag we had no idea how we were going to pay for when the bill came due.

Sure, credit cards are convenient and let you feel free to go on a spree, but there's no doubt about it. Credit cards are the bane of many Black women's existence. Credit cards can open the gateway to out-of-control debt. We all have good intentions of paying that bill, but, wow, life just gets in the way and that revolving credit balance starts to spin out of control. Plus, the more cards you have, the greater the chance that you will soon slide into a credit card crisis.

The average American consumer totes around seven pieces of plastic. Fair Issac, the company that calculates your credit scores, reports that a typical consumer has access to about $12,000 in credit. Get out your purse and count your cards.

Most families should have no more than two to four cards per adult—and preferably just two. And each card should have a specific purpose. One should be used for major purchases—with the goal to pay off the purchase in full within a very specific and tight period of time. (The shorter the period, the less amount of interest you will pay.) For this card, find the lowest interest rate available. The other card could be used for convenience purchases and must be paid off in full every month. This second card (which could be a debit card) should have no annual fee. One of these cards should offer perks such as frequent-flier miles. If you own your own business, you'll probably need a separate card for business purchases and tax-deductible expenses.

Although you may love the special offers or deals that retail stores (like Bloomingdale's or Macy's) offer their charge card holders, look carefully at the interest rates they charge if you do not plan to pay the bills in full each month. They can be outrageous—and cancel out even the juiciest discounts.

How to Read a Credit Card Offer or Statement

Annual percentage rate (APR): This is the finance charge, expressed as an annual figure, such as 13 percent. When comparing cards, the goal is to get the lowest APR available.

Cash advances: This tells you how much you've borrowed. Although that money may seem like free money, know the terms of this loan before you tap this source. Many cards charge a higher interest rate on a cash advance than on purchases. They may not offer a grace period. And some don't automatically apply your repayment to the cash advance debt. So track this balance until it's paid off in full.

Credit limit: The maximum amount you can borrow (cash advance) or charge to the card.

Due/pay by date: The date that your payment has to be recorded in the credit card company's computer—not the date of the postmark or when it arrives at the company. The typical bill cycle is twenty-nine to thirty-one days, and the payment is usually due twenty to thirty days from when the bill was printed. To be sure your bill arrives on time, mail payments ten days to two weeks before they are due, use online payment options, or better yet, pay your bill when it arrives. Remember, studies show that people who pay their bills immediately tend to be happier with their lives and feel in more control.

Fees:

Late fee: Penalty for paying your bill after the due date. These fees can average from $29 to $35 per month.

Over-limit fee: This is triggered when you make charges beyond your limit. Late fees also can take you over the limit. Expect to be hit with fees ranging from $29 to $39 a month until you bring your balance down to your allowed amount.

Miscellaneous fees: You may see fees that aren't clearly explained on the bill, such as credit insurance or debit card fees.

Grace period: How long a charge can be on your bill before you are charged interest. But take note: Some cards don't have grace periods for purchases or cash advances. Grace periods are getting shorter, and average about twenty days.

Finance charge: The interest charge on your outstanding credit card balance.

Minimum payment: The least amount you can pay on your bill. This will usually run from 2 percent to 2.5 percent to as high as 3 percent to 4 percent of your balance. If you can't pay the whole balance, double or triple the minimum payment whenever you can.

Payments and credits: Acknowledgment of payments and credit for returned items.

Previous balance: Amount owed before your last payment was recorded.

If you see an item you don't recognize, whether it's a charge or a fee, call the company and ask for an explanation.

Cashing in Your Get-out-of-Credit-Card Debt Chip

Although paying down your debt may seem like the impossible dream, having an action plan can make it easier. Pay the minimum on your credit card bills, and you could spend the next twenty years paying them off. That means you'll pay more than five times the actual debt in interest—even if you don't add a penny to the balance with new spending. But with a plan, you can reduce your payoff time to a single-digit number.

Let's say you have $8,000 in card debt like the average American family at a typical rate of 13.97 percent. By paying only the minimum 2.2 percent of the balance required each month, you will take thirty years to pay off that debt plus $10,000 in interest. If you paid $176, which was the minimum payment in the first month your debt hit $8,000, you'd cut your interest payments by two-thirds and be debt-free in less than six years.

How can *you* make a dent in your credit card debt? Follow this three-phase program.

Phase One: Get Real

Step 1: Write down every credit card you have and how much you owe. Start with your largest balance. Next to the amount, list the interest rate you're paying on that card.

Step 2: Develop a strategy to pay off this debt. Here's where the experts disagree. One camp believes you should pay off your small balances first, while continuing to pay the minimums on cards with larger balances. That might be the ideal if small victories inspire you to tackle tougher challenges. Other debt gurus like Jean Chatzky, author of *Pay It Down: From Debt to Wealth on $10 a Day*, insist that paying off the card with the highest interest rate first makes the most financial sense, since this debt costs you the most. Meanwhile you keep paying the minimum monthly amount on all other revolving bills. If you can't decide, try out the debt evaluation tool on www.msn.com to evaluate your situation.

Once the high-cost debt is eliminated, focus on the debt with the next highest rate. But keep this in mind: If your credit card has a low teaser rate that will go up after a few months, try to eliminate this balance before the low rate expires.

Step 3: Cut up the cards you no longer plan to use and call the companies to close out your account.

Step 4: Call the customer service lines of the credit cards you want to keep and negotiate lower interest rates. According to Consumer Action, a pioneering nonprofit advocacy and education organization (www.consumer-action.org), maintaining a $1,000 average balance on your 18 percent credit card will cost you more than $180 in interest over one year. If you switch that money to a 14 percent rate card you will save about $40. Yes, you can do this. Here's the deal.

Tell the customer service rep that you're shopping around for the lowest rate possible and when you find it you're planning to transfer your current balance to a new card with the lowest rate. Before you make good on your threat to transfer the account, read the pros and cons of transferring a balance in Phase Two, Step 8.

Step 5: Start using a debit card for more of your purchases. That way you have the convenience of not carrying around cash or the hassle of writing checks, but you're not piling on debt because the funds to pay for your purchase are being drawn directly from your account. Just remember to sign for the purchases, don't punch in your PIN.

Phase One sounds easy, huh? Taking charge isn't always a snap, but it will make you feel better. Still, you have some ways to go before you're on solid ground. Let's keep going.

Phase Two: Dialing for Dollars to Pay Down Your Debt

Step 6: Drastically reduce your spending. Chapter two focused on developing a realistic spending plan that included freeing up money to pay off outstanding credit card balances. Put that plan into action.

Step 7: Transfer your balances onto low-interest cards. But beware. Introductory or "teaser" rates can be unbelievably low, making it incredibly tempting to roll over your balance. First: If it sounds too good to be true, it probably is. Attractive rates often disappear after a few months, so read the fine print to find out the length of the introductory period and what rate will kick in at that time. If the rate goes up, you could be saddled with huge balances on high-rate cards. Second: Although you may be lowering your rate, you're also opening one more card. That means generating another outstanding open credit line that will show up on your credit report.

Before taking this route, find out all the fees involved in moving the balance or terminating your original account, as well as the fees and interest rates charged by the new account once the introductory period ends.

Step 8: Tap alternative sources for cash. If you will need more than three to five years to eliminate a debt, doubling or tripling the monthly minimums may not be enough. Here are four alternatives:

1. **Tap your home equity to pay off your credit cards.** With soaring real estate prices in some areas, this may seem like the slam-dunk solution to your credit woes. Here's how it works: If you replaced a 12 percent interest credit card balance with a home-equity loan at 8 percent you'll cut your interest costs by a third. In addition, the interest on a home equity loan may be fully deductible on your income tax return.

   But before you start dreaming of nothing but zeros on your credit card statements, tread carefully. True, the rates on home equity loans or lines of credit are typically lower than the rates charged on outstanding credit card balances. However, they both must be paid every month in addition to your mortgage. If you can't keep up, you may put your home at risk for that dream vacation, those fine furnishings, and the new wardrobe you charged over the past few years. Now, does that make sense? Plus, there's the danger of charging up those cards again, once the balance is paid off. This happens so often (70 percent of the time) that the banking industry has a term for it: *Reloading.*

A better choice may be a debt-management program. Say you have $20,000 in credit card fees. You can finish paying that off in three to four years and you'll probably pay $6,000 to $8,000 in fees and interest. With a home equity loan or credit line, you'll have to pay back the $20,000, but the fees and interest could run you an additional $18,000 by the time the loan is paid back.

2. **Refinance your existing mortgage** (For details on this transaction, see the Refinancing Home section, page 90).
3. **Borrow from your retirement savings plan** (See section in chapter four).
4. **Consolidate your student loans.** Under the Federal Direct Consolidation Loan Program, you can merge all of your federal student loans into one large loan with a reasonable interest rate. You can also extend the length of your payout from ten years to thirty years. Although this will lower your monthly payment, you will end up paying more in interest in the life of the loan. But the trade-off may be worth it to get rid of expensive credit-card debt.

Phase Three: Clean Up Your Score

Step 9: Get a copy of your credit report and credit score every year. Study both carefully so you can fix any mistakes and learn how to improve your score. By the end of 2005, you will be able to request one free credit report every year. To request your free report, go to www.creditreport.com or call 877-322-8228.

But if you are ready to start cleaning up your credit report right now, order a copy of your credit report from all three major credit bureaus: Experian (www.experian.com; 800-397-3742), Equifax (www.equifax.com; 800-997-2493), and Trans Union (www.experian.com; 800-888-4213). You can do this at once on any of the these Web sites for about $29.95, as well as www.myFICO.com, which is run by Fair Issac, the company behind the credit scoring. An individual report with your credit score will run you about

$14.95; $9.50 without. Reports are free if you've been turned down for credit, employment, or housing in the past sixty days. Not all creditors report to all three bureaus and you don't always know which bureau your lender, insurer, or potential employer is checking, so start with all three. The myFICO site offers a tool kit that will walk you through the entire process of evaluating your report and developing a letter to challenge mistakes and wrong information.

What's in Your Credit Report?

Most people don't have a clue about how credit reports work and how your credit score is calculated. This won't be you after reading this section. One common misperception is that married couples have a combined single score, according to a recent survey by the Consumer Federation of America. Not true. Everyone has her own score. For you single women, you need to know that marrying someone with better credit won't improve your rating.

A consumer credit report contains four types of information: Information that identifies who you are, credit information, public record information, and inquiries from potential creditors. This includes:

- Your name
- Your current and previous addresses
- Your Social Security number
- Your year of birth
- Your current and previous employers
- If you're married, your spouse's name
- Your banks
- Retailers where you have accounts
- Your credit card
- Your outstanding loans
- Bankruptcies
- Tax liens
- Monetary judgments
- Inquiries from creditors

What's in a Score?

Credit scores—which can range from 300 to above 800—help

creditors and lenders assess your credit risk. The higher the number, the better the score. Scores are based on mathematical models that evaluate your credit worthiness based on the following data:

Payment history on credit cards and installment loans such as mortgage and car notes. Late payments and nonpayment are two of the biggest contributors to bad credit ratings. These two factors account for about 35 percent of your score.

Current level of debt. Total amount owed and the ratio of what's owed to your credit limit are factored in for another 30 percent.

Credit history. How long have you been using credit? This includes when you opened your accounts and how long you have used each account. On average, this category determines about 15 percent of your score.

New credit applications/Number of credit inquiries. Too many accounts opened in the last twelve months may indicate that you are overextending yourself. This makes up 10 percent.

How many and what type of credit accounts you have. Accounts such as bankcards, department store cards, and installment loans are all considered. This category usually rates another 10 percent of your final credit score.

Personal details such as race, gender, and religion are definitely not considered when determining your score. Although each major credit bureau has its own method for calculating credit scores, scoring models are fairly standard, so a 600 score at one bureau is roughly equivalent to the same score at another.

WHAT'S A FAVORABLE SCORE?

The median credit score in the U.S. was 723 at the beginning of 2003. Overall, a score of 650 or above is a sign of very good credit. People with scores of 650 or higher probably have a good chance of obtaining loans or credit cards at the best interest rates. Scores of 620 to 650 indicate good credit, but may signal that there are potential problems. This could cause a creditor to request additional information before your credit request or loan will be approved. Scores below 620 signal a greater credit risk and as a result the loan process may be prolonged and involve more paperwork.

Possible reasons for low scores may include:

- Late payments
- Too much debt on existing accounts
- Past delinquency on accounts
- Too many accounts opened in the last twelve months
- Accounts that were forwarded to collection agencies
- Excessive number of accounts with balances owed
- No recent account history

Not only will a low credit score jeopardize your chances of getting a mortgage, if you do get approved, you'll pay dearly. Let's say your credit score was below 560. If you were able to qualify for a $150,000 mortgage, the rate for a thirty-year fixed-rate loan could be as high as 9.29 percent for a monthly payment of $1,238. However, if your credit score was over 720, you could have gotten a 5.72 percent rate with a monthly payment of just $877. Good credit could have saved you $4,392 in a year.

When you review your report, make sure of every piece of data, including such seemingly small matters as the spelling of your name or your correct street address. Make sure all of the information is about you. You don't want to suffer for anyone else's credit mishaps. Look for open lines of credit that you no longer need, such as credit cards you no longer use. Too much "potential debt" can prevent you from getting a loan. That's because when lenders review your report, they consider how much you owe and how much you may be able to rack up.

Positive credit information remains on your report indefinitely. If there is no new activity on an account after seven years, it will drop off the report. Most negative information will stay on the report for seven years. Bankruptcies can remain on your credit report for up to ten years. Other public record information can remain for up to seven years. Most inquiries stay on your credit report for up to two years.

Your credit report changes every day. The only way to repair a bad credit history is diligently paying down your outstanding debt, paying your bills on time, closing down unused accounts, and having erroneous information removed from the report.

To dispute errors on your credit report, you must write or call the credit bureau that issued the report and explain the problems. You can also consider going to a Web site like www.myFICO.com. For a fee, you can use their tool kit that clearly outlines what has contributed to your score being high, low, or average. It will also identify problems or errors that you may want to address and help you generate a letter to the credit bureau that outlines your concerns.

Dial Down My Debt Plan

This is easy. By now you should have a clear idea of your current debt load and understand why cash is still king. If you haven't reviewed your credit report within the last twelve months, make that a high priority. Use the form below to develop your debt action plan.

Debt Goal: ____________________

Major obstacles to achieving this goal: ____________________

____

What I need to do to achieve this goal: ____________________

____

Resources: ____________________

Timetable: ____________________

Step 1: ____________________

Step 2: ____________________

Step 3: ____________________

Plan Well: There's No Place like Home

Owning your home is the ultimate symbol of the American Dream, but if you're not prepared, buying it can be a nightmare. That's because, besides raising children, home ownership is probably the second biggest financial commitment you will ever make. By 2001, according to the U.S. Census, 56.3 percent of African American women, age thirty-five to fifty-nine, owned their own home. A study by the Fannie Mae Foundation revealed that 79 percent of African American women, ages 18 to 34, who now pay rent, were set on buying their own home some day.

So why is owning your own home such a cherished ideal?

1. The tax savings from home ownership is unbeatable. That's because you can deduct mortgage interest and property taxes from your federal tax and, in many places, your state income tax if you itemize your deductions.
2. Your housing expense could be set up to thirty years, depending on the type of mortgage loan you choose.
3. You can build up equity in your home. Your house can provide a source of money to be tapped when needed, like to help pay for your retirement or children's education.

Still, home ownership isn't for everyone. For instance, if your job has you moving around a lot over the next few years, this may not be time to buy. If you're not sure whether it's better to buy or continue renting right now, check out the comparison calculator at www.freddiemac.com.

With all the tools and advice available today—ranging from the Internet to books and magazines and online advice—you could consider buying your home without using any real estate professionals. But I don't recommend this. My husband and I bought a townhome last year and even though we've owned two other homes, our real estate agent (whose fee was picked up by the seller) and attorney were extremely helpful. Not only did they protect our rights throughout the process, our attorney negotiated thousands of dollars off our offer to cover repairs and replacing old appliances. Plus, the services of a well-connected Realtor can be amazing. For instance, Realtors with close ties to local lenders can help you smoothly navigate the loan process—even when there are problems with your application. Many seasoned pros know the best contractors and can put you at the top of their lists during busy home-improvement seasons.

Does owning your home make sense for you? It's your money and your sweat equity that will turn a house, condominium, or co-op into your home. So here are seven questions to ask yourself before you take the plunge, whether it's your first or fifth time buying a home.

1. **Am I ready to stay put for at least five years?**

   Buying a home is an emotionally charged financial transaction, so think through this question with your head and not your heart. Are you in line to be transferred to a new city in a few years? Are you thinking about going back to school? Or are you concerned about being downsized or suffering a drop in income that will make paying the mortgage difficult? Even in the hottest real estate markets, you can lose money if you sell any sooner than five years, especially when you factor in the cost of buying and selling a home. Plus, get this: You won't have to pay taxes on the profits from selling your home ($250,000 if you're single; $500,000 for married couples), if the house was your primary residency for two of the past five years. Sweet break, huh?

2. **Do I want the responsibilities and headaches of being a home owner?**

   Even owners of brand-new homes quickly get to know a local plumber, painter, electrician, contractor, handyman, window washer—the list goes on. Or, is your idea of living well to call the landlord to fix the broken faucet, repair a window, and replace the worn-out dishwasher? That's okay too. So whether you're buying your first home, or just need a change of scenery—think about whether owning or renting is more appealing at this stage of your life. And if home ownership is for you, does a single-family home or a townhome condominium, perhaps, make more sense for you?

3. **Can I afford my own home?**

   Paying the mortgage is just one hurdle of home ownership. The median price of a single-family home was $184,100 in 2004. A typical condominium would run you $193,600. This was the first year that the median price of a condo was more than a detached single-family home.

   Taxes, upkeep, and decorating can turn an otherwise affordable purchase into the ultimate money pit. Aim for a home that costs about two and a half times your gross annual salary—but many factors can change that guideline. Significant credit card debt or other financial obligations like many single parents face may force you to set your sights lower. To calculate how much house you can afford, go to Quicken.com (www.quicken.com) and Microsoft's HomeAdvisor (www.homeadvisor.com). The results are based on what banks look for in a mortgage borrower:

1. Your monthly housing costs, including mortgage principal and interest, property taxes, home owner's insurance, and private mortgage insurance if your down payment is less than 20 percent (for more on PMI, private mortgage insurance, see question 7 below), should equal no more than 28 percent of your gross monthly income.
2. That sum plus your minimum monthly payment on any long-term debts should equal no more than 36 percent of your gross income.

Buying the home is just the first phase. What will it cost to maintain your home? How about home insurance? Utilities? (You can call your utility company for an estimate of how much gas and electric cost the last owner each month.) Contactors will give you an estimate on what necessary repairs will cost before you make an offer on the house.

What about a condominium?

Traditionally, condominium apartments and townhomes were considered a cheaper alternative to home ownerships in most areas of the country compared to the cost of a single-family home. That trend reversed itself in 2004, when condos commanded an average price of $193,600 versus $184,100 for an average freestanding home. This may be due to the number of empty nesters downsizing their home to buy into luxury condo units complete with whirlpool spas and health club facilities in their complexes.

In a condominium, each owner owns her unit and pays a monthly fee to maintain shared areas like the lobby, walkways, or the pool. When major repairs are necessary, the condo board can assess fees to cover repairs. Before you buy a condo, review the common charges over the last five years to see if there have been any major assessments. Find out if there are any plans for major repairs in the future that may require an assessment. Ask what percentage of the residents actually own their units as opposed to just renting them (many condos include both). A complex with lots of renters has fewer owners who care about the upkeep, which may make it harder for you to get a mortgage on the property.

4. **Am I creditworthy?**

   Most likely you will need a mortgage to buy a house, so your credit history must be as clean as possible. Before you start house hunting, get copies of your credit reports—which list your credit scores—and scrutinize every entry. (See Dialing Down Your Debt for more information on credit reports, how to get them, and what to do to correct any errors.) The sooner you check your report, the better. Blemishes can delay or kill your chances for getting financing, so try to resolve problems right away. If the report is accurate but shows past problems, be prepared to explain them to a loan officer.

5. **Which type of mortgage is right for me?**

   Mortgage options can be overwhelming, and some can be downright risky, like the current *interest-only mortgage*. Many single women and young couples are using this loan to buy more house than they can afford now, with hopes of earning more in the future. For the first five or ten years of the loan, your payments are artificially low because you are only paying the interest, not the principal. Therefore, you're not building up any equity in the house during these years. If you don't sell or refinance within five or 10 years, the principal will come due and your interest rate may increase dramatically. As a result, your payments can balloon by 50% or more.

   For most home buyers, the oldies but goodies are a much better deal:

   Fixed-rate mortgages. Monthly payments in a fixed-rate mortgage never change. However, if the interest rate falls, you can either continue paying your higher preset rate, or you could refinance your loan, though that would mean paying additional closing costs. Typical terms for these mortgages run fifteen, twenty, or thirty years.

Adjustable-rate mortgages (ARMs). With an ARM, your interest rate and payments will be fixed for an initial period (usually one, three, or five years), then adjusts periodically based on market conditions, or more specifically, the rise or fall of a financial index, such as the one-year or three-year U.S. Treasury rate. Although the interest rate for ARMs typically have been less than a fixed-rate loan, this isn't always the case. Keep in mind that market conditions can cause the rate to jump quite a bit after the initial period ends. The terms of the loan should clearly state the cap, which will tell you just how high the rates can be adjusted.

ARMs appeal to buyers who:

- Need a larger loan amount than they can qualify for with a fixed-rate mortgage.
- Want to save money in the short term.
- Plan to move or refinance within a few years. Some home buyers choose an ARM, hoping to lock in to lower fixed-rates than were offered when they applied for the original mortgage. That's a gamble, so don't bet on it.

Which one is right for you? Creatures of habit who like the idea of a steady monthly payment and plan to stay in the house for more than five years should go with a fixed-rate loan. However, if you plan on being in your home for five years or less, the adjustable may be best. Unless interest rates go up significantly, you will pay less in the short term with an adjustable. No matter which mortgage you go for, keep the duration of the loan as short as you can. The monthly payments will be higher, but you will pay down the loan more quickly.

Karen, a single forty-five-year-old mother of two who plans to retire at sixty, wanted to buy a home, but living debt-free in retirement was very important to her. After using the calculators on her bank's Web site, she found the right solution. Karen could pay off her $100,000 mortgage by opting for a fifteen-year loan at 6.25 percent vs. a thirty-year loan at 6.50 percent. The payments would be $1,040, $125 more than the longer option. "But it's worth it, even though I now have to do my own hair most of the time," Karen explains. "What's a little sacrifice now, if I could burn my mortgage note at sixty years old?"

Balloon mortgages. With this mortgage, interest rates and payments are fixed for a set period (usually from five to seven years), followed by a single "balloon" payment of the entire remaining balance. This is good for people who want to keep their payments low and plan to sell their house in a few years (before the balloon payment becomes due). This could be extremely problematic if you want to stay in the house longer, because you'll need to cough up the remaining balance or refinance the loan—and you will not know what the interest rate will be at that time.

Loans for veterans, low-to moderate-income and first-time home buyers. The following four government-backed loan programs offered through local lenders may be the ideal solution for buyers with limited savings. The Federal Housing Administration, a part of the Department of Housing and Urban Development (HUD) (www.hud.gov), the Department of Veterans Affairs (www.va.gov), Freddie Mac (www.freddiemac.com), and Fannie Mae (www.fanniemae.com) mortgage programs offer:

- Low or no down payment requirements.
- Flexible income, debt, and credit requirements to help borrowers qualify.
- Down payment and closing costs may be funded by a gift or an unsecured loan.
- Fixed-rate and adjustable-rate loans.

6. Which lender is best for me?

Shop around. Shop around. Shop around. It's so important I had to say it three times. A little time researching which lender has the best rate could save you a lot of money in the long run. Scrutinize ads from mortgage lenders, call banks and credit unions, and surf the Internet. Some major corporations help employees trying to purchase a home. Check your employee benefits department to see what's available, including any special low-interest loan from selected lenders. Also unions like the National Education Association have developed great programs with lenders for lower fees than you may be able to find on your own.

7. **How much money will I need to close?**

   The first major home-buying hurdle is coming up with the cash for the down payment and closing costs—a major concern of Black women. Most lenders like to see at least 20 percent of the home's price as a down payment. If you can put down more than that, the lender may be willing to approve a larger loan. If you have less, you'll need to find loans that can accommodate you, like the government loans described earlier. If you qualify, it's possible to pay as little as 3 percent up front for a loan.

   Just remember: With a down payment under 20 percent, you'll probably pay for private mortgage insurance (PMI), a safety net protecting the bank in case you fail to make payments. PMI adds from 0.5 percent to 1.25 percent of the total loan amount at the closing, plus annual fees that will be built into your monthly mortgage payments.

   While doing your homework, don't forget the "points" or fees you may need to pay when you borrow. Usually, you pay from one to three points. Since one point equals 1 percent of the mortgage, one point on a $100,000 mortgage is $1,000, two points equal $2,000, and so on. If coming up with that much money in addition to your down payment and other closing fees will be tough, ask your lender to reduce the points in exchange for a higher interest rate.

   The longer you plan to stay in your home, the more you should consider paying points. For instance, a lender may offer an 8 percent loan at no points, or a 7.6 percent loan with two points. If you have a thirty-year, fixed-rate mortgage of $100,000, your monthly payment for a no-point loan would be $734; on the two-point loan, it would be $706.

That's a small difference, just $28 a month. But if you pay the points, you'll recoup the $2,000 you spent in a little under six years of payments. And over the life of the loan, you'll save $10,000. So in this case, if you planned to stay put for six years or more, it would make sense to go with the points.

Once you choose a lender, try to get "pre-qualified." This means that the lender has determined the maximum home price for which he will approve a loan. If the housing market in your area is very competitive, with homes selling just days after they go on the market, then you might also consider getting "pre-approved." This means the lender agrees to provide a mortgage even before you have selected a house. Not only will this help you move quickly to close on a home, it will give you an edge if others are competing to buy the same property. Pre-approval can cost $150 or more.

Closing costs may include the appraisal fee, loan fees, attorney's fees, inspection fees, and the cost of a title search. These fees (typically 2 percent to 7 percent of the loan) can easily add up to $5,000 to $7,000.

Most lenders frown on using borrowed money to meet the down payment. Banks will recognize that for what it is, a loan, and treat it as one of your debt obligations, not cash on hand. So tapping into your savings or using a windfall from a bonus, for instance, is the best way to come up with the down payment. If you're still short, here are two options:

- You can withdraw up to $10,000 without penalty from an individual retirement account (IRA), if you have one, though you must pay taxes on the amount.
- You may be able to tap your 401(k) or similar retirement plan for a loan from yourself.

Don't be so quick to pay down your mortgage.

If you pour all your cash into your mortgage, you'll have no cushion to fall back on. Once you've paid off your high interest credit card debt, consider using any cash—from a bonus for instance to make one extra payment a year or pay a little more on the principal each month. Just paying an extra $100 a month on a $100,000, thirty-year, 6.5 percent mortgage could shave 129 months off your term and—get this—save you $97,798 off the cost of the mortgage.

Refinancing, Home Equity Loans, and Lines of Credit

In the last section, we discussed paying off your debt by tapping into the equity of your home. You also can use this equity to renovate your home or help pay for college. You have three ways to leverage your home for cash: Refinance your mortgage, apply for a home equity line of credit (HELOC), or take out a home equity loan. There are many terms and fees to consider when taking out these loans, so comparison shop among lenders. If you are not comfortable finalizing this decision alone, ask a money-savvy friend to help you. You don't have to stay with your current mortgage lender, but customers in good standing may have more leverage to reduce fees and fast-track the application process. *Be wary of mortgage lenders who seem only to advertise on television in the middle of the night.* Some of these are lenders of last resort because their fees are often very high. Again, if it sounds too good to be true, it probably is.

When you *refinance your mortgage*, you're actually replacing it with a brand-new loan, which means going through the whole mortgage application process once again. Refinancing can make sound financial sense if you're looking to:

- Reduce your monthly payments by taking advantage of lower interest rates or extending the repayment period.
- Switch from an adjustable-rate to a fixed-rate loan or from a balloon mortgage to a fixed-rate loan.
- Reduce how much interest you'll pay over the life of your mortgage by taking advantage of lower rates or shortening the term of your loan.
- Pay off your mortgage faster (accelerating the buildup of equity) by shortening the term of your loan.
- Free up cash for major expenses or to consolidate debt.

When should you refinance? An article in the July 2004 issue of *MONEY* magazine, "101 Things Every Consumer Should Know!" offered this strategy: "You typically start thinking about refinancing when interest rates fall one percentage point below your rate. The decision then comes down to whether you'll save enough to cover the costs. If refinancing will cut your payment by $150 a month and closing costs are $5,000, you will need thirty-three months to break even. But don't forget to take into account how far you've paid down your mortgage. Refinancing a six-year-old loan with another thirty-year mortgage means that paying off your home will take thirty-six years and possibly cost you more in interest than if you'd stuck with the original loan. Another option is to refinance into a fifteen-year loan."

The calculators at bank sites and on www.money.com/refinancing can help you determine if the refi makes sense.

A *home equity line of credit* provides an ongoing access to your equity that can be tapped whenever you need money by using a check or credit card linked to your account. Monthly payments are determined by the amount of money you borrowed (up to the time of payment) and current interest rates. For instance, the monthly note for a $100,000 line of credit at 4.5 percent would be about $377. Because you can tap this pool of money whenever you want, carefully track what you spend. We all know how things get out of control when the currency seems to be plastic. Read all of the terms for the loan and scrutinize the fees. Ask for clarification whenever something does not make sense. Also ask whether you'll be charged a penalty for paying off the loan early.

Home equity loans provide funds in one lump sum. The monthly payments are predictable since they are based on the amount you borrowed and the interest rate at that time. Be very careful before signing on the dotted lines. You may be tempted with incredibly low payments that might just cover the interest on the loan. A large balloon payment due later on could be spelled out in the fine print. Another cause for concern: According to experts at the National Law Center, your monthly payments on a home equity loan may not cover all of the interest you owe. That means interest continues to accrue and the total amount you owe continues to rise, even though you're not borrowing any more money.

For Seniors Only

Older women who want to draw on the equity of their homes may want to consider a *reverse mortgage.* For women over sixty-two years old, a reverse mortgage can be a true blessing—but as with any financial transaction, you must be careful. Fees on this type of loan program can be enormous.

After you've spent years repaying the mortgage that allowed you to buy your home, a reverse mortgage lets you tap into that investment to draw out cash. You own your home as long as you live there, and you will never be forced to move. When you sell or move from your home, or when you pass away, the outstanding balance of your reverse mortgage will become due. You are guaranteed to have the money to pay it off because the loan is based on the equity you already have in your home. If the home's value is less than the outstanding balance, you or your heirs will not have to pay the difference to your lenders. On the other hand, if you sell the home for more than the loan balance at that time, you or your heirs will keep the difference.

To be eligible for a reverse mortgage, all owners listed on the home's title must be at least sixty-two years of age and occupy the home as their principal residence for the majority of the year. The property must be a single-family or a two-to-four-unit dwelling.

There are hundreds of scam artists trying to prey on older women, so go slowly. Plus these mortgages offer lots of choices—and not all of them are good. Having someone to protect your interests is important. Before talking to a lender about reverse mortgages, find a counseling agency approved by the Department of Housing and Urban Development (HUD) to work with you and an FHA approved lender in your area. Call HUD's Housing Counseling and Referral hotline: 800-569-4287. In some states you can only apply for the mortgage after you've consulted a counselor.

The American Association of Retired People offers free information on reverse mortgages: Call 800-209-8085.

Your Home Ownership Plan

After reading this section, think about your living situation and whether it's time to buy your first home or better leverage the equity in your current home to put you on solid financial ground. Are you still paying a high-interest rate on your mortgage set when you purchased your home fifteen years ago? Maybe it's time to shop around for better rates.

Home Ownership Goal: ______________________

Major obstacles to achieving this goal: ______________________

____

What I need to do to achieve this goal: ______________________

____

Resources: ______________________

Timetable: ______________________

Step 1: ______________________

Step 2: ______________________

Step 3: ______________________

Plan Well: Take Charge of Your Family Finances

When it comes to families and money, emotions rather than good financial sense often rule the coop. That's because money can mean very different things to the people closest to you—your spouse or partner, your children, your siblings and your parents. "We don't talk about money with our family in terms of goals and planning that often," says financial planner Gwendolyn Kirkland, "so we don't know whether our priorities are in keeping with the people who share our money."

Although there aren't any ironclad rules about how couples or families should manage their money, it's important that everyone with something at stake be brought into the conversation. "This is especially important if you're planning to change how the family spends or saves," says Hurston financial planner Cheryl Creuzot. "Carrying out your plans can be easier if everyone buys into the changes and knows what's in store. I even encourage my clients to include their children in the conversation. They don't need to know the details. Just help them understand why they may be eating out less or how your new financial priorities may affect how much money they will have to spend."

Let them know why you are making changes, like you need to save for their education or you want to buy a house. Then let them express their concerns and fears. It's good to air out as much as possible, even if you've already determined what needs to be done.

Couples and Money

For most couples, money represents power, status, self-worth. The hidden agenda is really about who controls whom, explains Howard Markman, author of *We Can Work It Out.*

Because money can be such a touchy subject, married couples aren't always up front with each other about the money they have and the purchases they make. Twenty-two percent of married people don't even discuss how much they earn with anyone, including their mates. That finding came from a survey I recently commissioned Mathew Greenwald & Associates to conduct for *MONEY* magazine. And 46 percent of spouses say they've lied about prices to their partner or hidden purchases outright. When women fail to mention a purchase or how much it costs, these items are usually for their children. When men hide what they buy or for how much, it's usually something for themselves.

Gina loved to shop for the kids, but her husband always complained about how much money she spent on their sneakers, jeans, and computer games. "He's always scolding me, telling me that I'm depositing our retirement account at the Bank of the Mall. What's up with that? I'm tired of sneaking shopping bags in the house when he's taking a nap," Gina explained to their financial adviser. "It's my money, why should he care?" Jeff was outraged: "What do you mean it's your money? I thought everything was ours together."

Although the debates about how much financial space couples should have rage on, most financial pros believe it's important for couples to strive for financial peace.

Learn how to discuss money in a neutral manner. Try to explore issues, concerns, or challenges before they come to a head. If you think you're going to have a blowup about money, try to fight fairly. One technique used by the Colorado-based Prevention and Relationship Enhancement Program (PREP) is to force couples to listen to each other by only allowing one person at a time to talk. The person with an object in his or her hand (say a stuffed animal or pillow—soft and fuzzy are the operative words here, and you'll see why) is permitted to talk while the other listens. You can click on the "tools for couples" button on the Web site (www.prepinc.com) to find a PREP workshop near you.

Discuss your money memories, fears, hopes, and dreams with your partner. Remember the roles of money outlined in the first chapter? Knowing how the other person feels about money can go a long way when it seems like you're both talking another language as you tread into uncomfortable territory in your financial life—like not having enough to pay bills, or expressing concern that your partner is spending too much money. Have your partner take the "What Does Money Means to You?" quiz in the first chapter and share your answers with each other. This may help you bring up topics that have been difficult to mention in the past.

Be committed to improving your finances, even if your partner is not interested in making necessary changes. Successful financial planning within a marriage or partnership usually takes two to tango, but you can't sacrifice your financial peace of mind if your spouse or partner won't dance. So do the best you can with the money that's under your control.

Discuss the pros and cons of separate financial accounts. Rest assured there is no right answer to this tough decision. Most couples have a joint account because it's just too complicated to pay the household bills and fund joint savings and investment accounts from separate accounts. (Remember, retirement savings accounts cannot be jointly owned.) A recent survey by the Raddon Financial Group in Oakbrook Terrace, Illinois, revealed that separate accounts are on the rise. In 2004, 48 percent of married couples had two or more checking accounts—that's up from 39 percent in 2001. One consultant who commented on the study felt this reflected a growing distrust between men and women.

Many couples keep separate (but not secret) accounts to fund their personal expenses and activities. And that's a good thing, according to experts who believe that even married people need a bit a financial privacy. Each partner also needs a credit card in his or her own name. Since half of all first marriages still end in divorce (and more than half of second marriages), every woman must establish a sound credit history in her own name.

THE FINANCIAL ANGLE OF DIVORCE

"Divorce is not fair," says Ginita Wall, cofounder of WIFE, Women's Institute for Financial Education. The San Diego author of *ABC's of Divorce for Women*, adds that too many women spend way too much money, emotion, and energy trying to make things fair. "Instead, she should be fighting for the assets that will help her financially, now and in the future. That means making hard choices. Most woman want the house, but we should also be eyeing the pension and retirement accounts," explains Wall. This is especially true for women in midlife. "It seems that the seven-year itch has been replaced by the twenty-year ditch," says Wall, noting that the breakup of long-term marriages is on the rise. In the very least, she warns, be prepared for the worst-case scenario before it happens. "You, not your attorney, must take control of your divorce and what happens to you."

Most attorneys are not equipped to work out the financial details involved when a couple parts. Alimony, child support, and proceeds from the sale of the family's home are the most common concerns, but depending on how complex your financial life is, the list could go on. As Wall notes above, dividing the retirement accounts, pensions, and Social Security is critical. That's why Gwendolyn Kirkland advises couples with substantial assets to consider a Certified Divorce Planner (CDP), in case of divorce. These financial professionals are specially trained to ensure that clients get their fair share of the marital assets. To find out more, go to www.cfp.net (certified financial planners), www.institutedfa.com (certified divorce financial analysts), and www.aicpa.org (forensic accountants).

CARING FOR AGING PARENTS

There are tons of resources, services, and agencies to help you care for aging parents who need assistance. It can be tough, though, helping out your folks when you don't know their full financial picture. Although it may be uncomfortable, find time to talk to your parents about their money situation before a crisis (with their health or their finances) occurs. For instance, we all know African American families who have lost valuable real estate because their older relatives were too proud to discuss their money problems until their homes were in foreclosure or confiscated due to unpaid taxes.

Talking to your parents or elderly family members may be the toughest money discussion you've ever had. But explaining your commitment to get your financial house in order as a starting point can help. Make sure your parents or other relatives understand that you are not interested in their money, you just want to make sure their needs are being covered. If you are having trouble broaching this sensitive subject, ask a trusted family friend, clergy member, or social service worker to help facilitate this conversation. For resources to help with aging relatives, contact the Eldercare Locator (www.eldercare.gov; 800-677-1116), the National Council on the Aging's benefits checkup site (www.benefitscheckup.org), the Family Caregiver Alliance (www.caregiver.org; 800-445-8106), or Children of Aging Parents (www.caps4caregivers.org; 800-227-7294).

The Importance of Wills and Guardians

Every adult—single or married, with or without children—needs a will. If you don't have a will in some states, the court may step in to determine how your assets will be distributed. A will is the best way to make sure the payout process (of your insurance death benefits, retirement accounts, etc.) or the transfer of your assets (such as your home) goes quickly and smoothly. Even if you're named beneficiaries for your retirement accounts or insurance, you still need a will.

Depending on the size and complexity of your financial situation, a will may run you a few hundred dollars to prepare to several thousand dollars. I wouldn't suggest a do-it-yourself will kit if you are truly concerned about the financial security of your family or fear that disgruntled family members may challenge the legality of the document.

Make sure your wishes are clearly stated in the will. Leave nothing to interpretation. Attach a letter to your will that outlines all of your accounts, investments, and insurance policies. Include account numbers and the location of all your financial documents, deeds, and policies.

Wills need to be updated periodically. Remember, you want your heirs to receive your assets. You don't want any money sitting around in unclaimed accounts. Make provisions for all your children, especially your minor daughters and sons. That's why the beneficiaries of your accounts and your will must be consistent and kept up to date. You probably don't want your money going to an ex-husband or your husband's children from another marriage who never gave you the time of day. Remember to remove any heirs or beneficiaries who have already passed away.

When identifying an executor of your will, find someone who is comfortable handling legal and financial affairs, especially if your family is depending on the proceeds from your estate to live on. This is not an easy job, so name someone reliable. Also name a guardian(s) for your children under age eighteen. You don't want your babies shuffled from family member to family member who may not have the interest, means, or space to adequately care for them. Discuss what you expect from your child's guardian with prospective candidates before making the final choice. Again, be specific. Discuss your concerns in terms of religious training, schooling, sports, activities, even rules about dating. You want to find someone who will raise your children as you would want them to be raised.

Finally, be careful about leaving money to minor children. If you do not appoint an executor to manage the money until he or she turns eighteen (or twenty-one in some states), the court will appoint one who will determine how the money will be spent.

Keep your will in a safe place—but do not put the original copy in a safe-deposit box. These boxes may be temporarily sealed when the bank learns of the owner's death, and therefore delay the distribution of your assets. Keep the original will at your attorney's office, but give your executor and another trusted family member or friend his or her contact information. You can keep copies in a locked file at home.

Take Charge of Your Family Finances Plan

After reading this section, think about your family's financial priorities and what you need to do to help your family better manage their money.

Family Financial Goal: ______________________________

Major obstacles to achieving this goal: ______________________

____

What I need to do to achieve this goal: ______________________

____

Resources: ______________________________

Timetable: ______________________________

Step 1: ______________________________

Step 2: ______________________________

Step 3: ______________________________

Protect Everything: The Five Policies You Can't Live Without

Health Insurance

Health insurance for you and your family is an absolute must these days. Fifty-one percent of the bankruptcies in this country are due to overburdened families struggling with medical debt. Although many working women are covered, the employees' share of the premiums is definitely on the rise.

Make sure you are using the health-care plan that makes sense for your family's needs. Work closely with your benefits department if you do not understand the different offerings. Make it a priority to attend the heath-care fairs and seminars offered by many companies in October and November, which is typically known as open enrollment season. That's the time when you can change policies. Consider benefits like the flexible spending account described in the Boosting Your Income section, as a way to cover your co-pays and unreimbursed medical expenses.

Buying health insurance on your own is daunting, as self-employed women all know. If you're not covered by your employer or you own your own business, investigate whether your local trade associations, chambers of commerce or local and national professional groups offer reduced rates to members. Also make sure you take the proper deductions on your federal income taxes.

If you are out of work, go back to the box "What Is COBRA?" that appeared earlier.

Life Insurance

"How much do I need?" is always a top question for women buying life insurance. The American Council of Life Insurers recommends five to seven times your annual earnings. But what's right for you can vary widely, depending on how old you are, the amount of your assets, and the ages of your dependents. At a minimum, get enough to cover big-ticket items, like your mortgage and your kids' college tuition. Two Web sites that will give you coverage estimates and rate quotes are www.quicken.com/insurance and www.accuquote.com. Even mothers who don't earn a dime outside the home should be covered. If you're a stay-at-home mom, think what it would take for your husband to pay for the home-keeping services you provide.

MONEY magazine's roster of financial experts often recommends term insurance rather than whole-life or permanent insurance. First of all, term is considered pure life insurance, which is why it's cheaper and provides more coverage for your dollar than whole-life. Whole-life combines investments and savings with a death benefit, but the fees and commissions are very high. Instead, many financial pros recommend funneling the money for these big premiums into a mutual fund each month. If you already have whole-life insurance, seek a second opinion from a financial planner or an insurance agent who will do a comparison of which one is better for you: Term vs. whole-life. But promise yourself not to bite if he or she puts on the full-court press to sell you something. Even if it seems like a great deal, do your own homework first. You would not believe how much money people waste trying to buy a better policy. You can make this comparison on your own using an insurance calculator at www.asec.com.

Typically, single women without dependents do not need insurance. However, if someone else has co-signed for your loans, and your assets won't cover the repayment, you should consider term insurance so that your co-signer will have the money to pay off your debts.

Many employees are covered by group life insurance policies, but this may not be enough. Your employer or professional association may offer better rates for additional coverage than you can get on the open market.

Disability

Only about 45 percent of workers have disability insurance through their employer. But think of this: You're much more likely to get sick or hurt and become disabled than to die prematurely. You should have enough disability insurance to replace 70 percent to 80 percent of your salary (most insurers won't sell you more because they want you to have an incentive to return to work). Even if you have coverage at work, it may not be enough. If that's the case, make up the difference with a gap, or residual, policy.

Auto and Home

Don't stay with your current insurer year after year just because it's easier or you're getting a discount as a longtime customer. Shop around for a policy that combines your auto and home coverage. Insurers often cut premiums up to 15 percent if you link the two because it's cheaper to service two policies from the same customer.

Raising your deductible from $500 to $1,000 will shave as much as 20 percent off your auto insurance bill; raising it to $2,000, 25 percent or more. Good grades and driving lessons will lower the hit of teenagers to your policy.

Pay close attention to your credit score too. The higher, the better. If you're not looking too good in that department, look for an insurer that pays more attention to other factors, such as your driving record. Don't forget to ask for discounts. For instance, safety precautions (like buying the Club for your car or installing a monitored security system in your home) can save you another 5 percent to 15 percent.

For the majority of single-family home owners, the most appropriate policy is the HO-3, sometimes called the special policy (in Texas, for some reason, it's known as the HO-B). It insures all major perils, except flood, earthquake, war, and nuclear accident. Ask for *traditional guaranteed replacement cost* that promises to pay whatever it takes to rebuild your home, even if it costs more than the original limits you purchased. Try to find one without a cap. If you rent, make sure you have renters insurance. Your landlord's policy doesn't cover your personal property, whether it was stolen or damaged due to flood or fire.

Insurance Goal: ______________________________

Major obstacles to achieving this goal: ______________

____

What I need to do to achieve this goal: ______________

____

Resources: ___________________________________

Timetable: ___________________________________

Step 1: ______________________________________

Step 2: ______________________________________

Step 3: ______________________________________

Chapter 4

SAVE MORE, INVEST WISELY, RETIRE IN STYLE

Every year my husband and I vow to cut our family's spending and increase how much we save. How often have you put savings on the top of your list of New Year's resolutions? But for way too many of us, those resolutions never see the light of day. Why can't we put away at least 10 percent of our income like the experts recommend?

WHY DON'T I SAVE MORE?

Transforming yourself from a spender to a saver requires discipline, a plan, and a strong conviction that savings will help you achieve financial goals that are more important than having, say, a new pair of killer pumps every season. Frivolous shopping isn't the only reason many Black women have problems building a nest egg. Our salaries are low. Life is expensive. Emergencies happen. Jobs are lost. Soaring medical bills alone account for 51 percent of bankruptcies in America.

All throughout these chapters, I've asked you to identify your financial goals and focus on what you need to achieve them. This time I'm going to do just the opposite. I want you to write down the reasons why you can't save. This should be easy since I'm sure you've repeated many of them to yourself many, many times.

Why I Can't Save

1. I can't save because ______________________________

____

2. I can't save because ______________________________

____

3. I can't save because ______________________________

____

4. I can't save because ______________________________

____

5. I can't save because ______________________________

____

Now that you've gotten these reasons off your chest, it's time to move on. I don't mean to be dismissive of your challenges, but as your financial coach, my job is to help you find ways to sock away as much as you can. So, where will the money come from? If you're still struggling to find enough money to cover the basic necessities —shelter, food, savings, and paying down debt—consider these everyday strategies:

Think about skipping one big expense this year. Postponing your family vacation or waiting to get a new car can jump-start your savings. Seems like a big sacrifice? It is. So make it a priority to find less expensive ways to relax or reward yourself.

Target your next raise as savings toward a specific goal. If you earn $40,000, for instance, a 5 percent raise will give you $2,000. Once you subtract FICA and tax withholdings, add what's left to your home down payment fund.

Hold a garage sale. Your castaways—from jewelry to clothes you no longer wear—may be just what your neighbors are craving.

Dine out less often—and look for less expensive restaurants for your special evenings on the town.

Take a tour of your closets and drawers. How about the clothes you don't wear because they need to be repaired? Wearing a skirt with a different top or adding a blazer is a great no-cost way to spruce up your wardrobe. Also check the labels to see what items you can launder at home instead of sending to the dry cleaners.

Taking a bus or subway instead of a cab or paying parking costs may shave significant dollars off your commuting costs.

Canceling some of your premium cable channels is an easy way to bring down your monthly expenses.

Consider offering your friends and family your services (like babysitting or helping them organize their closets or do their taxes) instead of buying expensive gifts you have trouble paying for.

Go the old change-in-the-jar route every night. Last summer I told my daughter she could have whatever she found in her father's drawers and a few small duffel bags he had stashed in the closet. She gathered up the money and asked a very strong friend to help her take it to the grocery store. Using the coin machine, she netted a cool $350. (Of course, I insisted half go in her savings account. Pay yourself first!)

Fill in your own ways to get extra cash to save:

____

____

____

Put Your Savings on Automatic

Once you've identified some pools of money, the easiest way to save is to put the process on autopilot and deposit your stash where you can't easily get at it. The biggest enemy of savers may very well be the automated teller machine (ATM). Sure it's convenient and easy to use. But that's just the problem. Your ATM gives you instant access to your money any time of the day or night, and the more you withdraw, the less you have left in your savings.

Banks and credit unions offer many types of automatic savings programs. I'm sure you've heard of Christmas or vacation clubs. All you do is set the amount, identify the checking or savings account the money is coming from, and, determine the place where it should go. If your employer offers direct deposit for your paycheck, you may be able to have your salary divided up and deposited into your checking, savings, and other types of accounts.

The Best Places to Park Your Cash

Short-term Goals and Emergency Funds

Planners like Gwendolyn Kirkland suggest putting this money in a money market account (offered by banks or credit unions) or money market mutual fund (at brokerage firms.) Interest rates for these savings vehicles aren't anything to sing about (ranging in the 1 percent to 2 percent range), but the rates are typically higher than a passbook savings account. Plus, your money is liquid, which means easy to access without any penalties.

If you have more than six months' worth of cash, consider certificates of deposit (CDs). The longer the term, the higher the interest rate. CDs are federally insured and carry penalties of up to six months' interest on early withdrawals. What a great incentive to keep your money tied up for saving!

Check your local newspapers for which banks, credit unions, or other financial institutions offer the highest interest rates for these savings vehicles.

Low-risk, Long-term Savings

Some companies offer U.S. savings bond payroll deduction plans. You designate a certain amount of money from every paycheck to invest in Series EE savings bonds. Because you don't get the interest until the bonds are redeemed, you're forced to save the earnings, too. Call your employee benefits department to see if your company participates in this program.

Don't Overlook the Great Rates at Credit Unions

Credit unions operate much like banks, and deposits are federally insured up to $100,000 by the National Credit Union Share Insurance Fund. However, credit unions are nonprofit, member-owned cooperatives whose members share something in common, such as a labor union, college alumni association, employer, or community. Members' immediate family may also be allowed to join.

Since credit unions return profits to their members, interest rates for savings and checking accounts at these institutions tend to be higher than at commercial banks, while fees and minimums tend to be lower. But a credit union may offer fewer services than a bank and it may have more restricted access to ATMs. To learn whether you are eligible to join a credit union, or to locate one near you, visit www.cuna.org or call 800-358-5710.

Saving and Paying for College

College can be expensive, but the investment in yourself and your children is enormous. Just review the Wage Gap Factor table in chapter one if you're not convinced. Every year we read that tuitions are on the rise, but the good news is that most students still attend colleges that charge less than $10,000 in annual tuition and fees. Nearly three-fourths of students attend public colleges and universities.

Counting on your children receiving full scholarships may be wishful thinking. So don't wait until your child's a senior before doing a little college planning. It's never too early to consider all of the alternatives for paying for higher education. You can start by going to www.collegeboard.com.

Two tax-smart ways to save money for your children are through 529 College Savings Plans and the Coverdell Education Savings Accounts. Although you won't receive federal tax breaks on your contributions, your money will grow tax free in these savings vehicles, meaning you won't pay taxes on the gains when you make withdrawals. Plus, in certain states you may qualify for state income tax deductions or credit on your contributions. The money may be used at any school you choose and must be used for qualified higher education expenses, including room and board. You can get great advice on 529 plans at www.collegesavings.org. To learn about the Coverdell Education Savings Plan and all of the federal tax breaks for students, go to www.irs.gov and search for IRS Publication 970 *Tax Benefits for Education.* For more on government-subsidized loans like the Stafford or Perkins Loans, log on to www.salliemae.com; www.nelliemae.com.

Invest Wisely

Mastering the fundamentals of investing isn't as hard as you think. Most of us aren't looking to make a killing, we just want to retire comfortably, travel to our favorite island, and occasionally buy the finer things in life. The sole purpose of investing is to make your money work harder for you than it can by sitting in a passbook savings account or a CD. Building a nest egg that needs to last thirty years or longer is a daunting task if you're only earning 1 or 2 percent interest. Many Black women would love to leave a legacy to their family. Imagine having enough money to live well and still pass on something to your kids.

Real estate continues to reign as the number-one investment choice of African Americans in 2004, reports the Ariel Mutual Funds and Charles Schwab annual study of Black investors. Ariel, based in Chicago, is the largest African American-owned mutual fund company in the world. The company's president, Mellody Hobson, wrote the forword for this section of the book. When asked which is the "better investment"—home improvements or stocks—76 percent of Blacks and 61 percent of whites chose home improvements, while only 20 percent of Blacks and 33 percent of whites chose stocks.

However, in 2003, 79 percent of whites had money in the market versus only 61 percent of Blacks (down from 74 percent in 2002), according to the study.

Investing in real estate can be extremely lucrative as long as you think of rental property like running a small business. That's because most landlords actively manage their real estate holdings. But putting your real estate holdings into most tax-sheltered retirement savings accounts is very complicated and that's why learning the basics of stocks, bonds, mutual funds, and annuities is a must for most retirement savers. I'll discuss more on how to save for retirement, later in this chapter.

One of the biggest money mistakes that Americans make, according to a 2004 *MONEY* magazine study, is trying to time the market by buying hot investments. Unfortunately, the Ariel study found that African Americans are twice as likely to consider "knowing how to time the market" a more important factor for successful investing than "being disciplined enough to invest regularly" or "being patient enough to see an investment through to the long term." It's no surprise that African Americans who did cite patience or discipline as important for investing success are two and a half times more likely to participate in the market than those who believe in the market timing myth.

To learn about investing, check out the retirement-planning seminars offered by your employer. Another ideal place to learn is your local college or community center, but be wary of signing up for or buying anything—investments or advice—from the person teaching the class. He or she should be there to teach and not to sell. If he starts pitching his products or services before, during, or after the class, be discerning about the information provided. Fair warning: Investment sessions held at restaurants are often fancy sales pitches by brokers and insurance agents looking for clients. Do your homework as outlined in chapter two to find a financial advisor or broker who's perfect for you.

The following four Web sites offer easy-to-follow self-tutorials: Black Enterprise's Investing channel at www.blackenterprise.com; Ariel Mutual Funds' Investing 101 at www.arielmutualfunds.com; the Women's Institute for a Secure Retirement (WISER) Savings and Investing channel at www.wiser.heinz.org; and *MONEY* magazine's Investing 101 at www.money.com.

Savings Goal:

Major obstacles to achieving this goal: ____________________

____

What I need to do to achieve this goal: ____________________

____

Resources: ____________________________________

Timetable: ____________________________________

Step 1: ______________________________________

Step 2: ______________________________________

Step 3: ______________________________________

Retire In Style

Who doesn't like to kick back, close their eyes, and imagine a time when your major decision for the day is whether you should go to the mall, visit friends to play bid whist, or spend catch-up time with an old classmate over lunch? Or perhaps your dream life includes carving out more time to help out at the after-school care program at church or volunteer at your local community center. Maybe you want to start your own part-time business selling one-of-a-kind jewelry you love to make or holding parties to sell beauty products.

Whatever you see when you look into your crystal ball, I'm sure it's not more full-time work, dealing with alarm clocks and the daily hassles of commuting, office politics, or complaining colleagues. Even if you love your job and worked hard building up a fulfilling career, most of us hope for a more relaxing life when we retire.

But for many African American women, turning those dreams into reality will be a lot tougher than we imagine. By the time the last of the boomer generation retires, far fewer people will be able to count on fat pensions from their jobs with full health-care coverage. If you were born after 1960, you won't be eligible for your full Social Security benefits until you are sixty-seven years old—and we all know these benefits won't be nearly enough to cover our basic living needs. Fortunately, for most boomers, drastic changes proposed for Social Security won't occur in time to affect us. But who knows what Medicaid will cover, as the program keeps evolving under each new presidential administration?

The Economic Policy Institute reports that 42.6 percent of African American women are covered by pensions, compared 51.8 percent of white women, 43.6 percent of African American men and 57.6 percent of white men. However, fewer than one in five African American women age sixty-five and older received private pensions, reports the U.S. Census Bureau in its 2003 Population Study. The Institute for Women's Policy Research published that same year "Gender and Economic Security in Retirement," revealed that half of all older women with income from a private pension receive less than $5,600 per year, compared with $10,340 per year for older men. The numbers are lower for Black men and women.

According to the 2003 AFL-CIO working-women survey, Social Security provides more than half of retirement income for 80 percent of unmarried older African American and Latina women. And the monthly payouts are paltry, reports the Social Security Administration: $659 in 2001 for unmarried Black women, compared with white women's $740. In addition to making less than men, we have considerably fewer years of service credits for Social Security benefits. That's because women are far more likely than men to take breaks to raise children and to care for family members. In fact, women retiring in 2002 had on average thirty-two years of service credits, compared with forty-four years for men.

President George Bush has advocated that America should be an ownership society and when it comes to your retirement—Guess what? You're already on your own. But for most working Black women, that doesn't mean you're without resources. Knowing how to play the retirement game is an absolute must if you want to be a winner and retire on your terms.

African American Women and Retirement

The 2004 Retirement Confidence Survey showed some positive signs that more African American women are taking charge of their retirement.

- Twenty-nine percent are very confident they will have enough money for basic expenses.
- Sixteen percent are very confident that they are doing a good job of preparing financially.
- Forty-two percent have personally saved money for retirement.
- Forty-four percent have tried to figure out how much money they will need to save by retirement.
- Twelve percent say they think retirement planning takes too much time and effort.

Major Reasons for Not Saving

(percentage reporting selected item as a major reason why they have not saved for retirement)

African American women

- Do not anticipate retiring . . . . .25 percent
- Children will help me out . . . . .7 percent

Current or Expected Major Sources of Income in Retirement

(percentage reporting selected item as a major reason why they have not saved for retirement):

African American women

- Social Security . . . . .47 percent
- Employer-provided Pension . . . . .43 percent

- Money Saved in a Work Plan . . . . .37 percent
- Other Personal Savings . . . . .14 percent
- Support from Children/Family . . . . .4 percent

Source: 2004 Retirement Confidence Survey

DETERMINE HOW MUCH YOU NEED TO RETIRE

In the past, experts felt that replacing about 70 percent of your annual income at retirement would adequately cover your needs. But most Americans don't plan to scale back their lifestyle when they finish working full-time, and in fact many hope to increase their travel, eat out more often, and enjoy the fruits of years of hard work. That will require you to replace 90 percent or more of your income. No wonder a recent AARP survey found that 79 percent of boomers these days plan to work at least part-time for several years after they retire from their current job. Only 25 percent of Black women, according to the 2004 Retirement Confidence Survey, plan to continue working.

Many people talk a good game about saving for retirement, but statistics don't lie. Americans aren't prepared to pay for the life of leisure we read about in magazine stories on retirement. You know, the ones with photos of couples walking on the beach, playing golf, or visiting family.

The problem with the picture-perfect retirement scene is that Black women will more than likely spend a significant part of their retirement alone. Nearly 60 percent of older women in America are single. The 2001 U.S. Census data showed that by age seventy-five, only about one in four women was still married compared to seven in ten men. The statistics are even worse for us. And the reality is that widowhood and divorce can sharply reduce our retirement income.

Divorce expert and certified financial planner Ginita Wall believes that one of the biggest mistakes divorced women make is not including their husbands' pension or pensions in the marital assets. "We always ask for the house," explains Wall. "But then a few years down the line, many of us realize that we can't afford the house and selling it won't always fund our retirement needs." For more on divorce, see the Family Finance section.

But now's not the time for a pity party. No matter how old you are or what shape your savings are in today, it's never too early or too late to start planning for your retirement. Of course, you know that the earlier you start, the more you have to work with. But if you're 45 to 55 years old and reading this book, you still can develop a kick-butt "Invest in Yourself Retirement Plan."

Figuring out how much you need to retire to keep your income at your pre-retiree level is a whole lot easier on the Web. To calculate what you need, go to the American Education Savings Council Web site (www.choosetosave.org) and use its Ballpark Estimate pre-retirement planning worksheet. Your bank, mutual fund company, or brokerage probably also offers calculators on its site. Your benefits counselor, financial planner, or tax preparer is also a good resource to help you do the calculations.

Let me warn you though. Some of these calculators can really produce whopping six-figure numbers in terms of what you need to save. But think of this as you consider how much money you have to save. Let's say you want to amass a retirement nest egg of $500,000. With an annual return of 8 percent, you'd have to save $875 a month to amass $500,000 in twenty years, $545 a month in twenty-five years, and $355 a month in thirty years.

Don't forget to consider Social Security and any pensions you may have from current and past employers when totaling up what will contribute to your monthly retirement income. More on these later.

Your Dream Retirement

What do you plan to do in retirement and where you do want to live? Moving to a less expensive area of the country could free up more cash to travel or to enjoy more evenings at the theater or concerts. Weather and family are two major factors that influence where retirees move. If working is still in the cards for you, think about the employment possibilities and where you want to live.

Perhaps you want to stay in your current home or downsize to a smaller place or move to a town home or condominium if you want to simplify your housekeeping chores. You may want to tap the equity of your home to boost your retirement income stream. Check out the reverse-mortgage-for-seniors information in the

Home Section. Have you considered house sharing with friends and family? Are you open to an active adult community? These complexes may offer cheaper or more expensive housing options than surrounding neighborhoods, depending on whether costs are subsidized and what amenities are provided.

Max Out Your Retirement Savings Plans

When is the last time someone offered you free money? That's just what you get when you put your money into tax-sheltered retirement savings accounts. How do these work? You put money into one or more accounts such as a 401(k) or an IRA, and you don't pay any taxes on earnings or dividends until you withdraw your money, usually when you retire. At that time you may be in a lower tax bracket. How cool is that? But there is a catch—and it's put in place for your own protection. If you withdraw the cash before you're 59 1/2 years old, you must pay income taxes on the earnings you withdraw and you may be subject to an additional 10 percent penalty. But that doesn't mean you can't access your money under the right circumstances.

Now I know all this sounds like a lot of financial gobbledygook—and I'm going to throw a lot more at you. Taking time to become familiar with the terms of these plans is critical if you want to be a more confident retirement saver. Even if you think you know the real deal about these accounts, it never hurts to take a refresher course. I cannot emphasize enough the importance of taking advantage of retirement accounts. To ignore them is like throwing away free money. And trust me, if you're reading this book, you can understand how these plans work.

Know the Terms

Before we get into details, there are two terms you need to understand:

- Contributions—the money you put into the account. In some plans, this money has not been taxed; in others this money has already been taxed by the government. Pre-tax contributions means the money has been taken out of your paycheck before the money has been taxed.

- Earnings (also known as capital gains). This is the amount of interest your account has made on the money you contribute.

Retirement Savings Plans At Work

Employer-sponsored retirement savings plans—401(k)s at private companies, 403(b)s at nonprofits, 457 plans at government agencies—are unbeatable for long-term savings. You invest a percentage of your pre-tax salary in stock, bonds, mutual funds, or annuities and your earnings grow tax-deferred until you withdraw your money.

I know there are Sisters out there who are downright afraid to put their money in their employers' retirement savings accounts. Unfortunately, this fear is keeping many women from taking advantage of this free money deal. Right now only 58 percent of eligible African American workers (versus 73 percent of the total population) participate in their employers' retirement savings plan—even when earnings levels are held constant. Experts are pondering why this is. One theory is that we may need the money to take care of family members outside of our household.

Some Sisters like to blame the retirement plan fiascos at companies such as Enron or WorldCom where employees lost much of their savings as their reason for opting out. What you need to understand about these disasters is that most of the money lost was invested in company stock. The stocks sank when the companies' businesses went under. When this happened, the savings of many workers also went down the tube.

Like all investment portfolios, your retirement savings plan must be diversified in various investments in case any one investment doesn't do well. Even if you love your company or your company stock is the darling of Wall Street, a retirement account consisting of primarily your company's stock is a disaster waiting to happen. We'll go into some retirement investing rules of thumb later on. For now, stay focused on the knockout features of these accounts to see why they are so powerful as savings vehicles.

In 2005, you can save up to $14,000 in these accounts; that number jumps to $15,000 in 2006. For women who have already celebrated their fiftieth birthday, the savings limits are even sweeter:

$18,000 in 2005 and $20,000 in 2006. These guidelines are set by federal law; however, your employer may set lower levels. That's because each employer must meet federal nondiscrimination tests that prevent highly paid employees from being able to save significantly more than lower-paid workers.

Imagine not having to pay tax on all this money. This may be more than you imagine ever saving in a year, but your goal should be to save as much as you can in these types of accounts. "If you can't afford to save the maximum amount, at least put in enough to get your company's matching contribution, advises Cheryl Creuzot, a Houston-based financial planner. "Many large companies and some nonprofits offer a match that's typically fifty cents on the dollar or dollar-for-dollar up to 6 percent of your salary."

Money.com offers a great example of how the match works:

- Your contributions: $3,000 (6 percent of $50,000 salary)
- Employer match: $1,500 (50 percent match on first 6 percent)
- Total investment: $4,500
- Taxes you save: $930 (assuming 31 percent combined federal and state tax bracket)
- Free Money: $2,430 (Employer match plus tax saving)

Your employee benefits department will help you determine what's the minimum you'll need to get the match. Be sure you know the vesting schedule—the number of years you must work for an organization before you become entitled to special benefits—of your plan (typically one to five years from when you first enroll). Although all the money you contribute is yours, you're only eligible to withdraw the match (in case you leave that job, for instance) when you're fully vested in the plan.

Unless your company has rules determining when you must withdraw the money, you may be able to leave it in place until you're 70 1/2. (The IRS doesn't allow you to touch it without penalty until you are 59 1/2 years old.) However, there is a provision in the tax laws, the 72(t) rule, which will let you withdraw earlier without penalty. But before you withdraw – beware. The rules are complicated, so you'll need your benefits counselor or tax professional to help you comply.

If you leave your job before you're 59 1/2, you may be able to keep your 401(k) at your old employer. That makes sense if your old company offers better investment options than your new employer. Two other options: Roll it over to your new company's plan or put the money into a traditional IRA (see below for more on this option).

But no matter what, do not be tempted to tap into this stash. You will be hit with ordinary income taxes and the 10 percent penalty, and you'll lose the advantage of compounded, tax-deferred earnings on the money you take out. Raiding your nest egg in this way even to pay down debt is not a good idea. (For better alternatives, check out the debt section.)

To keep temptation to a minimum and not make any mistakes that could trigger taxes or penalties, do a trustee-to-trustee rollover where the full amount of the check is made out by your old employer to your new employer or the bank or brokerage firm where you've set up your new account. If the check is made to you, your old company will hold 20 percent for tax purposes, which can be recouped when you file your federal income taxes, if you rolled the money into an IRA or another 401(k). The transfer must happen within sixty days if you don't want to incur penalties that will have to be paid at tax time.

A better way to access your 401(k) or 403(b) is through a loan. Most large companies and nonprofits allow you to borrow against your account and repay yourself with interest. Usually the amount is limited to no more than 50 percent of your vested account value. The loan is paid through deductions from your paycheck, usually within a set period of time. But remember, you will lose out on the compounding magic on the money you borrow. And the loan must be paid in full if you quit, get fired, or are laid off.

Some plans allow for qualified hardship withdrawals, though you'll still face a 10 percent penalty and owe income taxes. These usually include buying a first home, college expenses, medical costs not covered by your insurance, or money to prevent an eviction or a foreclosure.

Individual Retirement Accounts (IRAs)
Even with a generous match, according to the retirement experts at Fidelity Investments, the largest mutual fund company in America, your employer-sponsored retirement account probably will only cover part of your needs. As I discussed earlier, many people start saving late in the game or don't save enough to meet their full retirement needs. That's why it's important to take advantage of additional tax-sheltered savings in an individual retirement account.

If your employer does not offer a retirement savings plan or you meet certain income qualifications, you can open up an IRA at your bank, credit union, or brokerage firm. Eligibility is based on income guidelines set by the federal government. You can find them on www.irs.gov, or your financial planner, tax preparer, or the retirement expert at your bank can explain them to you.

Like 401(k)s, a traditional IRA offers tax-deferred growth. Contribution limits for IRAs are $4,000 in 2005 and $5,000 in 2006. That may not sound like a lot, but with compounded earnings you'd be surprised: In twenty years you can amass roughly $248,800 in your IRA, assuming an 8 percent annual return.

Before opening up a self-directed retirement account like an IRA, compare all fees that the institution may charge and be sure you have access to the type and range of investments you prefer. There are two types of IRAs to consider.

Traditional IRAs and Roth IRAs
Traditional IRAs. Contributions are deductible from your federal income taxes in the year that you make them. The earnings grow tax-free until you withdraw your money. You'll pay taxes on what you take out, based on your tax bracket at that time. (Nonworking spouses may also invest up to the federal limit in a spousal IRA and deduct the full amount if your combined earned income is within federal guidelines.)

Like with a 401(k), you will be taxed and will face a penalty if you start withdrawing your money from a traditional IRA before you turn 59 1/2. However, by law, you must start withdrawing money from this IRA in the year you turn 70 1/2.

Roth IRAs. These are basically for higher income earners who exceed the limits set for the traditional IRA. With a Roth IRA, you have to pay taxes on your contributions. Your money will grow tax-free as long as you keep it in your account for at least five years and you're older than 59 1/2 years old when you withdraw it. You'll be charged a 10 percent penalty if you withdraw any earnings before that age, but you can take out your contributions (the money you put into the account) without penalty at any time.

Self Employed Retirement Plans
Set up a self-employed or small business account if you're on your own or freelance. There are several types of tax-sheltered retirement plans for small business owners, self-employed people, and free-lancers. The solo 401(k), simple IRA, and Keogh are the most popular. They operate pretty much the same ways as the ones described above, but the savings potential could be higher. Again, these can be set up at most financial institutions like banks, credit unions, or brokerage firms. As with any self-directed retirement account, compare all fees and be sure you have access to the type and range of investments you prefer.

Social Security and Pensions
Stay current with your Social Security and pension benefits. Face it now. It's going to be tough retiring on your Social Security alone—but when combined with other savings, these dollars can make a big difference in how well you live. By now you should be receiving an annual summary of the Social Security benefits you've accumulated so far. Carefully check these statements: Your name, address, all employers, and the dates you and your employers made FICA payments. (If you are not receiving this statement, call 800-772-1213 or log on to www.ssa.gov for instructions on what to do.)

If you were born between 1943 and 1959, you can collect full benefits at age 66. If you were born in 1960 or later, that number pops up to 67. Each year you wait after you're eligible, your check grows by 4.5 percent.

Some employers provide similar benefits statements—on paper or on your employee Intranet Web site. If this is not available, contact your benefits administrator and see if he or she would crunch the numbers for you to help you start planning. This is especially important if you're only a few years from retirement.

If you are expecting a pension from a former employer, keep the company up to date in terms of your contact information. Also, ask that benefit administrator to determine the amount of payout you should expect.

Retirement Versus College
Think about this: Your child may be eligible for scholarships, financial aid, or loans to pay for college. There are no such programs for retirees. Although it is a good thing to want to help pay for your children's education, you may not be able to foot most of the bill. That's okay. Most families contributing to their children's education pay about one-third of their college expenses. (For the best ways to save for college, see the Savings section.)

Countdown to Retirement

So now that you know where to put your savings for retirement and how to check Social Security benefits, what's your timetable?

35 to 40 Years Old
Save as much as you can and be aggressive. As much as 90 percent of your retirement savings should be in stocks or stock mutual funds. The rest should be in bonds or bond funds. (Remember, keep your company stock to 10 percent of your portfolio.)

40-something Years Old
Keep saving, but ratchet down the stocks and put more into bonds —70 percent stocks vs. 30 percent bonds. Don't tap into your retirement funds, if you can help it. Almost 20 percent of 401(k) participants in their forties have outstanding loans from the plan. This is the time when downsizing and age discrimination increase chances of job loss, which means that the loan would come fully due. Roll over your 401(k) into an IRA if you change jobs. Set your retirement goals using a Ballpark Estimator calculator (www.choosetosave.org) to determine what you'll need.

50-something Years Old
By the time you hit fifty, it's time to save harder to make up for any lost time. Remember, the limits for 401(k)s and IRAs are higher for this age bracket (recheck the limits mentioned earlier). Now your

mix of retirement investments should be 60 percent stocks and 40 percent bonds.

YOUR INVEST IN YOURSELF RETIREMENT PLAN

After reading this section, think about your retirement priorities and what you need to do to retire comfortably.

Retirement Goal:

Major obstacles to achieving this goal: ______________________

____

What I need to do to achieve this goal: ______________________

____

Resources: ______________________

Timetable: ______________________

Step 1: ______________________

Step 2: ______________________

Step 3: ______________________

READY, SET...INVEST IN YOURSELF

Throughout the past four chapters, I've asked you to do a complete emotional and financial audit of your life. Where do you stand in terms of the six pillars of sound money management: Earn, plan, protect, save, invest, and spend? How did you feel during this period of self-discovery? Were you shocked? Surprised? Disappointed? Pleased? Concerned? Content? Uncomfortable? Satisfied?

More importantly, are you inspired to rethink your relationship with money, the roles it plays in your life, and how you can take charge? Your first step may be to pay your bills on time, but always keep in mind the more lofty financial state of mind you want to achieve:

- Financial integrity?
- Financial security?

- Financial happiness?
- Financial serenity?
- Financial peace of mind?

These are rather tall orders for someone who's never thought that she has had two wooden nickels to rub together. Right?

You bet. And yes, you deserve to attain and enjoy each and every one of them.

There's no way you can tackle every one of the goals you've identified in these chapters. You certainly can't do them all at once. You're probably feeling overwhelmed just thinking about them. So take a deep breath. Relax. It's time to set your priorities. Work your way through what's urgent, what's important, what will make you happy, and ultimately, what will help you realize the financial state of mind you crave. You have the tools, you've reviewed the strategies, you've identified the resources you need, and you've established your timetable. What's left? Nothing. Just do it.

If you're an African American woman in your 30s, 40s, 50s or 60s, your time is now. Today is the day you start putting in the hours, the effort and the imagination to rid yourself of money losing habits so you can kick start your financial life into high gear. Wishing and wanting are not enough. Remember: It's all about *your* money GOALS, Girl!

HEALTH

Vivian Pinn, MD

LIVING LONGER, LIVING BETTER: MAKING INFORMED HEALTH DECISIONS

Kendra Lee

WELLNESS: A CONSCIOUS CHOICE

OBESITY AND STRESS: THE #1 THREAT TO BLACK WOMEN'S WELLNESS

12 STEPS TO A WELLTHIER YOU

LIVING LONGER, LIVING BETTER: MAKING INFORMED HEALTH DECISIONS

BY VIVIAN PINN, MD

Not only must we be informed caregivers, we must be 'self-caregivers' giving care to others while daring to nurture ourselves– making health our living legacy.

From my earliest remembrances, I wanted to help the sick feel better and all those dear to me to live forever—so I would never lose them. Ah, the dreams of youth! I couldn't bear to see anyone sick or hurting—and there was a lot of illness around me as a child: diabetes, kidney disease, cancer, and heart disease (thought back then to be the result of indigestion from eating cold beans!). It became clear that my greatest joy came from helping members of my family or even complete strangers feel better.

When I was a teenager my mother's complaints about her pain were not taken seriously by her physician. Instead of diagnosing bone cancer in time to save her life, I watched with horror and helplessness as he sternly and authoritatively treated her with gold shots and oxford shoes for what he decided was a 'posture' problem. While she suffered a premature and perhaps unnecessary death, I learned some painful but invaluable lessons that shaped my life and attitudes. Foremost—that health care providers must pay attention to what we say about our health concerns; that African American women MUST have doctors or other health care providers that treat them with respect and sensitivity, not arrogance and simplistic authority; and, that we really need more health research about women. Such research will provide the answers that can help us determine if Black women are getting the best health care available. If we are better informed, then we can take better care of ourselves, and those around us.

Black women want to know why some of us live long, healthy and active lives, while others suffer from conditions or diseases that result in a poor quality of life or premature death. Black women can no longer passively accept authoritative edicts that we don't understand or that don't seem to relate to our life experience.

If we are better educated, we can have knowledgeable expectations of all those to whom we entrust our health care. Today, the scientific and health care communities are responding to women's health because we are beginning to hold the health care system accountable.

Clinical trials are now designed to include African American women. This represents a significant breakthrough and a concrete way for Black women to partner with science in clarifying the health issues relevant to them. Biomedical researchers seek to answer questions about how the human body functions, what causes it to function well, and how to prevent or cure diseases. Scientists have recognized for some time now that in order for research to apply to everyone, it must include both men and women for sex/gender comparisons and must address the conditions of diverse minority groups so that health disparities can be determined.

It was this desire to make sure that women and women of different ethnic and racial heritage are studied that led to the establishment of the Office of Research on Women's Health (ORWH) at the National Institutes of Health. It is through the policies and programs of this office that we can now learn more about the health and diseases of African American women and determine specific and proven ways to preserve wellness.

As Director of the ORWH, recalling my early dedication to supporting research that would provide more answers to what ails us, it has been exciting to oversee setting a 21st Century research agenda for women's health. For so many years, most health standards had been set based upon what was known about men or about non-minority populations. Ultimately, it is the results of research studies that determine how health care is delivered, how public health policy is formed, and what we can do to stay well. They also give us the information we need to make realistic medical decisions and to understand what we have a right to expect from medical professionals.

Today, African American women benefit from the fruits of studies that have the potential to cure, and prevent diseases. Such a new research agenda presents expanded concepts of Black women's health and addresses the issues of most concern, from the genetic basis of diseases to how behaviors can prevent illness. These studies help us learn how to prevent conditions that can affect our quality of life, minimize disabilities, preserve mental and physical abilities, and help us live longer.

...All is not grim for African American women's health. There are bright windows of hope...

One of the most important health developments in recent years has been the knowledge that we can actually preserve our own health through simple changes in our lifestyles and personal behaviors. We have learned that for many diseases or conditions, there are factors over which we have some control. We can prevent potential health threats from becoming serious conditions that shorten our lives or our ability to live well. And as Black women learn to recognize these major health threats we can begin to adopt preventive health behaviors that will protect us from unnecessary illnesses. Mature Black women can now continue to live their lives as perennials enjoying the same verve, wellness, and pizzazz that they planted in their hearts in their twenties.

The medical and research communities bear responsibility for finding better ways to prevent, treat or cure those conditions and diseases that may affect our minds and our bodies. However, we, as proud and capable Black women, must make sure that we learn about those findings, and use them to make informed decisions to preserve our own health while we spread our love and assistance to those around us. We must become better informed, and then inform others of the *real* facts about living longer and living better. Some say, 'knowledge is power.' But knowledge does not become powerful until we *act* on what we know can improve our health. Recognition of this truth is the foundation of NCNW's "Invest in Yourself" message.

African American women have shorter lives than all American women combined. Deaths from heart attacks are the leading killer of all women, but for African American women at ages 45-54 they are about triple the number for white women, and two and a half times as many at ages 55-64. Stroke and lung cancer are also leading causes of death. While breast cancer occurs less often in African American women, our survival rate is less, primarily because of later detection or deferred treatment. For African

American women, serious chronic diseases such as asthma, arthritis, cancer, diabetes, high blood pressure, obesity, or depression compromise our health.

You can make a difference in your own health.

However, all is not grim for African American women's health. There are bright windows of hope that the NCNW portrait of women in the five targeted cities has brought forward. If we consider the many factors that lead to disparities in health—including education, environment, access to health care, and cultural traditions, in addition to biologic and other scientific contributors, these data demonstrate that Black women are making progress. The question is—how can we learn more about and build on this exciting breakthrough?

There are some very obvious things that women can do to lessen the likelihood of having serious problems from these conditions, beginning with taking time for your health care in spite of all other responsibilities that occupy your time. Taking time to care about yourself can make a great difference in your ability to take care of others! If you smoke, you can quit; if you are overweight or have high blood pressure, you can change your diet to reduce your weight and blood pressure level; and you must make time for daily physical activity in your life. If you are ignoring the stresses of being tired while taking care of professional and family responsibilities, you must reconsider your priorities and develop ways to relax. Learn to take a few minutes for yourself each day, and deal with life circumstances so that your own health is not compromised.

Not only can you set examples for younger girls and women by embracing healthy behaviors, you can also set priorities for living that will prolong your life and the lives of your family members. You can set specific times for your health screenings—such as using your birthday as the time to schedule your annual physical and gynecological examinations and mammograms. You can also participate in research studies that can expand what we know about the health of African American women.

We have come a long way toward improving our individual and collective health and wellness, but a long way is not far enough. We cannot afford to be passive or blind regarding the fate of our bodies and our minds. We must become proactive, insistent with our environment and ourselves and claim our right to wellness. Why should you care about embracing wellness? Because the statistics tell us that it is a life or death choice.

Wellness is a process that demands your ongoing attention. It requires that health becomes one of your core life values. Healthy lifestyles are based upon informed decisions about proven strategies for prevention of diseases and preservation of wellness. Prioritizing wellness means asking questions of your doctors if you don't understand your health issues. Prioritizing your wellness means taking responsibility to be active in community based and national political efforts to improve health policies and health services with related economic and educational efforts. Prioritizing wellness means making informed choices and taking steps that allow these choices to influence every day of your life.

We, as African American women, take pride in being strong, and we ARE! Our historical legacy has been one of caregiving—taking care of everyone around us. However, if we are to continue the legacy of our ancestors, we must commit to becoming INFORMED caregivers. We must realize that if we take care of everyone else—our families, our friends, our communities—and don't take care of ourselves, we will not be able to help those who most depend upon us. Not only must we be informed caregivers, we must be *'self-caregivers'* giving care to others while daring to nurture ourselves—making health our living legacy. This of course will be a radical act, but it is the revolution in consciousness that will guarantee the wellness that all Black women so truly deserve.

Vivian W. Pinn, MD, is the Director, Office of Research on Women's Health at the National Institutes of Health (NIH). She led a national effort to reexamine priorities for the women's health research agenda for the 21st Century, involving over 1,500 advocates, scientists, policy makers, educators and health care providers. Her recent focus has been to raise awareness about the importance of sex and gender factors in basic science, clinical research, and health care.

Dr. Pinn has received numerous honors, awards, and recognitions, and has been granted eight Honorary Degrees of Laws and Science. She was cited by *Ladies Home Journal* as one of the Top 10 Researchers in Women's Health, among "50 Women Who Are Shaping Our World" by *Essence* magazine, and as one of its 16 "Superstars of Medicine" by *More* magazine. In 2004, Dr. Pinn received The Dr. Dorothy I. Height Leadership Award for Carrying the Torch of the Earth Shaker and Dream Maker.

Chapter 5

WELLNESS: A CONSCIOUS CHOICE

"Health is a state of being. Wellness is the process of getting there."

At the dawn of the 21st Century, we, African American women, have an incredible opportunity to redefine our futures. There was a time when you had to grow old to gain wisdom, but thanks to scientific breakthroughs and improved women's health research, we no longer have to delay. This generation of Black women at middle life—ages 35 to 59—has something the generations before us never had: The opportunity to get healthy and stay that way. However, getting the 6.1 million Black women in this age group to embrace a *wellness lifestyle* that will allow us to live to the fullest—physically, emotionally, mentally, and spiritually—requires making a choice, a commitment, and a plan.

I already hear you saying, "Sister, we already *know about our health issues.*" Yes, there *is* a general awareness of what we need to do to be healthy. You'd have to be living on another planet to have avoided the barrage of media messages to get moving, change our diets, put down that pack of cigarettes, perform monthly breast self-exams, or get tested for HIV. However, hearing these messages, and putting them into practice are very different things. And, Sister, we've been talking the talk for far too long. Now is the time for us to stop our health lip service and begin *walking the wellness walk.*

Yes, the wisdom of our mothers, grandmothers, and great-grandmothers lives within us. Because of their struggles, we have countless opportunities that they could never dream of. Because of their perseverance, Black women have emerged as the "just do it" girls of the 21st Century. We are strong—we have to be to juggle kids and career, to balance significant others with family and community caregiving—all while being dressed to the nines, nails done, hair *amazing.* We're resilient, talented, and competent. We teach school, take care of the sick, run our own businesses and major corporations, win academy awards, advocate for peace and the poor—all while facing down blatant stereotypes and discrimination. We take care of business.

Surely women who can handle all of this, look good, and be mothers, daughters, sisters, wives, lovers, and friends must be doing well, too. In fact, according to the NCNW focus groups and survey research, when middle life Black women were asked about their health, 81 percent reported that they were in good or excellent health. This self-reported information differs significantly from the real picture of Black women's health.

While research shows that Black women *in general* may not be doing so well on the health front, when we focus on specific age groups—such as middle aged Black women—a new and different portrait emerges. NCNW began to suspect—based on its interactions with its constituents—that the stereotypical portrait of Black women as broke, sick, depressed, and hopeless was a distortion and only a small part of our story. The organization began to question the countless dire reports about Black women's health, and pointed out that allowing *all* Black women's health to be defined by our weakest link is not only distorted, it's destructive. Since middle life Black women self-report their health status as being at least good, this perception creates a real opportunity for maximizing lifestyle changes.

So following in the grand tradition of Mary McLeod Bethune, the organization she founded has picked up the mantle to explore a new awareness and possibilities for a new generation. *Tomorrow Begins Today* dares Black women to seize the time to value their health, make intentional choices, and chart a path to wellness.

One of the first steps in achieving wellness is to examine what we know, what we are learning about the status of Black women's health, and what we can do about it. In the table on page 133, heart disease is ranked as the number one killer for Black females of all ages, as it is for all American women. But if we segment out middle life Black women ages 35 to 64, we see that contrary to "what we know" cancer is actually the leading cause of death. Heart disease (at 33.7 percent) doesn't become the major cause of death for Black women until we reach age 65 (which is considered old age).

We cannot overestimate the value of knowing accurate age-related health information. Segmenting health data by race, gender, and age helps us focus on our unique and specific health conditions. It can also guide us to change our behaviors and reduce our risks. This perspective is important to all women who are disproportionately affected by one-size-fits-all health solutions.

Leading Causes of Death for Black Females by Age Group, 2001

Rank	Black Females All Ages; Percent	35-44 years	45-54 years	55-64 years	65+ years
1	Heart Disease 28.7%	Cancer 20.6%	Cancer 28.8%	Cancer 32.2%	Heart 33.7%
2	Cancer 20.8%	Heart Disease 15.9%	Heart Disease 21.7%	Heart Disease 26.6%	Cancer 19.1%
3	Stroke 7.8%	HIV 12.3%	Stroke 6.4%	Diabetes 6.5%	Stroke 9.3%
4	Diabetes 5.1%	Unintentional Injuries 8.0%	HIV 4.5%	Stroke 6.1%	Diabetes 5.6%

Source: National Center for Health Statistics, 2001.

The groundbreaking NCNW research also reveals that not only are Black women ages 35 to 59 more optimistic about their health and hopeful about their future, but many of these women have adopted increasingly healthier lifestyles, gained access to health resources, including insurance coverage, and have made conscious choices for wellness in their lives. This is good news. Recent studies confirm that optimism plays an important role in your well-being; it can even help you survive a serious illness or improve the quality of your life in the face of a debilitating disease.

So what does all this mean to you? It's simple. You can work to maximize the education/income/age-related advantages highlighted in the NCNW research and create successful health outcomes for now and later life, or you can do nothing and become a tragic statistic and be at greater risk of a chronic illness or premature death. The key—and it is a crucial one—is to take stock of the various aspects of your life now to determine where you are functioning well and where you need to devote serious attention and effort.

The following Black women's vitalities and vulnerabilities chart was inspired by our focus group research.The implication is that often the things that we identify as our greatest strengths can end up becoming our greatest weaknesses. As you reflect on your current level of wellness, you need to be aware of that paradox. The box, below, identifies some of those strengths and how, if taken too far, they can cause serious damage to your health.

Black Women's Vitalities and Vulnerabilities

Vitality	Vulnerability
Optimistic	Unrealistic
Strong sense of family	Lost sense of self
Interest in health information	We don't know how to ask the right health questions
Strong	False sense of "superwoman" abilities
Positive body image	Don't recognize the health threat of being overweight and obese
"Can-do" attitude	Don't recognize our human limitations
Invincible	The "victim" mentality
"We can handle everything"	"We can't handle anything"
We don't look our age	We feel our age and ignore our bodies' response to high stress

Claiming Wellness as a Core Value

When the sun, moon, and stars align, everything is right with the world. So, too, it is with wellness. When the sum of all your parts—mind, body, spirit—come together as if by some celestial agreement, you've achieved wellness perfection, a sort of health nirvana, if you will. The truth is, however, wellness—the development of your whole self—isn't achieved by some celestial manipulation; it's found within you.

Wellness is the process of becoming aware of and making intentional choices that support your total well-being. Wellness means taking responsibility to create a positive lifestyle that supports the fulfillment of your potential through the balanced integration of the eight key dimensions of life—the social, cultural, physical, mental, emotional, spiritual, environmental, and occupational arenas.

Wellness philosophy once resided on the outskirts of the American sensibility, but today with scientific confirmation of the body-mind-spirit connection, wellness dominates our definition of healthy living. Wellness recognizes the whole person; it acknowledges that so-called physical health is never established in isolation. Seeking and achieving wellness means that you must become conscious of the multiple dimensions of your life and recognize the need to make choices that cultivate your capacities in each arena.

What's the payoff for adopting wellness as a core value in middle life? By balancing and integrating life's competing demands, your general level of well-being will improve. A wellness lifestyle also has the potential to reduce your risk of premature death from preventable, lifestyle-related disease. Research has confirmed that *"as much as 70 percent of all chronic disease in the United States, from diabetes and high blood pressure to cardiac disease and even some cancers can be controlled by timely and sensible changes in lifestyle behavior."*

To live long and prosper requires more than low blood pressure or physical fitness—although such assets will certainly help. Successful living requires a willingness to understand that no matter how fast life is moving, we are human beings and not machines, and it is the healthy interaction between each dimension of our experience that will grant us a satisfying life.

Lessons in wellness are in evidence throughout every moment of our daily lives. Wellness can translate into eating right and exercising or discovering new meaning and purpose in your life from an unexpected source. Wellness can blossom by keeping your mind stimulated through lifelong learning or connecting with a *higher source* through meditation. Wellness can emerge through satisfying work that reflects your interests, values, and skills. Loving and being loved in relationships that satisfy your heart and soul can boost your wellness, too.

The art of living well rests in the practice of being awake, alive, and accountable for your choices and being in touch with your greatest passion and your deepest yearning.

This is why African American women cannot afford to cultivate one single aspect of wellness at the expense of the others. Your challenge in middle life is to increase your wellness quotient by taking a new step every day, because small steps taken consistently will result in the giant steps required to achieve the permanent gains that you seek.

Ready or Not

Instead of taking on the challenge to be well, too many of us are content to define our health in terms of not being sick: *"If I'm not sick, I must be well."* But "not being sick" and "seeking wellness" are two concepts that are often separated by a wide gulf.

Claiming wellness is a new concept to Black women. We're socialized to think that putting our own well-being first is, at best, something that takes time away from performing our obligations and responsibilities, and, at worst, somehow a selfish act. Joanne Banks-Wallace, Ph.D., an associate professor at the University of Missouri-Columbia's Sinclair School of Nursing, discovered this during a hypertension study.

"One of the major components of the study was having women think about what they were doing every day and the impact those things had on their overall health and well-being, particularly in relation to their hypertension," Banks-Wallace said. "The women told us, 'I get up every day, and I do all these things, and you are requiring me to stop and think about what I'm doing? If I think about [all those things], I won't be able to do them. That means that my kids won't have a place to live, and I won't be able to put food on the table.'"

Not only do we buy into this mentality, but our families and friends do, too. One woman in Banks-Wallace's study retired from her job due to a disability. "But [the fact that she had to stop working because of disability] didn't have anything to do with her family and community obligations," Banks-Wallace said. "In fact, they said, 'Good, now you've got more time for us.'"

We have unwittingly accepted the false notion that poor health is inevitable for African Americans. We say: "My grandmother had diabetes, all my aunts and uncles had diabetes, I'll probably get it, too. And if I do get it, I'll just have to deal with it. I'll just enjoy life while I can, because what's going to happen to me is going to happen." Buried within this unconscious fatalism is the unspoken fear that we can't do anything to change the situation.

But we can do something. It is now time for Black women to put their health front and center. We can change our complacent attitudes, and understand that our physical and mental declines and general life dissatisfactions are not solely the product of heredity, aging, or luck. In fact, we must own the truth that wellness is the result of the personal choices we make every day–in what we eat, what activities we engage in, the quality of our relationships, and our ability to deal with life's stresses. Wellness resides equally in the choices we make to cope with our rapidly changing lifestyles and family dynamics. We have clung too long to the outdated myths and stereotypes about our health, aging, families, and soul food. It's time to gain a new perspective that builds on the best of our cultural and our personal values and the best of our new social and scientific knowledge.

To contemplate adopting a healthy lifestyle, you'll need to establish your wellness baseline. The following quiz will help you determine how "wellthy" you really are.

What's Your Wellness Quotient?

Rate your level of wellness on each of the following dimensions on a scale of 1 to 4 (1=never, 2=occasionally, 3=often, 4=always)

Physical Health	Never (1)	Occasionally (2)	Often (3)	Always (4)
I maintain a healthy weight.				
I walk briskly.				
I do muscle and joint strengthening exercises.				
I stretch before and after exercising.				
I feel good about my body.				
I get seven to eight hours of sleep each night.				
I don't catch infectious diseases.				
I heal quickly when I am sick.				
I have lots of energy and don't get tired.				
If I feel sick, I go to the doctor.				

Emotional Health	Never (1)	Occasionally (2)	Often (3)	Always (4)
I laugh easily about my life.				
I don't use alcohol to help me forget my troubles.				

Emotional Health (cont.)	Never (1)	Occasionally (2)	Often (3)	Always (4)
I have no difficulty expressing my feelings.				
When I am angry, I don't lash out at people.				
I don't worry a lot.				
I know when I'm stressed.				
I feel good about myself.				
When I am upset, I try to work through my problems with the help of others.				
I adapt well to change.				
My friends think I'm well-adjusted and stable.				

Mental Health	Never (1)	Occasionally (2)	Often (3)	Always (4)
I am not impulsive and I think about the consequences of my actions.				
I learn from my mistakes.				
I follow directions to stay safe.				
I weigh alternatives when making decisions.				

Mental Health (cont.)	Never (1)	Occasionally (2)	Often (3)	Always (4)
I respond to life's challenges in thoughtful ways.				
I don't let my emotions get the better of me.				
I learn what I can about products before making a decision to buy them.				
I manage time well.				
Loved ones trust my judgment				
I listen to my inner voice and examine my feelings.				

Spiritual Health	Never (1)	Occasionally (2)	Often (3)	Always (4)
I am grateful for the gift of life.				
I make time to connect with nature and the beauty in the world around me.				
I reflect on my life, who I am and why I am here.				
I have faith in a higher power.				
I engage in acts of loving kindness without expecting anything in return.				

Spiritual Health (cont.)	Never (1)	Occasionally (2)	Often (3)	Always (4)
I feel compassion for those who suffer.				
I strive to touch the lives of others in a positive way.				
I make meaningful contributions to my community and the world at large.				
I love and accept who I am.				
I live my life to the fullest.				

Source: Adapted from the "How Wellthy Are You" questionnaire from the Mckinley Health Center, University of Illinois at Urbana-Champaign

Rate Your Wellness

Tally your score in each section. The ideal score for each section is 40. How did you do?

35-40: Terrific! You are aware that this area is important to your overall wellness. You also practice good health habits, setting an example for others.

30-35: Good. But there is room for improvement. Take a look at items to which you gave a low score, and ask what changes you can make to improve your score.

20-30: So-So. You need to change your behaviors in order to lower your health risks.

Less than 20: Poor. You are putting yourself—and maybe those around you—in jeopardy.

Your Wellness Scores:

Physical Health _____ Emotional Health _____

Mental Health _____ Spiritual Health _____

Doing the Denial Dance

When wellness isn't one of your core values, your well-being can often get lost in the shuffle. Roselyn is a classic example of the battle of wills between optimism and realism. Roselyn's doctor found "something suspicious" in her left breast during her annual physical ten years ago, and he sent her to have a mammogram. The diagnosis was "an aggressively malignant tumor" that needed to come out "right away."

In fact, Roselyn said, the technician suggested that she schedule surgery that day. "That wasn't what I wanted to hear," she said. "I was forty, I worked out religiously, and I felt fine. And as far as I knew, there had been no breast cancer in my family." So Roselyn sought a second opinion. When that doctor gave her the same diagnosis, she went for a third opinion. And then a fourth. "I spent ten months trying to find a doctor who would tell me that I didn't have breast cancer, and when I couldn't find him, I tried to find one who would tell me I didn't need to have a radical mastectomy."

Finally her older sister refused to drive her to any more appointments. "She told me in no uncertain terms that my 'foolishness' was going to get me killed," Roselyn said. "We had a huge argument about it. But I finally scheduled my surgery." From the initial diagnosis to the surgery, Roselyn's cancer had progressed from stage II to stage III, and Roselyn is convinced that happened because she was in denial for so long. "I'm fine now, but I would've had a much easier go of it—and a much better prognosis—had I gone for treatment after my second opinion."

Taking a more proactive approach to her well-being helped Patricia, 58, catch her breast cancer at an early stage. A couple of months of unusual exhaustion was a sign to the retired federal government worker that something was amiss. "There was nothing different about my schedule," she said. "I couldn't blame being so tired on work or the kids. But I knew something was wrong, so I forced the issue with my doctor." Her doctor, however, suggested it was all in Patricia's head and told her to try getting more rest.

"He had the nerve to remind me that he was the doctor. He made me mad," Patricia said. "But I wasn't imagining how tired I felt. I know my body well enough to know when something isn't quite right. So I found another doctor and scheduled an appointment with him." Far from blaming Patricia's overactive imagination, the new doctor listened to her concerns. "The first thing he asked me, after looking over my medical records, was if I'd been performing my monthly breast exams. I had been, but hadn't felt anything strange. He needed to do further testing, but he let me know my input was important."

The tests turned up a cancerous lump in Patricia's left breast. After a lumpectomy and chemotherapy, Patricia was fine, and her cancer has not recurred in eight years. "But what if I hadn't listened to what my body was telling me? What if I hadn't gone to another doctor? I hate to think what might have happened. When it comes to your health, you have to take matters into your own hands," she said.

Invest in Yourself

Wellness is both a conscious choice and an intentional action. The choices you make each day, and the actions you take on those choices, can lead to a healthier lifestyle. Making positive choices in the areas of physical fitness, stress, work, relationships, nutrition and medication—and then acting on those choices—can ensure both a sense of accomplishment and well-being.

Embracing wellness is like breaking in a new pair of shoes: They might pinch your toes a little at first and chafe your heels, but you want to wear them anyway because they look so good. After the initial discomfort, those shoes will fit like a pair of the finest kid-skin gloves. Like those shoes, declaring wellness as a value may feel uncomfortable at first, but once you break it in, Sisters, you can strut your stuff.

So how do you confront your patterns of resistance, weak excuses, or longstanding indulgences—I used to be able to eat everything and now I can't eat anything!" How do you get rid of your "poor me" attitude? How do you make wellness a core life value? First, you have to examine your lifestyle choices and activities. Then you must determine what you value, and how you want to live. Finally you must find the support necessary to build the "wellthy" life you want.

You already know that you make time for what's important to you. For instance, if you value quality time with loved ones, you prioritize your family and friends. If you value career achievements, you put in the work to get that promotion. If you value looking good, you find the time—and the money—to squeeze in a weekly hair appointment. That's how it works with your wellness, too. Make the time to invest in your wellness.

INVESTING IN YOUR WELLNESS PAYS DIVIDENDS TODAY AND TOMORROW

Research shows that your actions today can affect you thirty years down the road. So that obesity at age 37 can turn into diabetes at age 67. A stressed out woman of 45 can be felled by a stroke by 75. The 50-year-old who still smokes and refuses to quit can be living with an oxygen tank at 80. But it doesn't have to be this way.

Here are some examples of steps you can take right now that will help you reap immediate results and lasting future benefits:

Quit smoking. Since inhaling her last cigarette, Jeanette, 35, experienced a drop in her heart rate, improved circulation, and a decreased risk of heart attack and stroke. If she continues not smoking, she'll be less likely to contract lung cancer, a Black woman's highest cancer risk, when she reaches age 65.

Change Your Diet. Diane, 40, eliminated sugar and highly refined carbohydrates from her diet, and has lost fifteen pounds over the last six months. Changing her diet and eating smart has helped lower her risk of developing heart disease and cancer, and helped her to manage her blood sugar level better. If she hits her target goal of thirty lost pounds, she can lower her moderately high blood pressure by ten points. A 5 to 7 percent weight loss now is a sound insurance policy for preventing diabetes and its complications—including blindness, amputation and kidney disease—when she reaches 70.

Get physical. Within eight weeks of beginning a walking program, Evelyn, 53, noticed changes in her body. Her love handles diminished and her legs were much more toned. Even better: The stiffness in her knees lessened and she was no longer winded after bringing in the groceries. The changes in Evelyn are real because even small amounts of physical activity can translate into better health. The best news? The Nurses' Health Study found that walking just one to three hours a week can lead to a 25 percent reduction in Evelyn's risk of developing breast cancer over the next thirty years. And daily exercise—combined with a healthy diet—can cut her risk of heart disease and stroke in half.

When you strive to make wellness a core value, it gets easier to create new habits and the boundaries necessary to achieve this goal. This progress, combined with self-care and self-responsibility, is the prescription for living well throughout our entire lives.

When we make wellness a core value, we no longer have to settle for amputations because we haven't been monitoring our diabetes status. We do not have to settle for being so obese that just leaving the house is a challenge, flying is all but impossible, and we're embarrassed to be seen. We do not have to settle for a stroke or brain aneurysm because we skipped our blood pressure medication. And once you've made the decision to choose wellness, good health can be one more glass of water and one less can of soda away. Good health means leaving the car at the far end of the mall and walking, no matter what the weather. Good health is pushing back from the table before that second helping. Good health means being here to take care of the husband, children, parents, and friends we love so much.

Making wellness a core value demands that you recognize the health gains we've made over the past thirty years. For instance, we are less likely to succumb to infectious diseases. There are better treatments for heart disease; there have been large gains in cancer survival rates and other chronic diseases. And our life expectancy at 75.5 years is higher than that of our mothers and grandmothers.

Life Expectancy by Sex and Race

Gender	Race	Life Expectancy
Female	White	80.2
Female	Black	75.5
Male	Black	68.6
Male	White	75

Source: National Center for Health Statistics, 2001.

We must build on these gains, however minimal. We must put a halt to being at high risk of succumbing to the number one threat to Black women's wellness—obesity and stress.

Chapter 6

Obesity and Stress: The #1 Threat to Black Women's Wellness

Sound the alarms. There is a health crisis in our community. We're a nation of fat people—with African American women carrying the heaviest burden of all—and our health is a mess because of it. Sisters, being big isn't beautiful; it's deadly. Obesity and stress are the number one threat to Black women's wellness.

It hasn't always been this way. But for the last twenty years, the percentage of overweight people has been steadily increasing. Incredibly, in the two years between 1998 and 2000, despite growing attention to the fat epidemic in America, the average dress size for Black women *increased* from 18 to 20!

The reasons for this most recent weight explosion among Black women are varied, but include factors such as our cultural values (we praise thick over thin), our sometimes low incomes, physical inactivity, and a fondness for high-fat, low-fiber diets. Physicians worry that obesity is on pace to overtake tobacco as the leading cause of preventable deaths.

Nevertheless, we continue to pack on the pounds, all the while hiding behind insane rationalizations. Instead of acknowledging that we're as super-sized as the McDonald's meals we're eating, we use terms like "big-boned" or "full-figured" or "pleasingly plump" or (my personal favorite) "thick." We say, "My man likes me with a little meat on my bones." We argue that we won't be held to the European ideal of beauty (read: Skin and bones). We flaunt our big, beautiful behinds, saying "J-Lo ain't got nothin' on me," ignoring the fact that J-Lo wears a size 6, not a size 26. We hide behind a—get this—"healthy" self-esteem, which is a great thing to have, but not at the expense of our lives.

Though we've heard that carrying extra weight contributes to heart disease, certain cancers, high blood pressure, diabetes, fibroids, infertility, arthritis, and dementia, scientists don't know why being obese makes us more likely to get these diseases, but the links are there. Too many of us haven't made the connection between being overweight and our health. As NCNW focus groups confirmed, Black women recognize overweight and obesity as a problem—we just don't see excess weight as a health issue. And not making the connection is killing us.

There's no simpler way to put it: Keeping your weight under control reduces your chances of developing illnesses. And there are only two good ways to manage your weight—eat better and start moving. We have to stop thinking being overweight or obese is OK. Being thirty pounds overweight is not OK, because it interferes with your path to wellness. In fact, being Black and obese increases your risk of death by 36 percent; extremely obese Black women have a 60 percent greater risk of death. So understand that I'm not talking about losing weight for vanity's sake or to fit into an outfit for a special occasion. This isn't about how you *look* but how you *live*.

Overweight and Obesity

The American Heart Association defines obesity as too much body fat. Obesity and overweight represent a fundamental energy imbalance—too many calories and not enough physical activity.

Recent studies from the Centers for Disease Control and Prevention and the University of Pittsburgh profiling overweight and obesity revealed the extent of the obesity problem for all women, and offered specific statistics for African American women, who face the highest health risk of any ethnic group.

Increase in Overweight and Obesity Prevalence (%) Among Women by Racial/Ethnic Group

Racial/Ethnic Group	Overweight (BMI ≥ 25)	Obesity (BMI ≥ 30)
Black (non-Hispanic)	78%	50.8%
Mexican American	71.8%	40.1%
White (non-Hispanic)	57.5%	30.6%

Source: CDC, National Center for Health Statistics, 2002

These statistics confirm the obesity crisis in our community and the need for intervention. This is why NCNW has taken on the mission of educating Black women about the dangers of obesity and stress and its role as the number # 1 health threat for Black women as they strive to maintain their present middle life health advantages.

Deciphering Your Body Mass Index

There is a direct association between excess body weight and deaths from all causes in women ages 35-55. When the body mass index (BMI) exceeds thirty, the relative risk of death related to obesity increases by 50 percent. To measure obesity, researchers assess body fat based on weight and height through the BMI, the ratio of weight to height squared. There are four categories of BMI which provides a more accurate measure of obesity or being overweight than your weight alone.

Body Mass Index

Healthy	Ideal Weight	BMI ≥ 18.5
Overweight	20 lbs more than ideal weight	BMI ≥ 25
Obese	25 percent more than ideal weight	BMI ≥ 30
Extremely obese	100 lbs more than ideal weight	BMI ≥ 40

Of course, with a significant number of us having a BMI higher than 25, we've stuck our heads in the sand about this fat-measuring tool. We like to think it's not designed for Black women's bodies. We have discussions, sometimes heated, with our friends about how BMI doesn't apply to us. Before you dismiss the BMI as a tool that can't work for you, your family, and your friends, find out what the BMI really says about your measurements. And pay attention to the experts' debate on this topic.

At the 2005 annual meeting of the National Medical Association, Anne E. Sumner, M.D., an investigator at the National Institutes of Health, questioned whether a BMI below 25 is beneficial for Black women. "Low BMI promotes osteoporosis, decreased muscle reserve, eating disorders, and general dissatisfaction with appearance," she said. She suggested that there might be a difference between the BMI number above which there is an increase in poor health outcomes in Blacks and whites.

Although obesity has increased for all women of all age groups at a minimum of two percentage points per year since 1960, the greatest increase has occurred among middle aged women over the past decade. Data from the National Health and Nutrition Examination Survey found that "life lost secondary to obesity occur…in white women when BMI is greater than 28…but in African American women, a BMI greater than 38 was necessary to show years of life lost secondary to obesity." Research from the American Cancer Society pointed to similar findings, but the point is that excess fat will kill you. A BMI of 27 might be a little bit high, but one of 38 is close to extremely obese (100 pounds or more over the ideal weight for your height).

The BMI is based on your height and weight. As you lose weight, your BMI will change. You can't change your height, but you can change your weight. How do you rate? Calculate your BMI using the chart below.

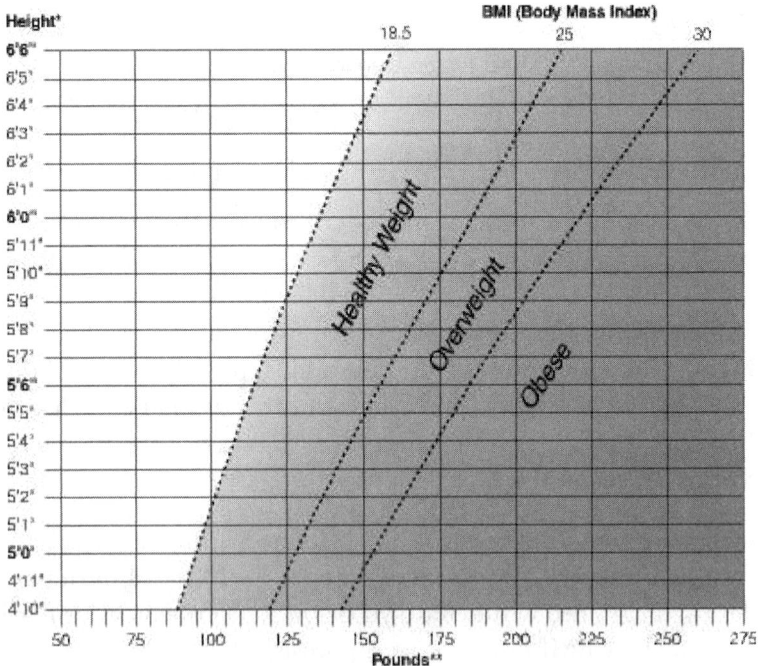

Obesity Causes Excessive Physical Stress on the Body

Obesity plays a major role in causing poor health and premature death in more than half of adult U.S. women who are overweight, and more than one-third who are obese. The life expectancy of women in the U.S. is approaching eighty years, and more women than ever are expected to turn sixty-five in the second decade of the new millennium. The need to establish prevention and early treatment of obesity as a priority is crucial to ensuring a healthy population of women of all ages.

There are many obesity-related conditions that uniquely affect women. Obesity has a direct link to at least fifteen compromising health conditions. Deciding to "invest in your health" by making a few easy, personal choices will reduce your risk of many of these illnesses and health conditions and improve your chances of living successfully today and in the future.

Obesity Risks and Related Health Conditions

Arthritis

Osteoarthritis (OA)

- Associated with the development of OA of the hand, hip, back and especially the knee.
- At a Body Mass Index (BMI) of > 25, the incidence of OA has been shown to steadily increase.
- Modest weight loss of 10 to 15 pounds is likely to relieve symptoms and delay disease progression of knee OA.

Rheumatoid Arthritis (RA)

- Related to RA in both men and women.

Birth Defects

- Maternal obesity (BMI > 29) has been associated with an increased incidence of neural tube defects (NTD) in several studies.
- Folate intake, which decreases the risk of NTD's, was found in one study to have a reduced effect with higher pre-pregnancy weight.

Cancers

Breast Cancer

- Postmenopausal women with obesity have a higher risk of

developing breast cancer. In addition, weight gain after menopause may also increase breast cancer risk.

- Women who gain nearly 45 pounds or more after age 18 are twice as likely to develop breast cancer after menopause than those who remain weight stable.
- High BMI has been associated with a decreased risk of breast cancer before menopause.
- Premenopausal women diagnosed with breast cancer who are overweight appear to have a shorter life span than women with lower BMI.
- The risk of breast cancer in men is also increased by obesity.

Cancers of the Esophagus and Gastric Cardia

- Strongly associated with risk becoming higher with increasing BMI.
- The risk for gastric cardia cancer rises moderately with increasing BMI.

Colorectal Cancer

- High BMI, high calorie intake, and low physical activity are independent risk factors.
- Larger waist size (abdominal obesity) is associated with colorectal cancer.

Endometrial Cancer (EC)

- Three to four times the risk of EC than women with lower BMI.
- Women with obesity and diabetes are reported to have a 3-fold increase in risk for EC above the risk of obesity alone.
- Body size is a risk factor for EC regardless of where fat is distributed in the body.

Renal Cell Cancer

- Associate obesity with renal cell cancer, especially in women.

- Excess weight was reported in one study to account for 21% of renal cell cancer cases.

Cardiovascular Disease (CVD)

- Increases CVD risk due to its effect on blood lipid levels.
- Weight loss improves blood lipid levels by lowering triglycerides and LDL ("bad") cholesterol and increasing HDL ("good") cholesterol.
- Weight loss of 5% to 10% can reduce total blood cholesterol.
- Effects of obesity on cardiovascular health can begin in childhood, which increases the risk of developing CVD as an adult.
- Increases the risk of illness and death associated with coronary heart disease.
- Major risk factor for heart attack.

Carpal Tunnel Syndrome (CTS)

- Established as a risk factor for CTS.
- Four times greater than that of a non-obese patient.
- Found in one study to be a stronger risk factor for CTS than workplace activity that requires repetitive and forceful hand use.
- 70% of persons in a recent CTS study were overweight or obese.

Daytime Sleepiness

- Frequently complain of daytime sleepiness and fatigue, two probable causes of accidents.
- Associated with increased daytime sleepiness even in the absence of sleep apnea or other breathing disorders.

Deep Vein Thrombosis (DVT)

- Increases the risk of DVT, a condition that disrupts the normal process of blood clotting.
- Increased risk of DVT after surgery.

Diabetes (Type 2)

- As many as 90% of individuals with type 2 diabetes are reported to be overweight or obese.
- Found to be the largest environmental influence on the prevalence of diabetes in a population.
- Complicates the management of type 2 diabetes by increasing insulin resistance and glucose intolerance, which makes drug treatment for type 2 diabetes less effective.
- A weight loss of as little as 5% can reduce high blood sugar.

End Stage Renal Disease (ESRD)

- Direct or indirect factor in the initiation or progression of renal disease, as suggested in preliminary data.

Gallbladder Disease

- Established predictor of gallbladder disease.
- Obesity and rapid weight loss in obese persons are known risk factors for gallstones.
- Gallstones appear in persons with obesity at a rate of 30% versus 10% in non-obese.

Gout

- Contributes to the cause of gout—the deposit of uric acid crystals in joints and tissue.
- Associated with increased production of uric acid and decreased elimination from the body.

Heat Disorders

- Found to be a risk factor for heat injury and heat disorders.
- Poor heat tolerance is often associated with obesity.

Hypertension

- Over 75% of hypertension cases are reported to be directly attributed to obesity.
- Weight or BMI in association with age is the strongest indicator of blood pressure in humans.
- Association between obesity and high blood pressure has been observed in virtually all societies, ages, ethnic groups,

and in both genders.

- Risk of developing hypertension is five to six times greater in obese adult Americans, age 20 to 45, compared to non-obese individuals of the same age.

Impaired Immune Response

- Found to decrease the body's resistance to harmful organisms.
- A decrease in the activity of scavenger cells, that destroy bacteria and foreign organisms in the body, has been observed in patients with obesity.

Impaired Respiratory Function

- Associated with impairment in respiratory function.
- Found to increase respiratory resistance, which in turn may cause breathlessness.
- Decreases in lung volume with increasing obesity have been reported.

Infections Following Wounds

- Associated with the increased incidence of wound infection.
- Burn patients with obesity are reported to develop pneumonia and wound infection with twice the frequency of non-obese.

Infertility

- Increases the risk for several reproductive disorders, negatively affecting normal menstrual function and fertility.
- Weight loss of about 10% of initial weight is effective in improving menstrual regularity, ovulation, hormonal profiles and pregnancy rates.

Liver Disease

- Excess weight is reported to be an independent risk factor for the development of alcohol related liver diseases including cirrhosis and acute hepatitis.
- Most common factor of progressive liver disease.

Low Back Pain

- Plays a part in aggravating a simple low back problem, and contribute to a long-lasting or recurring condition.

- Large waist size is risk factor for low back pain.

Obstetric and Gynecologic Complications

- Women with severe obesity have a menstrual disturbance rate three times higher than that of women with normal weight.
- High pre-pregnancy weight is associated with an increased risk during pregnancy of hypertension, gestational diabetes, urinary infection, Cesarean section and toxemia.
- Reportedly associated with the increased incidence of overdue births, induced labor and longer labors.
- Higher incidence of blood loss during delivery, infection and wound complication after surgery, and more Cesarean deliveries.
- Complications after childbirth associated with obesity include an increased risk of endometrial infection and inflammation, urinary tract infection and urinary incontinence.

Pain

- Bodily pain is a prevalent problem among persons with obesity.
- Greater disability, due to bodily pain, has been reported by persons with obesity compared to persons with other chronic medical conditions.
- Known to be associated with musculoskeletal or joint-related pain.
- Foot pain located at the heel, known as Sever's disease, is commonly associated with obesity.

Pancreatitis

- Predictive factor of outcome in acute pancreatitis.
- Found to have a higher body-fat percentage and larger waist size than patients with mild pancreatitis.

Sleep Apnea

- Most significant risk factor for obstructive sleep apnea.

- 12 to 30-fold higher incidence of obstructive sleep apnea among morbidly obese patients compared to the general population.
- Among patients with obstructive sleep apnea, at least 60% to 70% are obese.

Stroke

- Elevated BMI is reported to increase the risk of ischemic stroke independent of other risk factors including age and systolic blood pressure.
- Abdominal obesity appears to predict the risk of stroke in men.
- Risk factors for ischemic and total stroke in women.

Surgical Complications

- Risk factor for complications after a surgery.
- Surgical patients with obesity demonstrate a higher number and incidence of hospital acquired infections compared to normal weight patients.

Urinary Stress Incontinence

- Well-documented risk factor for urinary stress incontinence, involuntary urine loss, as well as urge incontinence and urgency among women.
- Srong risk factor for several urinary symptoms after pregnancy and delivery, continuing as much as 6 to 18 months after childbirth.

Source: Reprinted with permission from the American Obesity Association.

Focus on Disease

The chart, above, talks about a number of obesity risks and related health conditions, but in the following section, I'll pay special attention to five diseases—cancer, heart disease, high blood cholesterol, stroke, and diabetes—most affecting the health of Black women at middle life and their connection to obesity. We'll discuss the factors that put you most at risk of developing the diseases and what you can do to minimize those risks.

Cancer

Because cancer affects men and women of all races, it has not always been easy to know the kinds of cancer that affect Black women the most. But we do know that many cancers affect us disproportionately especially in middle life. However, research shows that cancers of the colon, lung, breast, kidney, and esophagus are associated with obesity.

What Is the Risk?

Some studies have found links between obesity and cancers of the gallbladder, ovaries, and pancreas. The causes of these increased cancer risks, include genetics, poor diet, smoking, stress, and lack of physical activity.

Lung. Lung cancer is the leading cause of cancer death for middle-age Black women, accounting for 21 percent of our cancer deaths and has the second highest incidence rate.

Breast. Obese women die from breast cancer more often than other women because their tumors are more difficult to find and more likely to be detected at a later stage. A recent report showed that African American women who have a high BMI are more likely to have an advanced stage of breast cancer at diagnosis. The distribution of body fat may also affect breast cancer risk. Women with a large amount of belly fat have a greater breast cancer risk than those with fat hips, butts, and thighs.

We're less likely to be diagnosed, and more likely to die from breast cancer at 35.9 percent compared to White women at 27.2 percent. And our five-year survival rate is fourteen percentage points lower than that of white women.

Colon. Colorectal cancer is the most commonly diagnosed cancer for middle age Black women, and our third-leading cause of cancer death.

What You Can Do Right Now.

Making these changes can cut your cancer risk by 25 percent:

- Walk thirty to ninety minutes every day.
- Eat fruits and vegetables daily—remember nine servings is the

optimum. Cut back on red meat, and reduce sugar intake.
- Stop smoking.

Heart Disease

Heart disease used to be thought of as a man's disease; yet it is the leading cause of death for American women. Through initiatives such as the Red Dress Campaign, women are getting the message that heart disease is also a woman's disease. In fact, nearly twice as many women die of heart disease and stroke than from cancer, including breast cancer. And obese Black women are at greater risk.

What Is the Risk?
Black women younger than fifty-five have twice the risk of getting coronary heart disease as their white counterparts. This is because of a higher incidence of high blood pressure in obese women—and one-third of all Black women have elevated blood pressure. Also, if you are 20 percent or more over your desired body weight (as many of us are), you are more likely to develop heart disease. Even if you have no other risk factors or behaviors that increase your chances of developing a disease—such as smoking, diabetes, or high blood pressure—you're still at risk.

What You Can Do Right Now:
- Quit smoking. You may want to seek help from professionals; research shows that, though we are more likely to kick the habit than women of other races, we are also more likely to relapse.
- Lose weight. Even losing twenty pounds improves your health outcome.
- Check and control your cholesterol.
- Moderate your alcohol consumption.

Facing Heart Disease: Nichele's Story

A friend told me I had been complaining about chest pains on exertion for maybe a month or so, but I don't remember those chest pains or telling her about them. My M.O. was to push myself physically harder than I needed to. I just pushed through. I thought this is what happens when you're not in shape.

On the day of the Avon two-day walk for breast cancer [in 2003],

I did the first part, and it was fine. In the early hours of the next morning, it was really cold, and we were sleeping in a tent. At 3:30 a.m., I woke up with pretty classic symptoms of a heart attack—chest pains, jaw and neck pain. Generalized shoulder pain. Numbness in my left hand and arm. Nausea. And anxiety, which I didn't realize was a symptom. I said to myself, "These are symptoms of a heart attack, but I'm not having a heart attack."

So I did not seek medical attention. I was thinking everybody was probably asleep. Nobody was in the medical tent at the time. I was in a field in the middle of the night in Maryland. Plus, I didn't think I was having a heart attack, because I had just walked thirteen miles! My mom and dad don't have heart disease. And I was in pretty good shape. I had the mistaken impression that people who had heart attacks were people like Jim Fixx obsessive runners, or corpulent, 500-pound people. And besides, I'm young—I was thirty-six at the time. I had read about how African Americans are at higher risk for contracting heart disease, it just wasn't something that I felt was a pressing risk.

And after going to the bathroom, I felt better. The next morning, I walked ten miles. Though I didn't seek medical attention at the time, I did pledge to myself to find out what was going on. I made an appointment with my doctor and he did an electrocardiogram (EKG). This was about a week after the Avon event. The doctor said, "You're really young and your EKG looks fine. It's probably just gas, but let's schedule you for a stress test."

But I didn't think it was gas. A lot of women just get the gas pills because a lot of doctors don't get that we get heart disease. I'm thankful my doctor at least had the good sense to schedule me for the stress test.

I had the stress test a week later, and it didn't show anything, either—which is typical for women. But I was having pains during the stress test. Since I was having chest pains, the lab staff decided to schedule another stress test. I was in a daze; I was by myself. I was about to walk to the elevator—astonished and numb as I've ever been—and I thought, "I don't know what the hell is going on." I went back to talk to the lab people to ask them to go over what they'd said again. They gave me two options: Wait until the following week for another stress test or get an angioplasty that day. I opted for the angio, which revealed a blockage in one artery.

The working arteries were all pearly. But the blocked one looked crazy; it was all lumpy. So the surgeons put in three stents. I was there for two or three days. And my doctor said I could go back to work right away—half-days. I did, and in retrospect, that was a bad idea. It took a week for my brain to catch up to what was going on with my body. I was thinking, "Can you get fired for being a fitness magazine editor and having heart problems?" And I knew I was overweight. I'd gained twenty pounds during that last year.

My doctor said I had to lose weight, but he wasn't really firm about the diet. I'm not sure if that's because he thought I wasn't going to change it anyway or if it was because my diet wasn't all that bad to begin with. I asked him if I needed to do rehab, and he said, "Yeah, if you want." I was a little surprised he didn't recommend rehab more strongly. But since then I've discovered stats that say women, particularly Black women, don't get rehab as often as white men.

The Nightmare Continues

About eight months later, I started working out much more—cardio and lifting. One afternoon I ran thirty minutes on the treadmill and went back to work. Then I went to dinner with a friend. Then I went to see a guy I was dating, and that night I started feeling chest pains. They were a mild version of what I'd felt earlier that year. I had a nitroglycerin spray with me. It didn't give me a lot of relief, so I went to the hospital. I told them emergency room staff that I was having chest pains—which is the magic phrase. I tell anybody, if they think they're having a heart attack but their symptoms aren't the classic ones , say, "I'm having chest pains." They admitted me immediately and checked me out. After an overnight stay, they did another angioplasty and discovered a blockage in another artery that hadn't been there in the spring. So I got three more stents.

Life Goes On, Only Different

It turns out, my heart problem stems from elevated cholesterol. I'm genetically predisposed to elevated cholesterol. A genetic problem, weight gain, and stress. The genetic problem was always going to be there, but if the weight gain and the stress hadn't happened, I probably wouldn't have known about the genetic issue.

No one has ever said it, but I can imagine people are thinking, "You were one of the most fit people, the most active people I knew, and then you end up with a heart problem? I ain't even bothering." In many ways I'm lucky this surfaced, because if I had not been in the shape I was in, I may not have seen this problem for another five years, and it may not have been after a thirteen-mile walk. It may have been in the middle of the night, and I may not have awakened from it. Being somewhat fit helped in the recovery and in ameliorating the symptoms.

So I've made changes. I try to eat more vegetables. I can't take birth control pills anymore. I won't say I exercise as much as I should, but exercise is more important and losing weight is more important. I also take fish oil tablets. I asked my doctor about it, and he said, "Yeah, that's not a bad idea." He also said it wouldn't be a bad idea if I became a vegetarian. He was kind of vague about the lifestyle changes. But I know my changes ought to be weight loss and weight management.

I also stopped working at a stressful job. I started concentrating on dealing with stress better. And I'm taking a bunch of drugs, including Plavix, which makes me bruise really easily.

And I joined WomenHeart: The National Coalition for Women with Heart Disease (www.womenheart.org). Joining that was really good for my physical and mental health, because I was able to talk to other women who are in my situation. I was also able to speak at events nationwide, help other women avoid getting heart disease or live with heart disease in a more informed way.

There's more: What I didn't know was that depression—for which I've been treated since 1997, because I was going through a divorce—increases your risk for heart disease. I can attribute my weight gain to depression, but no one told me I'd better be careful on the heart front. No one ever told me about the link between heart disease and depression. There's a lot of anecdotal evidence that having heart disease can lead to depression but not the reverse. Even my doctor says there's less info out there about the causal relationship depression has on heart disease.

HIGH BLOOD CHOLESTEROL

Cholesterol, the waxy fatlike substance found naturally in your body, can clog your arteries, putting you at increased risk of a heart attack or stroke.

What Is the Risk?

Just being a woman past age 45 puts you at increased risk of high cholesterol—which one in four women has—as does carrying extra weight. High levels of low-density lipoprotein (LDL) cholesterol, the bad cholesterol, raise the risk for women.

What You Can Do Right Now:

- Limit your cholesterol intake to 300 milligrams per day if you're healthy, less if you've been told you have high cholesterol or heart disease.
- Do your cholesterol homework. Know your good and bad cholesterol numbers. Saturated fats (found mostly in food that comes from animals, though the content in palm oil, palm kernel oil, and coconut oil is fairly high, as well) raises blood cholesterol the most.
- Learn which foods—such as ribs, chit'lins, oxtail, and egg yolks—are the most dangerous on the cholesterol front and avoid them.

AM I HAVING A HEART ATTACK?

Women don't always experience the "classic" heart attack symptoms—crushing chest pressure, pain shooting down the left arm—that men do. Warning signs in women include:

- *Unusual fatigue.*
- *Unusual shortness of breath.*
- *Nausea.*
- *Dizziness.*
- *Lower-chest discomfort.*
- *Back pain.*
- *Pain spreading to the shoulders, arm, neck, and jaw.*
- *Indigestion or gas-like pain.*
- *Excessive perspiration.*

What You Can Do Long-Term:

Get your cholesterol measured every five years. If your cholesterol level is high, or you are at risk of developing high cholesterol you'll need more frequent testing.

Stroke

A stroke occurs when a blood vessel, which carries oxygen and nutrients to the brain, is either blocked by a clot or bursts in an artery, preventing oxygen from getting to the brain.

What Is the Risk?

Every forty-five seconds someone in this country suffers a stroke. More often than not, that person is Black. We are two times as likely to suffer a stroke as white people. We are also 1.8 times more likely to die of stroke. Though age is a factor (being older than fifty-five is its own risk factor), younger African Americans, those 35 to 54, are four times more likely to die from the disease than whites the same ages. In addition to age and obesity, other stroke risk factors include heart disease, high blood pressure, diabetes, and sickle cell anemia. The more risk factors you have, the more likely it is you'll suffer a stroke.

What You Can Do Right Now:

Know the symptoms of stroke:

- Sudden numbness or weakness of the face, arm, or leg, especially if it's located on one side of the body.
- Sudden confusion, trouble speaking or understanding.
- Sudden trouble seeing.
- Sudden dizziness, loss of balance or coordination.
- Sudden severe headache with no known cause.
- Brief loss of consciousness.
- Sudden nausea associated with a headache.

Get your blood pressure checked. If it's high, moderate daily activity can reduce it. In addition, a study published in the January 2005 *American Journal of Hypertension* found that stress-reduction techniques, including meditation, may lower high blood pressure. You should also adopt the Dietary Approaches to Stop Hypertension (DASH) eating plan—which emphasizes eating fiber (35 grams per day), fruits, and vegetables—and decrease your daily intake of salt.

Diabetes

Diabetes is a disease in which the body does not produce or properly use insulin, a hormone your body needs to convert suger, starches and other food into energy. In Type 2 diabetes, the body either doesn't produce enough insulin or the cells ignore insulin. In Type 1 diabetes, usually diagnosed in children and young adults, the body doesn't produce insulin at all.

What Is Your Risk?

The fourth leading cause of death for all Black women, and at age 55 and older, as we age, it becomes the third leading cause of death for Black women. Black women's risk is increased due to high blood pressure, high cholesterol, and obesity. One of the more troubling aspects of the disease is that, while the number of us it affects is significant, we are often not aware we have it until we develop one or more of its life-threatening complications—kidney failure, amputations, blindness, and heart disease. There is no cure. But lifestyle changes reduce the risk of diabetes by 58 percent.

What You Can Do Right Now:

- If you are 45 or older, get tested for diabetes to determine if you are insulin resistant.
- Start exercising. Obesity, combined with a sedentary lifestyle, can play a major part in the development of Type 2 diabetes. Physical activity and a small weight loss—just five to seven percent—will help decrease your chances of developing Type 2 diabetes and its complications.
- Partner with your physician. If you have diabetes, manage the "ABCs":
- A stands for the A1C test, which measures average blood sugar levels? over the past three months. The test result should be less than seven and the test should be given at least twice a year.
- B stands for blood pressure, which should be below 130/80 and measured at every doctor's visit.
- C stands for cholesterol. The LDL, or "bad" cholesterol level, should be below one hundred and checked once a year.
- Have your triglyceride levels tested once a year. Triglyceride is a type of fat in your blood stream, and your levels should be less than 150mg.
- Take a multivitamin. This helps your body process food better and control your blood sugar levels.

SHIRIKI KUMANYIKA, PH.D.

Professor of Epidemiology
Associate Dean for Health Promotion and Disease Prevention
University of Pennsylvania

HCNW'S research analysis of middle life Black women (ages thirty-five to fifty-nine) found 90 percent of the participants to be free of diabetes. This means that only 10 percent have been diagnosed with this condition. But I don't see that number as low. If you start with the idea that the percentage should be close to zero and look at the percentage of some other groups, then ten percent could be considered high. I'm certainly glad it's no higher than that, because diabetes, once you have it, turns a woman's risk of heart disease into a man's risk. If not controlled, it can also lead to kidney failure, amputations, and blindness. So, it's really important to try to avoid getting diabetes.

According to data from the National Health and Nutritional Examination Study (NHANES), about 20 to 25 percent of women with BMI over thirty will develop diabetes within a 15- to 17-year period. As African American women get heavier, chances of them developing diabetes increase. We haven't seen the full impact yet. I don't want to be an alarmist, but I don't think we're in good shape. That 10 percent is twice as high as the percentage of white women of the same age range with diabetes.

Also, researchers have found that half of the diabetes cases are undiagnosed. In many people Type 2 diabetes onset is a little bit later. People tend to get it at ages sixty to seventy. Ages thirty-five to forty-four are not the highest period of chronic disease risk. So if you're begin carrying a lot of extra weight in your late thirties, diabetes might take ten years to show up

We don't seem to have made the link between excess weight and this disease. The predominant view of diabetes, historically, was the Type 1 that affects thin people. Those were the people you knew had it because you might have seen them taking insulin. One of the reasons many people don't associate diabetes with weight is because they adults they grew up around may have had diabetes and were very thin. The other reason is that some people feel that talking about the disease is giving in to it. It's not the same as denial, but they don't want to be preoccupied with it. So a lot of women with diabetes—with community and family responsibilities—are not catered to or treated as if they have a chronic disease.

Put it in the overall context of how people look at their health, many Black women don't realize the severity of the disease. They know about diabetes—they know something could go wrong and they could take injections or be able to control it with pills. So they may think it's not severe.

In general, the way the medical community looks at the health of the Black community is not the prevailing way in which we understand our health. Most people with diabetes have never taken many classes to understand the disease. Once diagnosed they might get one or two classes; they might talk to a dietitian. But there is not a lot of understanding by doctors about conceptions Black women have about the disease. So it doesn't surprise me that Black women haven't understood/digested the information they've received. Once diagnosed, a physician typically prescribes medication and tells the patient the status of her sugar levels. But the medical community could do a better job of educating not only people *with* the disease but also the rest of the community.

For example, the medical community could provide better information on how to control diabetes. It could learn to spot patients who are less likely to take control and then give them extra support. The medical community could also screen patients more routinely. Without routine screening, it's likely that many people will go undiagnosed.

Black women could also learn more about prevention. The best advice the medical establishment currently knows to give Black women is to control your weight. If we could get more overweight or obese women to lose weight, we'd make significant gains. It's also important to understand how diabetes progresses. For example, the methods you use to control your condition today may differ in five years. We really don't know how to arrest the disease and stabilize it once people have the diagnosis. Again, weight loss is the only thing that seems to help with controlling diabetes. But we don't know if that deals with all the disease's complications.

Prevention and Maintenance

There is evidence that genetics might be partly responsible for our expanding waistlines. Indeed, a University of Pennsylvania Medical Center study found that overweight Black women burn one hundred fewer daily calories than overweight white women. Recent research also reveals that we have much higher levels of ghrelin, a hunger hormone, and leptin, an obesity-related hormone. But blaming Great Grandma Bessie and hard-to-pronounce hormones for our weight problems is another form of denial.

Once we stop denying that many of us need to do something about our weight problem, solving the obesity epidemic really is as simple as watching what you eat and being more physically active. Yet for many of us those two things require a major lifestyle change, and that's not always so simple. We make grand plans to change in a week, get on the weight-loss bandwagon, and then beat ourselves up when we fall off that wagon. That plan is designed for failure. The key is to start smart and small. As you start to make progress, you can always add more intensity to your workouts and make additional dietary changes.

Nutrition Makeovers: Maintaining a Healthy Diet

Telling Black women to eat a well-balanced, healthy diet can be like speaking a foreign language. The standard dietary messages often don't work for us, in spite of the federal government's most recent dietary guidelines recommending that everyone limit fat and sugar intake; increase consumption of fruits, veggies, and fiber; exercise; and lose weight. Officials say that the mypyramid.gov interactive Web site and its increased attention to calorie control and fitness is a direct reaction to the nation's obesity epidemic. This suggests that since African American women are the heaviest, we stand to gain the most from following the guidelines. However, don't attempt a complete overhaul of your diet right away; you're less likely to stick with the changes. Instead, decide your goal ("I'm going to lose twenty pounds") and start by making manageable changes.

Manageable Change #1: Become Portion Savvy

During the first week of your nutrition makeover, commit to cutting your food portions by a third. Over the last two decades, the average American's total daily caloric intake has risen from 1,854 calories to 2,002 calories. *That increase works out to an extra fifteen pounds a year.* Eating smaller portions of food is one of the easiest ways to cut back on calories, but it's also one of the most challenging methods, since "supersize it" is one of today's most-used phrases. All-you-can-eat-buffets, extra-large "single servings" of candy bars and snack foods, and jumbo muffins contribute to overeating. So, too, does piling your plate high at home. Many people think the *kind* of food you eat is more important than the *amount.* This notion troubles many nutritionists who have long questioned the wisdom behind "low-fat" and "no carb" messages, which cast a shadow over the more important concern of total caloric intake. The question is, do you know a reasonable portion of food when you see it?

A good way to understand portion sizes is to translate the more abstract information represented by the serving size into something more easily remembered. Instead of measuring ounces, cups, and tablespoons, compare the serving sizes of particular foods to familiar physical objects. For example:

1 ounce of meat = a matchbox

3 ounces of meat = a bar of soap
(this is the recommended portion for a meal)

8 ounces of meat = a thin paperback book

3 ounces of fish = a checkbook

1 cup of pasta = a tennis ball

1 medium potato = a computer mouse

1 cup of raw vegetables = a baseball

1 pancake = one compact disc

2 tablespoons of peanut butter = a ping pong ball

1 ounce of cheese = four dice

1 average-sized bagel = a hockey puck

1 teaspoon of margarine = a postage stamp

2 tablespoons of salad dressing = an ice cube

Portion tricks:

- Load up on veggies. Weight gain is caused by bigger portions of foods high in fat, sugar and calories, junk foods, and highly refined carbohydrates. So increase your intake of vegetables, fruits, whole grains, and other foods high in water and fiber. You'll fill up before you fill out.

- Don't eat from the bag. Prevent overeating by placing a few chips, crackers, or cookies in a bowl.
- Go single. Buy single portions of snack foods so you're not tempted to keep returning to the whole box.
- Use less. If you like butter and sour cream on your baked potato and cream cheese on your bagel, use one-third less than the amount you usually do. Cut additional calories by using lower-fat varieties.
- Size matters. Use breakfast saucers instead of dinner plates at meals.

Portion tricks for eating out:

- Chose a regular or kid-sized serving. Choosing the kiddie meal, a children's hamburger at your favorite fast-food joint, saves you about 150 calories. Small fries save about 300 calories.
- Order the small soda. It has about 150 fewer calories than the larger ones.
- Share an entrée with a friend when you go to a restaurant.
- Eat your salad first; it fills you up so you eat less of the entrée.
- Order thin-crust veggie pizza, and eat only one slice.
- Ask for half your meal to be packed in a doggie bank, and eat it for lunch the next day.
- Know this: Most people underestimate the number of calories they consume each day, and guestimate appropriate portion sizes. If you really want to come correct about portion control, *practice, practice, practice*—buy a scale and weigh your food.

Payoff: Smaller portion sizes are a direct path to weight loss.

Manageable Change #2: Read Labels

Your goal is to decrease calories, sodium, sugar, cholesterol and fat, while increasing fiber, vitamins A and C, calcium, and iron. During the first week of your new nutrition lifestyle, learn your way around the labels on food packages and record your key discoveries in your Invest in Yourself journal:

1. Check the serving size, which is provided in a familiar unit, such as cups or pieces. Make a note of how many servings are in the package. This influences how many calories and other nutrients you are consuming. If the package contains two servings, and you eat the entire package, you've doubled the amount of calories and other nutrients you've eaten.
2. Next look at the calories, which measure how much energy you are getting from a particular food. Eating too many calories is linked to overweight and obesity, so follow the Food and Drug Administration's general guide to calories: A food equaling 40 calories is low, 100 calories is moderate, and 400 calories or more is high.
3. Review the label nutrients list, which can include fat, cholesterol, sodium, fiber, vitamins A and C, calcium and iron. Make a note of the values in the column titled "% Daily Value." Your goal is to have less than 65 total grams of fat (but at least 25 grams), less than 300 total milligrams of cholesterol and less than 2,400 total milligrams of sodium each day.

During week two of your nutrition makeover, keep a log of how many calories you're eating. In week three, make a note of how much sugar you're ingesting. Week four should be devoted to keeping track of the fat. By keeping track of these things, you'll familiarize yourself with what you're eating.

Calorie-control tips. You can trim at least 100 calories a day easily:

- Drink one less regular soda each day.
- Use cooking spray instead of a tablespoon of olive oil.
- Remove visible fat and skin from meats; better yet, buy only extra-lean cuts.
- Put one less tablespoon of butter on your toast in the morning.

Sugar-control tips. Did you know that an eight-ounce serving of regular soda can have more sugar—and more calories—than a slice of cake? You may have suspected that carbonated drinks contained lots of sugar. But other foods—some you may even believe are good for you (juice, for instance)—contain loads of hidden sugar. Also, when making fat-free foods many manufacturers replace fat with sugar to maintain flavor. And even when a package says there's "no sugar added," if you see any of these words on the ingredients list—

brown sugar, concentrated grape juice, corn syrup, dextrose, fructose, galactose, glucose, honey, lactose, malto dextrins, maltose, molasses, sorghum, sucrose—you're getting some form of sugar.

Payoff: When you're more conscious of what you're eating, you can transform old habits.

Demystifying Insulin Resistance and Metabolic Syndrome

People who have insulin resistance do not use insulin properly, causing excess glucose to build up in their bloodstreams. Genetics are partially responsible for the problem—insulin resistance tends to run in families—as are excess weight and an inactive lifestyle. People who are obese and who have insulin resistance, high blood pressure, and high levels of cholesterol are at an increased risk of developing metabolic resistance syndrome (formerly called syndrome X).

The syndrome works like this: Low-fat foods may be low in fat, but they are typically high in hidden sugars. Years of ingesting all this sugar causes insulin resistance. In fact, metabolic syndrome—also known as insulin resistance syndrome—is a group of symptoms, including high blood pressure, high blood glucose, and obesity.

In addition, being obese, eating a diet high in carbohydrates, and having a sedentary lifestyle can trigger the onset of metabolic syndrome. If you have metabolic syndrome, your cells are resistant to the effects of insulin. This, in turn, increases your risk of developing heart disease and Type 2 diabetes. Metabolic syndrome is the mid-point between normal blood sugar control and diabetes. According to researchers, the syndrome may be caused by nutritional deficiencies. So changing your diet and your lifestyle could head it off at the pass—before it turns into full-fledged diabetes.

What You Can Do:

1. Reduce your sugar intake.
2. Avoid refined carbohydrates, like white bread, white rice, and starchy vegetables, such as white potatoes.
3. Eat more high-fiber, slow sugar releasing foods, such as vegetables, beans, and whole grains.

4. Replace saturated fats and transfatty acids with monounsaturated or polyunsaturated fats. Also, be mindful of hidden sugars in low-fat foods.
5. Get thirty minutes of physical activity each day; it makes your body tissues more sensitive to insulin.
6. Take a multivitamin to help your body process food better and control your blood sugar levels.

Manageable Change #3: Learn to Tweak What You Eat

Contrary to popular belief, you don't have to sacrifice the foods you love for the rest of your life to achieve the optimal diet. In fact, you can still have many of the foods you love. You just have to do a little recipe manipulation to eliminate some of the sugar, fat, and calories. Try these healthy twists on some of the most-popular soul-food dishes:

- Macaroni and cheese—use low-fat cheese and 1 percent or skim milk.
- Greens—use skin-free smoked turkey, liquid smoke, fat-free bacon bits, or low-fat bacon instead of fatty meats.
- Gravies or sauces—skim the fat off pan drippings. For cream or white sauces, use skim milk and soft-tub margarine.
- Stuffing—substitute broth or skimmed fat drippings for lard or butter. Use herbs and spices for flavor.
- Biscuits—use vegetable oil instead of lard or butter, and skim milk or 1 percent buttermilk instead of regular milk.
- Sweet potato pie—mash the sweet potatoes with orange juice concentrate, nutmeg, vanilla, cinnamon, and only one egg. Skip the butter.
- Cakes, cookies, pancakes—use egg whites or egg substitute instead of whole eggs. Use applesauce as a sweetener.

Payoff: When you know you don't have to deprive yourself of good food, you're more likely to maintain your new nutrition lifestyle.

Manageable Change #4: Use Food to Fight Disease

Some foods help fight disease, and you should include as many of them in your meal plan as possible:

- Broccoli. Who knew the little green "trees" could be such

powerhouses? It and other cruciferous vegetables—cauliflower, bok choy—contain phytochemicals that guard against colon cancer.

- Tomatoes. The cooked kind—spaghetti sauce, stewed, juice—have cancer-fighting properties. Seven or more weekly servings also lower the risk of cardiovascular disease.
- Salmon. Omega-3 fatty acids found in salmon and other fish have drawn attention recently for providing protection against heart disease. Recent studies show omega-3 fatty acids may also fight depression. Other heart-healthy fish include tuna, mackerel and sardines.
- Walnuts. If you're no seafood lover, go a little nutty; walnuts pack plenty of omega-3 fatty acids.
- Sweet potatoes and carrots. Yes, your mother was right when she told you to eat your carrots. Yellow-orange veggies and fruits help protect your eyes.
- Berries. They may be little, but their benefits are large. Blueberries, cranberries, strawberries, and raspberries are rich in phytochemicals that prevent cancer, diabetes, heart disease, and ulcers. They also help lower cholesterol levels. Forego the juices and the muffins: Berries are most effective when eaten in their raw, whole-fruit form.
- Beans. The silly rhyme from elementary school had it right: Beans—pinto, kidney, Black, garbanzo and lentils—really are good for the heart. A serving of the naturally fat-free food four times a week can lower your risk of heart disease by 22 percent.

Payoff: Increase your servings of healthy fruits and vegetables and fight disease at the same time.

Make Fitness Part of Your Lifestyle

A federal research study found that 67 percent of African American women don't exercise. Some fitness experts believe that figure is low, however. Keep in mind that even modest amounts of activity can impact your weight and improve your health outcomes. Ideally you should choose something you enjoy doing, that way you're more inclined to continue doing it. Start with walking; you can do it anywhere and at anytime. It's also easy on your joints. Start small.

Don't try to run a marathon if the last time you exercised was twenty-five years ago in tenth grade gym class. Get a partner. And know that you won't see changes after the first day—or even the first week. It takes about eight weeks of regular physical activity to notice differences.

Once you've incorporated physical activity into your life, however, make sure your fitness plan is well-rounded. Incorporate the following suggestions into your routine:

- Cardio. Endurance exercises get your heart pumping and rev up your breathing to build stamina and improve cardiovascular health. Dancing, walking, cycling, in-line skating, swimming, and even gardening are considered good cardio choices.
- Strength or resistance training. These tone muscles, build new muscle mass, and improve bone health. The best program works all of your major muscle groups at least twice a week and includes weight-lifting or resistance-band stretching.
- Flexibility. Stretching exercises, such as trying to touch your toes or doing a side hip rotation, yoga and improve your freedom of movement and flexibility. Do these after your muscles are warmed up.

Ma and Me Workouts: The Importance of an Exercise Buddy

I'll admit it here in print: I hate exercising. I don't hate it for the reasons you might think. It has nothing to do with "sweatin' my hair back," because I do the wash-and-wear style. Time constraints really aren't a factor, either. Though I'm a workaholic with an impossible schedule and often work odd hours, there's a 24-hour-access exercise facility a hundred or so paces from my front door. If I'm totally honest, I have to say exercise bores me. I find nothing even remotely interesting about walking briskly down the sidewalks of my neighborhood. Those boot camp classes with the drill-sergeant instructors make me more angry than motivated. And hike through the woods? With spiders, ticks, mosquitoes, and snakes? Are you kidding me?

So, yes, I need a partner to push me, cajole me, guilt me into getting this jiggly body to the gym. My friend Lynae has a similarly crazy schedule—and an equal dislike of Stairmasters, weights, and walking—so we thought it would be good to pair up and give each other the necessary motivation.

Right idea, wrong person. When it rained, Lynae and I had no problem keeping dry. At home. If I had a rough day at work and wanted to bag the gym, it didn't take much to convince Lynae we should postpone our workout until the next week. Or the next month. On days she was too pooped to do pushups, I'd just as soon crawl into my own bed. And I often did. On the rare occasions we did manage to find thirty minutes to devote to fitness, we frequently congratulated ourselves post workout at the Taco Bell across the street from the gym.

But research shows pairing up with a partner can help stave off exercise boredom and keep you committed to your regimen. Having a workout partner can also make you more accountable: When someone else is depending on you, you're less likely to forego a session. An exercise buddy can give you the push you need to do those last few crunches or climb that last hill. And a partner can act as a "coach" by making sure you're performing your workout properly.

A fitness partnership can even improve your love life. An online survey by the Women's Sports Foundation found 90 percent of women who exercise with their significant others say they experienced greater satisfaction in those relationships, including better sex and improved communication.

Finding a workout buddy is simple. Just ask a friend or family member who shares your fitness goals. That's what I did two years ago when it became clear Lynae and I didn't have what it takes to help each other stay the course. I made the decision to recruit my mom, because I knew she'd be just the pit bull I needed to make me maintain my focus. Now three days a week, rain or shine, tired or not, no matter what excuse I concoct, she's there, knocking on my front door, sneakers on, ready to go, keeping me committed. And you know what? We're so busy gossiping about the latest goings on in the family and at church while we pace ourselves on the treadmill that I forget all about my boredom!

What's My Motivation? Exercise's Impact on Disease

Physical activity not only helps you lose weight and get in shape, recent research shows it can also help you live longer. Moderate exercise for thirty minutes at least three times a week:

- Cuts the risk of developing pre-diabetes.

- Increases insulin sensitivity.
- Decreases blood glucose levels.
- Decreases anxiety.
- Lowers cholesterol.
- Reduces heart disease risk.
- Helps manage stress.
- Lowers blood pressure.
- Improves circulation.
- Relieves depression.
- Improves mobility.
- Increases your energy.

These benefits hold true even for people at higher risk of heart attack and stroke, as Beverly, who has high blood pressure, discovered once she got moving. Beverly thought she was looking cute. But at 5'4" she was tipping the scales at 189 pounds. "I had been wearing a size 14, but when I went to get my usher uniform, I had to get a size 16-1/2, and I said, I can't stand this. I am very vain about some things, and my weight is one. So I decided that something had to be done."

The thing was that Beverly had been walking five miles a day and figured she was in pretty good shape. But a hysterectomy changed all that. "After I had the hysterectomy I gained weight. The doctor didn't tell me that when you have a hysterectomy you gain weight," she said. "I had this little red suit and that was *my* suit. I looked some kind of good in it. It was a size 12, and I got too big for my little red suit."

Pictures of herself also shined a light on her weighty issues: "I looked like a fat black rat," she said. Then a newly slim co-worker told her about Weight Watchers, and Beverly joined. Her enthusiasm for the program hooked other people in her office, and they started having a Weight Watchers class every Wednesday at lunch.

"We learned that it's more than just weight loss," she says. "It's really a health issue. Your pressure goes down. You're not afraid of becoming diabetic. Your cholesterol is lower. It becomes a way of life."

Beverly's life definitely changed. She began to eat healthier, measuring her food and increasing her intake of vegetables and fruits each day. She cut out fried foods and doesn't keep potato chips and peanuts (her weak spot) in her house anymore. And she started working out for an hour and a half four days a week. "I read the nutritional value on the back of the food now. At one time I didn't pay any attention to that. I learned about the transfats and the good fats. I thought if I got down to a size 10, I'd be doing good," she said. Instead, she dropped fifty pounds in nine months and now wears a size 6.

And she's kept the weight off for more than a year. "I'm proud of myself, and I mean, I look good. I'm just as cute and tiny," she says with a laugh. She still has high blood pressure, but it has been under control since she lost the weight, and her energy level is much higher. But maintaining takes vigilance. "I'm not going to say I enjoy it all the time, but I know it's good for my health. Sometimes you get tired. You want to go back to the old habits of eating. But if you start eating like that, it's hard to stop."

When she gets tempted to backslide, Beverly keeps two things in mind: "I can't afford to buy another whole new wardrobe," she says. "Not only that, I'm taking care of God's temple. That keeps me motivated. I want to be around for a while. If you don't take care of your body, anything is subject to happen. It's not just weight loss. It's a health issue. This is my lifestyle. And this is the way it's going to be, with God's help, for the rest of my life. I don't ever intend to go back to where I used to be."

Obstacles to Exercise

Like the best defense attorneys, we can provide all kinds of arguments against working out. Our excuses range from "it's too expensive" to "it's too late for me to get physically active." Below are the best excuses and tips to get over the hump.

1. "I don't have time." Set realistic goals. If thirty minutes of continuous exercise isn't possible, break up the recommended thirty minutes of exercise into ten-or fifteen-minute blocks.

   Multitask. Lift dumbbells while you watch TV. Stretch while talking on the phone. Walk your dog. Kill two birds with one stone: Use a push mower to cut your grass. Get up a little earlier than usual to make time for exercise.

2. "A gym membership costs too much." Walk in the park or at the mall. Run up the stairs at your house. Play volleyball or Frisbee with your kids at the beach. Jog around the track at a local school. All these activities are free.
3. "I don't want to mess up my hair." It's time for a new hairstyle. Try braids or go wash and wear. Purchase a wig.
4. "I hate exercising." Find an activity you like and do it. Don't like running but love to dance? Turn on your favorite dance music.
5. "I can't stay motivated." Change your routine—something new with more intensity—every four to six weeks to combat boredom.
6. "I'm not seeing the benefits fast enough." If you're expecting overnight results, forget it. It took you longer than that to gain the excess weight. To see realistic results, give yourself eight to twelve weeks.

If you find that you need additional help, check out the walking programs developed by these organizations to find (or start) a walking club or a support group: Weight Control Information Network (WIN) www.win.niddk.nih.gov and the Black Women's Health Imperative www.blackwomenshealth.org.

Stress and Obesity

Black women are often stressed but unaware of it. Or perhaps worse, as the participants in the NCNW focus groups stated, "We know we're incredibly stressed, but we accept it as just a part of life." *Stress develops when the demands of your life exceed your ability to cope with them.*

Stress has countless external causes—deadlines, kids and aging parents, overdue car notes and crazed finances, traffic jams, being passed over for a promotion at work. But it is actually caused not by what happens to you, but how you react to it. Stress can be positive (the birth of a child, a promotion, buying a new house, getting married) or negative (trouble at work, illness, fights with your partner, insufficient funds). All of these events make your body react—to fight, to run, or to hold it in.

SPECIAL INSIGHT

KIMBERLY GARRISON
Certified personal Trainer
Owner, One on One Ultimate Fitness, Philadelphia

There is no such thing as one "ultimate workout" for women in each decade of their lives. It depends on what level that woman is when she starts her exercise program. Age is truly a number, and it doesn't necessarily reflect anything. The first thing an out of shape person should do is go to the doctor and get a checkup. A lot of times people jump out there, and they think, "I'm young; I can do this," and they end up injuring themselves, or they have a pre-existing condition and make themselves sick.

Once you've been cleared by a doctor, you should start out gingerly with a walking program. Say, "I'm going to walk for fifteen minutes or thirty minutes, or until I feel fatigued." Then add increments of five minutes until you get up to an hour. Take baby steps. When you feel ready to do a little bit more, work up to a jog. Slow and steady wins the race, instead of crashing and burning—which is what most people do. I say crawl, walk, run.

You have to focus on what I call the fitness square: Cardiovascular conditioning, which is what I just talked about with the walking and jogging. Next is strength and conditioning. That is so important, but women tend to neglect their strength. If you don't have dumbbells, use soup cans or fill up water jugs. But you can get a set of dumbbells for about $10 and work out the entire body. Exercise bands also provide different levels of resistance. The third part of the square would be flexibility, which a lot of people neglect. They just like to run on the treadmill, and then they have tight hamstrings and lower-back pain. Incorporate yoga for flexibility. The fourth component is nutrition, which is where most people fall off the wagon.

Making Your Workout More Intense
If you're using the stairs, run up the steps two at a time, do walking lunges, hop on one leg or change the speed at which

you're taking the steps. Jumping rope is also good. You can do different combinations—jumping backwards, a figure eight, hopping on one foot. If you jog, work up to a run. Anything below six miles an hour is a jog. Once you get past six miles an hour, it's a run.

Also, it's important to understand that you don't have to have gym equipment; they're just bigger toys. Jumping rope is the best single cardiovascular all-body workout you can do. It burns more calories than any big piece of gym equipment, including the treadmill. It works every single muscle in the body. If you did 140 revolutions per minute for thirty minutes, you'd burn 600 calories. It's also low impact. You can get a rope for about ten bucks, and it's portable, so you can take it with you when you travel.

You can do body-weight exercises. Pushups, pull-ups, dips, handstand pushups—these really work the shoulders-and squats. All these exercises can be done using your own body weight. Use the steps in your house. Most big cities have some sort of monument that has a lot of steps; in Philly it's the Museum of Art. Go up and down those. All of these things are available at no cost.

The Missing Fitness Link

I'm seeing more Sisters in the gym, and that's good. That's progress. But I think what happens is a lot of people applaud the fact that they're coming to the gym, and after a while the quality of their routine starts to diminish. So they'll go to a step class for five years, and it's no longer productive. They know the routine better than the instructor. People get in their comfort zone and they stay there. In order to continue to grow, you have to get out of your comfort zone. The point of fitness is to keep progressing. You have to raise the bar. If you're comfortable, you need to change your routine. The body grows through the struggle. For example, if you're trying to lift weights, and it's tough, so you really have to focus, you're making progress.

SPECIAL INSIGHT

What's My Motivation?

We come up with all kinds of excuses. The number one reason is denial. We stubbornly stick our heads in the sand. And we procrastinate. A person can be obese, but she'll say, "I know I'm a little chubby." A little chubby is ten pounds, not one hundred pounds. We also get hung up with the term and say: "Obese. I don't like that word!" Like I made up the word. We don't want to say obese; we don't want to say overweight. We want to come up with cutesy camouflage words. No one is saying if you're overweight you have to hate yourself. But we are saying that you're damaging your health.

We typically put a lot of emphasis on our outward appearance. I'm not saying people aren't entitled to having their favorite hairstyles. People say, "Oh those gyms are expensive." I say, no, a weave is expensive. Having triple bypass surgery is expensive. They say, "You want me to change my eating habits? That's radical!" I say having someone cut you from your neck to your navel to unclog some arteries is radical. Why don't we think that's radical? If doing one more pushup can save your life, let's do that.

I have a client who was doing really well—she'd lost about thirty-five pounds—and then she was diagnosed with kidney disease and had to have a kidney removed. We're the same age—early forties—but she was one hundred pounds overweight. Since her surgery, she hasn't recommitted herself to working out. She has the equipment at her house, but she's not using it. But when I tell you she's faithfully getting her nails done and her hair done.... We often wait until something tragic happens—until it's too late—to get motivated.

We're not making the connection. On purpose. We roll into the office building and take the elevator. Soon we'll all be on scooters. Our bodies are designed for movement. They're like cars. If you don't use the car, it starts to rust. That's what happens to us.

We're doing this stuff at our own peril. It has nothing to do with racism. It's not about money. It's not about where you live. Affluent African Americans have the same health problems as those who live in the 'hood.

To deal with this denial, I get women to think about themselves and that, really, we have to make ourselves the number one priority. A lot of women I train are mothers. They are the ambassadors of health and fitness in their families. I tell them, "You have to be the example. You make the meals healthier and the children are going to follow suit." I make them think about what it's costing them not to do this. I ask, "Do you have the energy to do all the things you want to do in your life?" Once they start answering those questions, they start to think maybe they do need to prioritize. The best thing you can do for your family is to take care of yourself, so you can be there for that family.

When a client comes to me, I first do a fitness evaluation. Then I have her give me goals. Quantifiable goals, not "I want to lose some weight." Are we talking fifteen pounds? Twenty pounds? One hundred pounds? Then we break that down into manageable goals. We shoot for one pound a week. For women who can't do a pushup, we'll start with a modified pushup. Then we work from a modified pushup to a standard pushup. Then we go from one pushup to five, to ten. And then I let them exceed their expectations. I can't tell you the elation that a woman who could not do a pushup feels when she can suddenly do one. Next, I have my clients try doing clap pushups. Once they master these, we're in the bonus round! I keep people motivated by helping them exceed their expectations, and it overflows into the rest of their lives. The confidence blossoms. And they think, "I can do some pushups, I can ask for a raise. I can ask that guy out. I can leave this loser I'm with."

SPECIAL INSIGHT

MARILYN MARTIN, MD

Psychiatrist

Medical Director, Maryland Health Partners

In Search of the Stress-Free Black Woman

The stressless Black woman doesn't exist.

Whether the source of stress is trying to learn a new computer application in order to hold on to a job or from trying to convince your seventeen-year-old that you actually *have* gained knowledge during your years on this earth, stress is a given in our lives. Stress is any demand put on us, whether it is positive—your daughter's tenth birthday party—or negative—an unexpected $450 cell phone bill. It is any demand to which your body or mind has to adjust.

What should be different from decades past, however, is our approach to the reality of stress. Our mothers and grandmothers pretty much resigned themselves to the fact that life would be filled with burdens. They eked out the longest life expectancies they could against tremendous odds. When they could, they "got away" to the beauty parlor or had a friend press their hair. They attended church regularly. But few had the time or resources to deal with internal struggles, such as unresolved grief from siblings lost in childhood or unspoken sexual assaults.

What Black women in this new millennium need to know is that to be truly healthy and to manage stress successfully, we must have an organized plan. This is not to take anything away from our sisters who went before us. In fact, this is one of our arguments against developing a plan. We think, "My mother and grandmother bore up, why can't I?" We need to recognize that they did the best they could and represented us well. We must know that we are not abandoning our past by making new choices. We are, in fact, honoring their contributions and now carrying our people into the next round. Each generation of women should become stronger in their physical, emotional and spiritual, and economic health. Our stress management plans must address this fact.

The Plan

Preparation is the key to successful stress management. We must build into our lives ways we will deal with it on a regular basis. We must also recognize that stress will come from without and from within. Oftentimes, we minimize the stress from within. We may have thought we'd gotten beyond the death of our mother last year until her birthday rolls around this year, and we suddenly find ourselves crying. That's an internal stress that creeps back in for which we didn't plan. Or we find ourselves being angry with our fifteen-year-old son for everything. Then we remember that was the age of the cousin who molested us so many years ago, and we never told anyone about it. We may find stress presents as a headache or backache every month when we are premenstrual and don't handle life's demands as well.

For these and other reasons, we need to develop a plan for effective stress management. Developing a plan does not have to be burdensome, but it should address several important areas:

- *Physical activity is a must.* This may be the major factor that can save our lives, particularly as it relates to chronic illnesses, such as diabetes, heart disease, depression and stress. While brief daily periods of physical activity are most effective, several intense workouts a week are also helpful as respites from stressful schedules. It helps if you begin to think of physical activity as a reward instead of punishment.
- *A support system is essential.* Sisters who live in connection with others live longer and healthier lives than those who

live in isolation. That means giving to others as well as allowing them to give to you.

- *Build relaxation into your schedule.* If you have children, sign up to take a class with them. That way you get to spend time with them, learn a skill together, and teach them the importance of taking care of themselves. Try yoga, tai chi, karate, or meditation classes at your church, school, or local community center.
- *Anger management skills are particularly important.* Many of us never learned how to deal assertively with others. Numerous resources are available to help women learn to assert themselves appropriately without harming others.
- *Time management and prioritizing are a major part of stress management.* Being able to say "no" is a major dilemma for many Black women. Too many of us have found ourselves in the emergency room with uncontrolled hypertension. We try to be nice to everyone else, but say "no" to ourselves too often. We still struggle with differentiating between "self-care" and "selfish."
- *Read all about it.* More and more self-help books are being written by Black professionals who understand the steps to making a difference in your life. These books and tapes can teach us techniques—such as journaling, visualization, and humor—that can help you manage stress.
- *Learn when to ask for help.* There are times when you may need professional help. For instance, if you keep having the same problem with all of your relationships, you are unable to complete school successfully, or you can't keep or advance in your job, a psychologist or other therapist may be able to help you find solutions. Or if you find you think about death all of the time or about hurting yourself or someone else.

With the right plan, we can get stress under control before stress gets us. But before you develop your stress management plan, ask yourself how vulnerable you are to stress. The quiz on page 188 will test your coping skills and indicate areas you can improve the ways in which you deal with stress.

For many Black women who struggle to survive, persistent stress exacts an emotional and physical toll that increases our risk for panic attacks, heart disease, high blood pressure, ulcers, upper-respiratory infections and obesity. Stressed pregnant women can go into premature labor. Long-term chronic stress can compromise our immune systems.

"Black women appear to handle stress somewhat differently from men or white women," says psychologist Angela Neal-Barnett, author of *Soothe Your Nerves: the Black Woman's Guide to Understanding and Overcoming Anxiety, Panic and Fear.* "Black women's stress responses are intriguing; *we tend, befriend, mend and keep it in*.... Strong Black Women will keep on giving even when they should stop. It is as if we feel that to acknowledge we are stressed out or need to rest is akin to giving up our membership in the Strong Black Woman Club.... A Strong Black Woman refuses to admit she's stressed and keeps her feeling and emotions bottled up inside while she helps everyone else."

Overeating is a major response to stress. And research now confirms that there is a direct link between stress and obesity. For many strong Black women, food has become the drug of choice. The fact that one out of every two Black women in America is obese may be telling us something that we don't want to hear—Black women may not be handling their stress very well at all. For many Black women food is a tool for relieving anxiety, frustration, deprivation, anger, and guilt. Many obese women may use food as a way to regain a lost or fragile sense of self-control.

Recent research findings from the Study of Women's Health Across the Nation (SWAN) by Dr. Tené Lewis, a health psychologist at Chicago's Rush University Medical Center, suggests that the stresses of middle age, especially the kind caused by unhappy life events—divorce, ailing parents, and bad jobs—cause weight gain. "Women who faced lots of stresses weighed significantly more than the less stressed. The link between personal trouble and weight gain held up for all middle aged women, regardless of race, income, or education," Lewis said.

How Stressed Are You?

Rate your level of stress by indicating how much of the time each of the following statements applies to you on a scale of 1 (Never) to 4 (always).

	Never (1)	Occasionally (2)	Often (3)	Always (4)
1. I eat three balanced meals per day.				
2. I get seven hours of sleep each night.				
3. I give and receive affection regularly.				
4. I am happy with my career/job.				
5. I exercise at least three times a week.				
6. I do not smoke.				
7. I do not drink alcohol.				
8. I am the appropriate weight for my height.				
9. I have an income that adequately meets my basic expenses.				
10. I get strength from my beliefs.				
11. I regularly spend time on hobbies.				
12. I have a network of friends, acquaintances, and co-workers.				

	Never (1)	Occasionally (2)	Often (3)	Always (4)
13. I embrace change.				
14. I take care of my personal hygiene and am in good health.				
15. I am able to speak openly about my feelings.				
16. I have regular conversations with the people in my house about domestic issues.				
17. I can praise myself and acknowledge my successes.				
18. I set goals and organize my time effectively.				
19. I do not drink coffee, tea or cola that has caffeine.				
20. I make quiet time for myself during the day.				

Tally Your Score.

The ideal score is 70-80. How did you do? ___________

70-80: Congratulations. You are living a balanced life and are prioritizing your physical and emotional well-being.

60-70: Good. You can do even better and reap greater rewards. Example the 1s and 2s that you checked and create an action plan for changing them into 3s and 4s.

50-60: So-so. Make reducing your stress a top priority. Focus on changing all of your 1s and 2s to 2s and 3s.

Below 50: Indicates you are extremely venerable to stress and are putting your health and emotional well-being in jeopardy.

Adapted from the "Vulnerability to Stress Test" by B. Beuermann-King, 2004.

In a recent interview for USA Today, Dr. Elissa Epel, a psychologist at the University of California, San Francisco's School of Medicine, agreed that stress can cause excess abdominal weight gain in women in middle life. This is particularly worrisome because fat stored in the abdomen has been linked to heart disease. "Stress may be particularly lethal after menopause," Epel said. "You just don't crave carrots when you're stressed. You want comfort foods that are high in fat and sugar."

Overeating, as a way of coping with constant stress, won't protect you from it. Instead, it may make you even more vulnerable to life-threatening health problems. Fortunately, you can develop new skills to avoid some stressors and limit the effects of others. You'll be less fatigued, have more peace of mind, and—perhaps—a longer, healthier life.

Athena Rising

Three months into her new job as the public information officer for a major urban school system, Athena fainted before a big press conference. "I have low blood sugar," she said. "And I hadn't been paying attention to how I was eating. It wasn't unusual for me to have a cup of coffee first thing in the morning, and nothing else. I'd carry a banana and yogurt with me with every intention of eating them, but I'd never find the time to eat them."

She was so busy with the job, however, that she didn't attribute the fainting spell—or her inability to schedule time for meals—to stress. Her days typically started at 7:30 a.m. and often ran well past 10:00 p.m. And that was on a day when nothing out of the ordinary—a fire in one of the system's 197 schools, a dead body on school grounds, the death of a student, a teacher-student sex scandal—happened. "I was dealing with everyone from administrators to teachers to students to elected officials to community groups to the press. And on any given day, they could all come at me at once. One year, we lost a student to a tragic death every month. It was a whirlwind. And there was never any consistency or time to plan," she said. It might've helped if her district had more employees; comparable-sized school systems had four employees to handle the job Athena, age thirty-seven, did single handedly.

After a serious bout with bronchitis followed by more of the same two months later, Athena still didn't recognize the effects of stress on her body. "I just thought I wasn't getting enough rest. Stress is so elusive that it can do things to you and you don't realize that it's stress that's causing it. My hair started to gray in patches. Then I started to lose my hair in patches. When my beautician discovered that I had not just lost hair, but it had come out in a perfect circle, she asked, 'Are you stressed?'"

Finally, a breakthrough: Her beautician's observation prompted Athena to assess her life. "I added up what was happening daily," she said. "Not being able to turn my cell phone off. Ever. Going from having just a cell phone to a cell phone and a Blackberry. It's around the clock access to your life. It's your job to respond to crises. That means getting calls at 1:30 in the morning. Teachers fighting teachers. Being called when you're on vacations, at conferences, during illnesses. During all of this, my mom was diagnosed with cancer, and she died. And I worked through her entire illness. I didn't take time off until the last two weeks of her life. And then I went right back to work."

Athena also exhibited other physical signs: "I had asthma attacks. I started getting more headaches than I'd ever had. I had skin ailments and anxiety. I had mood swings, bouts with sleeplessness. And I gained weight, because I never had time to eat anything except whatever someone stuck in front of me, which was usually junk. I started having problems with my eyes," she said. She also found herself spending huge sums of money trying to feel better. "I'm almost ashamed to admit I probably have $10,000 worth of shoes in my closet. Shopping felt good while I was doing it, but when I got home, I didn't feel any differently. It must be how a drug addict feels. You take the hit, and it feels good, but once it wears off, you're looking for the next one."

Four years into the job—a position no one else had ever held longer than eighteen months—Athena started to get angry. "I didn't like having to adjust my life to the job. The job would cause things, and I'd have to make an adjustment. You're supposed to live and the job is secondary. In my life, I was living for the job," she said. So she quit.

"I had to get my life back," she said. And she has. "My hair has grown back. I'm eating properly. I'm exercising. My skin is clear. I have no reason to go to the doctor except for scheduled exams. I left for my life."

Learn Your Stress Triggers and Eliminate Them

Like Athena, you'll have to learn how to recognize what triggers negative stress in your life. You can manage your stress levels by developing a wellness plan that includes the following:

- *Just say no.* Accepting every challenge that comes your way might make you seem invincible, but it comes at a price, usually exhaustion. Use the "pick your battles" theory and start by choosing one thing a day that you won't do, and then don't do it.
- *Learn to delegate.* Share responsibilities and plan what you need to accomplish each day. Don't be afraid to delegate.
- *Eat right.* Poor nutrition contributes to the mental fog created by stress. Make sure you have a balanced diet, and don't skip meals. Limit your caffeine intake.
- *Exercise.* Physical activity lowers stress and boosts energy.
- *Nurture yourself.* Get plenty of sleep, massages, and bubble baths.
- *Change your environment.* Pay attention to your surroundings when you are stressed. Ask yourself what patterns you see—how you felt about a situation and your reaction to it—or take steps to remove yourself from that environment.
- *Take time out.* Find a few minutes each day just for you. Even if you're at work, close your eyes, and go on a mental vacation.
- *Get enough sleep.* Sleep is essential for you to perform at your maximum level during the day.
- *Rest.* Recognize your limits; give up trying to prove your superwomanhood.
- *Avoid conflict.* It is OK to agree with someone—once in a while. Or keep quiet, you don't always have to have an answer or be confrontational.
- *Stay connected.* Make time to keep up with friends and maintain an active social life.

We know that staying healthy can be a struggle, even under the best conditions. And when you throw the troublesome duo of obesity and stress into the mix, you have the ingredients for a toxic recipe that threatens wellness. As we've shown in this chapter, carrying extra weight and being chronically stressed can have a major impact on your physical well-being, as well as your emotional health. But it doesn't have to be this way. We're not asking you to change the world, just learn to make small changes and prioritize your wellness. Just keep in mind that the goals you set to deal with being overweight or obese and to manage your stress are important, but they will take time and perseverance. Learning to live with less stress is a step-by-step process. Don't give up. In the next chapter learn how to recognize the signs and lighten the load.

Chapter 7

12 STEPS TO A *WELL*THIER YOU

It's easy to point the finger at inadequate healthcare professionals, rising insurance premiums, the economy, the political party in power and Black men on the down low for the growing numbers of unhealthy Black women. But we can't blame anyone but ourselves for our sedentary lifestyles. We can't place having unprotected sex at someone else's doorstep. We can no longer proclaim that we're "phat" and fine and lovin' it, in light of the crushing obesity epidemic. At some point, we have to take responsibility for our health. More than 70 percent of the major health risks African American women face as they age can be prevented or reversed by making conscious lifestyle choices and making our health and wellness a priority.

As you go about your plan and develop a "wellthier" lifestyle, one of the things you will notice immediately is when something is going wrong with your body. When you start taking responsibility to stay in tune with yourself—body, mind, and spirit—you stop living in denial.

Do you value your own well-being? Well, if you are like many American women, you haven't set your personal health priorities. You read magazines and listen to news briefs, and like the women in the NCNW focus groups, you readily admitted health is important, but you have neither the time nor the motivation to take care of your health. These sentiments confirm the results of other surveys that say women place a greater priority on the health of their families than on their personal health. Women's inclination to put others first clearly affects their perceptions of their own health status and their perceptions about aging well.

Because African American women refuse to acknowledge that even Superwoman can be vulnerable. We have to stop being in denial about the actual state of our health and stop suffering in silence. We must begin to place a high priority on achieving and maintaining wellness.

Perhaps you don't know where to begin. Just the thought of it may seem overwhelming. That's where this chapter comes in. Over the next year, we encourage you to invest in yourself by taking each of the following twelve steps—one a month—to a "wellthier" you!

Take these steps in any order you want, depending on where you are at this particular stage of your life. What is critical, however, is recognizing that middle life is the time to establish concrete wellness goals and to prioritize your health. For far too long, wellness has eluded Black women. Now is the time to take stock of your life (remember the wellness quiz in chapter five), figure out what you're doing well and what areas need work. In fact, I'll make you a promise right now: Commit to taking one of these steps a month for the next year, and there's no doubt that you're going to be in a much better place twelve months from now.

In this chapter, we'll discuss the following wellness goals:

1. Do your health homework.
2. Establish a relationship with a primary care physician.
3. Ask the right health-care questions.
4. Evaluate your insurance coverage.
5. Schedule health screenings.
6. Get a baseline for sexual and reproductive health.
7. Know your HIV status and practice safer sex.
8. Stop smoking.
9. Lose weight.
10. Maintain your emotional well-being.
11. Get comfortable with your sexuality.
12. Don't ignore the warning signs.

Before you dive in, create an "Invest in Yourself" wellness journal. Write down which of these goals you'll tackle every month and your strategy for accomplishing them. Then track how well you're doing. For example, if "lose weight" is your goal, decide how you'll reach that goal. Be specific: How much weight do you want to lose? How much will you try to lose each week? Your strategy will be to cut 400 calories from your diet each day and to get thirty minutes of exercise three times a week. Keep track of your fitness activities (e.g., brisk walking, thirty minutes) and nutritional intake (e.g., one banana, fifty calories). At the end of the week, note how well you've done. Now let's get started.

1. Do Your Health Homework

Goal: Be more proactive—commit to your wellness. Seek out and evaluate relevant health information.

What you should know: You cannot enjoy successful living without identifying your vitalities and vulnerabilities. In other words, if you skip your homework, you flunk this test, and this test is your life. There is no better time to assess your health status than at middle life, when, as the information from the NCNW research we presented to you in chapter 6 suggests, you still have time to adjust your wellness path.

What you should do:

- Do your research—learn about the health conditions and issues that most impact African American women.
- Find out your real age (take the real age test at www.realage.com).
- Know your blood type.
- Know your blood pressure.
- Know your cholesterol level.
- Know and understand your body mass index (BMI).
- Get a health buddy.
- Ask friends and loved ones to support your wellness.
- Learn how to evaluate health information.

We're in a position to take better care of ourselves because we have access to better health information. Yet we don't always take advantage of that access. Just as we buy fashion magazines because we want to look good, we need to take the same initiative about our health. Listen to health reports on TV and radio, read health newsletters and magazines. Stay on top of the latest developments by signing up for one online health newsletter—a good one to try is from the Black Women's Health Imperative (BWHI) at www.bwhp.org. It's a good starting point for health issues of Black women. Another good general health information resource is www.americanheart.org, the American Heart Association's Web site.

Keeping abreast of health news can be tricky because we're often deluged with information. And sometimes the medical community seems as confused as we are. Today we're touting complex carbohydrates. Tomorrow we'll condemn sugar. A decade ago we targeted fat. Every day we're inundated with health news: Eat more cheese. Lower your cheese intake. Good fat versus bad fat versus transfat. So how do you survive the waist-deep pile of data and determine if the information you're hearing about your health is credible? Consider these things:

- Do you have the same health issue as the people in the study? Health news will be most relevant to you if you are like the people being talked about in reports. If the study includes people the same age and gender as you, that's even better.
- If your information is more than three years old, try to find more recent information to go along with it.
- A good health study should involve a large sample of patients, especially if the illness is a common one.
- Any treatment that promises or advertises one hundred percent success is probably not on the up and up.
- Get opinions on different sides of the issue before making a decision.
- Don't just look for information on effectiveness of treatments, but also for information on side effects. And keep in mind that sometimes forgoing treatment may be better in the long run than having it.
- If a therapy has been used successfully for hundreds of years, it's reasonable to believe that it works. Similarly, a therapy that has been used successfully across several cultures also speaks to its effectiveness.
- Although you may conduct an exhaustive search, there may not be a lot of information or the perfect article for your situation. Sometimes you have to work with the best evidence available.

- Learn how to distinguish between traditional advertising (no matter how hip), advertorials—part ad and part "real people" testimonials— and credible authority-based information.

Rating Web Sites

The Internet—and its easy access to information—has opened a whole different jar of bumblebees. The number of Web sites offering health-related resources grows daily. The information provided by many sites is valuable, but others may have information that is unreliable or misleading. To evaluate medical information on the Web, ask the following questions:

Who runs this site? Good health-related Web sites should make it easy for you to learn who is responsible for the site and its information. Web addresses ending in ".gov" are federal government-sponsored sites. Those ending in ".org" are organization sponsored. If a site ends in ".com," it is typically a commercial site. I've found credible information at www.diabetes.org (American Diabetes Association), www.cancer.org (American Cancer Society), www.nih.gov (National Institutes of Health), and www.bwhp.org (Black Women's Health Imperative).

Where does the information on the site come from? Many health and medical sites post information from other Web sites or sources. If the person or organization in charge of the site did not create the information, the original source should be labeled.

What is the basis of the information? In addition to identifying who wrote the material, the site should describe the evidence the material is based on. Medical facts should have references, for example, to articles in medical journals. Opinions or advice should be set apart from information based on research results.

Is the information current? Web sites should be reviewed and updated regularly. The most recent update or review date should be posted. Even if the information has not changed, you should know whether the site owners have reviewed it recently to ensure it is still valid. WebMD's site, www.webmd.com, typically posts the dates of article updates at the bottom of the page, and the articles are reviewed and updated regularly.

Reward: You know that you can make a difference in your own health. In the words of Dr. Vivian Pinn, when you've done your health homework, "you become an informed *self*-caregiver."

2. Establish a Relationship with a Primary Care Physician

Far too often we wait until there's a health crisis to seek care, and then we have to race to the emergency room for treatment. This is true even for Black women who have health insurance. But using the emergency room instead of building a relationship with a physician you know and trust can have serious consequences, including a lack of access to follow-up care for chronic conditions; fewer routine tests such as mammography, diabetes screening, cholesterol testing, prenatal care, and high blood pressure screening; and limited or no access to medications.

Goal: Find a good primary care doctor for regular or annual checkups. If your obstetrician/gynecologist is your primary care physician, use the time when you're getting your annual pap smear to address other health issues.

What you should know: As you age, more things go wrong with your body. During annual checkups you get preventive care, which catches problems, such as high cholesterol or high blood pressure, before they get out of control and wreak havoc on your body. If you already have a chronic illness, such as diabetes, your primary care doctor will be familiar with you. He or she will know if you have medicine allergies, when you last received a tetanus shot, and your family's health history.

How to Find a Primary Care Physician

Choosing and trusting a doctor can be intimidating. Don't let it be. First, compile a list of names of physicians in your area (or check the list of participating providers on your health insurance plan). Ask friends or relatives if they know a physician on your list who has given quality care in the past. If you've recently moved to a new town, ask your former physician for a recommendation of someone in your new location. You can also try local medical societies; these usually have a physician referral service and will give you names based on your geographical area or the type of physician you need.

Before you make a decision about a physician, however, schedule an appointment to meet with the doctor. It is best to meet when nothing is urgently wrong. This meeting will help you determine whether you are comfortable with the physician, the support staff, and the facilities. Ask the following questions:

- Are you accepting new patients?
- Which insurance plans do you accept?
- At which hospitals do you have staff privileges?
- Are there any limitations on your privileges?
- Do you practice alone, or are you part of a group?
- How many members are there in your group?
- Who provides care for your patients in your absence?
- Will I have long or short wait times when I come to see you?
- Are you board certified? Which board? In what specialty area?
- How long have you been in practice? (Years in practice are one measure of experience, but the numbers of procedures performed and people treated are also important. Also keep in mind that older doctors may have the years of experience, but they may not be as familiar with the latest techniques and advances as younger physicians.)

Obstacles to care: One big roadblock to visiting a primary care physician is fear of the medical system.

Reward: Creation of a healthy doctor-patient relationship, one that allows you to trust and feel more comfortable with your doctor.

3. Ask the Right Questions

Goal: To get all of your healthcare questions answered in a way that you can understand, so that you can make informed decisions.

What you should know: When you go to the doctor's office, do you feel rushed? Do you understand the information he or she gives you? Do you get to ask questions? Does the doctor answer those questions to your satisfaction? Your relationship with your healthcare provider affects the quality of care you receive. The

> **FEAR OF THE SYSTEM**
>
> *For African Americans, mistrust of the medical community can be summed up in three words: Tuskegee Syphilis Study. In the forty-year study, researchers withheld medical treatment from poor, Black men infected with syphilis who died without treatment so researchers could study the natural progression of the disease. However, much has changed since Tuskegee. In government-sponsored trials today, volunteer community advisory boards now monitor safety, and informed consent is required from all participants. Nevertheless, the damage done by Tuskegee has come to symbolize racism, misconduct, and abuse of Black people. The experiment has had long-lasting effects, hindering current efforts to fight diseases such as cancer, diabetes, and AIDS. This fear of the system and physicians has also kept many of us from participating in the medical system and scientific research studies.*
>
> *The specter of intentional minority malpractice was raised again in May 2005. An Associated Press report based on Liam Schef's article "The House that AIDS Built,"*

best relationship is one where you and your doctor work together to make the best decisions about your health.

What you should do: To communicate more effectively:

- Go prepared. The average visit to a doctor's office is fifteen minutes, so you'll need to make the most of the time you have with him or her. Write down any questions you have before you go. Have a list of symptoms you've been experiencing. Also make a list of medications you take, including vitamins, herbs, and supplements. Bring a pen and paper to take notes. If this is your first visit, have your medical records sent in advance. Remember to bring your insurance card.
- Speak up. If you don't understand something your doctor is saying, ask her to explain it again. In a study on high blood pressure in Black women conducted by Joanne Banks-Wallace, Ph.D., at the University of Missouri-Columbia, some of the women knew they had high blood pressure and that it was related to numbers, but they had no idea what the numbers meant.

"They didn't know what systolic meant," Banks-Wallace said. And they hadn't told their doctors they didn't understand. If there are issues you want to discuss that a doctor doesn't mention, raise them yourself. Don't be afraid to push doctors to discuss matters such as weight, stress, diet, sexual practices, insomnia, or substance abuse. Ask if there are tests, such as a mammogram or a colonoscopy, you might need because of your age. Don't leave the doctor's office without understanding everything she said.

- Be honest. The more information your doctor has about you, the better he'll be able to figure out what's wrong and how to treat you.
- Take someone with you. A companion can provide more than moral support. She can remind you of questions you may have forgotten and help you remember what the doctor said.

If a doctor ignores your questions or rushes you out of the office before you've had ample time to address your concerns, find a new practitioner.

revealed that government-funded researchers conducted fourdozen studies inseven states. They allegedly tested AIDS drugs on hundreds of poor and minority foster children over the past two decades. The antiretroviral drugs created questionable side effects and "disturbingly" higher death rates among children who received the experimental higher dosages of medications. Most of these studies were carried out without the oversight of required independent advocates.

According to the experts, one way to combat African Americans' fear of the medical system is through education. The increased active participation of knowledgeable Black patients who hold physicians, researchers, and scientists accountable for providing quality health care and humane research is another way. To ensure that you create the health outcomes you need with your doctor, engage the support of a healthcare partner—an advocate, such as a knowledgeable friend or family member—who knows your health history and who is willing to help you manage your health and make the best wellness decisions.

Questions for Your Doctor

Make a copy of this list, and take it with you when you go to the doctor.

- What is wrong with me?
- What caused this problem?
- Will I need tests?
- What tests do I need? Why do I need them?
- What do the tests involve?
- How do I prepare for the tests?
- When will I get the results?
- Will my insurance cover the cost?
- What are my treatment options?
- What are the benefits of each treatment?
- What are the risks of the treatments?
- Are there side effects?
- What is the most common treatment for my illness?
- What is the plan if the treatment doesn't work?
- Do I need to see a specialist?
- Should I have a second opinion?
- Will I need to take medication? For how long?
- What does the medication do?
- What are the side effects to this medication?
- What should I do if I experience side effects?
- Is there a generic version of this medicine and can I take that?
- Will the medicine interact with other medications I'm taking?
- Are there any activities or foods I should avoid while I'm taking this medication?
- Will I need to schedule a follow-up visit?

Reward: More control over your health and well-being and a feeling of empowerment in your relationship with your doctor.

4. Evaluate Your Insurance Coverage

Goal: Find out your insurance status. How much coverage do you have? If you don't have any—or if the insurance you have is insufficient—learn your options.

What you should know: People with health insurance are more likely to have a regular source of medical care and to use preventive care, while people without health insurance are more likely to have unmet medical needs and to use hospital emergency rooms for routine care. Being without coverage means going without health care when you need it. Yet some forty-five million Americans—22.2 percent of them Black women, one out of every three of us—don't have health insurance. And as the economy continues to fluctuate and medical costs skyrocket (a 2004 study by Families USA found that 14.3 million Americans lost more than a quarter of their income to healthcare costs), experts predict that more women will continue losing coverage that is already sketchy, unpredictable, and expensive. According to the Kaiser Family Foundation, women use the health system in a different way than men and have a greater overall need for health services. We tend to make more doctors' visits and have higher health costs, especially during our reproductive years. We are also more likely to have chronic conditions with fewer financial resources with which to purchase healthcare coverage.

Having health insurance is especially important in middle life. During this phase, many Black women will develop chronic illnesses and have to rely on prescription medications. A Kaiser Family Foundation survey of nearly 4,000 women in 2001 (and updated in 2004) found that nearly 50 percent of Black women in middle life reported having chronic conditions—including hypertension, asthma, arthritis, and diabetes—requiring ongoing medical treatment.

The NCNW study confirms that 82 percent of Black women who are employed full time have health insurance coverage. Research shows, however, that even when we do have insurance, we face health risks because our plans may not pay for needed services, may have high cost-sharing provisions, and may have benefit caps that limit our access to emergency care. The major health insurance vulnerability that Black women face occurs through unemployment, a shift to part-time work, or loss of a spouse's employer-sponsored coverage through divorce or death. In addition, many companies are cutting back on the coverage they offer employees or eliminating coverage altogether. Increasing costs of medical care are making worker contributions to health-benefit plans rise. Individual coverage through employers is averaging $508 per year; families are forking over an annual $2,412. Private insurance can range from $200 to $600 per month for individual coverage and $800 to $1,200 per month for family coverage.

Stephanie, a 41-year-old independent consultant, has navigated without health insurance for more than four years. When she left her last full-time job, she found she couldn't afford the premiums, and insurance took a back seat to paying her mortgage and her other more immediate financial obligations—her car note, the electric bill, and groceries. This means that every winter, she has had to avoid catching whatever cold or stomach flu is making its rounds. "I was always washing my hands. People probably think I'm obsessive-compulsive," she joked.

Last year, however, she wasn't so lucky. All the hand washing in the world didn't keep Stephanie from falling down a flight of stairs and breaking her left leg in three places. After surgery, she spent three weeks in a rehabilitation facility; her stay should've been two weeks longer, but she couldn't afford it. The bills—which she says are still trickling in—wiped out her savings. She even pulled the money from the 401(k) she had from her last job—in spite of the hefty penalty for early withdrawal—because she saw no other choice. If you don't have health insurance, even a minor ailment can lead to medical bills that take years to pay.

What you should do: Learn your options. Should you suddenly find yourself without adequate coverage, there are alternatives.

Individual Coverage

More insurers offer individual policies in response to the expanding numbers of uninsured. But you'll need to do your homework before signing on the dotted line. The policies with the lowest premiums usually have the highest deductibles and co-payments. Some don't cover prescription medications, maternity care, dental care, or mental health treatment. Do you want an insurance plan that pays for routine medical expenses or one that takes care of major illnesses? If you can pay routine health-care costs, you can save on premiums by choosing a plan with a high deductible. But if you can't afford those out-of-pocket expenses, you're better off picking a policy that carries a lower deductible and a higher premium. Also, if you have pre-existing health issues or are older, you'll pay more.

Short-term Coverage

If you're between jobs or waiting for your probationary period at a new job to come to a close, you could find yourself temporarily without insurance. You can close the gap with COBRA (the federal law that requires your former employer to allow you to continue your medical coverage), short-term private insurance, or state high-risk plans.

- If you lose your job, you can be covered for at least eighteen months under COBRA. You'll pay the full cost of the premiums, plus an administrative fee.
- Some insurers offer short-term coverage for six to twelve months. The eligibility requirements aren't as tight as they are for long-term policies, and the premiums are often substantially less than COBRA's.
- Many states offer insurance, called state high-risk plans, to people who aren't able to get coverage anywhere else. To qualify for a state high-risk plan you need to be a resident of the state and prove that you've been turned down for private insurance coverage. The premiums are expensive and there might be a waiting list, but if you have a major illness, a state high-risk plan could be the only way for you to have coverage.

Organizations and Associations

Many trade and professional organizations, civic groups and churches include group health insurance as a member benefit. The premiums for this type of coverage are calculated based on characteristics of the group as a whole. Typically, all eligible members of the group can purchase coverage under the plan, regardless of age or physical condition. Review the health benefits of any organizations to which you belong.

If you're uninsured and can't afford one of the above health insurance options, check out a local community health clinic to find out about low-cost primary health care. For help with prescription medication costs, go to www.needymeds.com, an online source that provides information about patient assistance programs.

Medical Bankruptcy: Is Your Insurance Adequate?
A recent study reported that medical-related bankruptcies jumped an astronomical 2,200 percent in the twenty-year period between 1981 and 2001, making it the second-leading reason, behind job loss, that people declare personal bankruptcy. Perhaps more startling to the researchers than the jump, however, was the realization that ninety percent of all medical bankruptcies were among the middle class. Poor, uninsured, and underinsured people have always borne the brunt of health-care disparities in this country, but this study found that educated, middle-income Americans with steady jobs aren't immune to medical financial burdens. According to the study, more than three-quarters of the people who found themselves living this nightmare were insured at the start of the illness that forced them to declare bankruptcy.

Reward: When you know how much insurance you have—or where to go to get insurance if you're uninsured—you're more likely to get the treatment you need when a health problem arises.

5. Schedule Screenings

Goal: Make sure you don't have a disease, such as diabetes or cancer, that you don't know you have; if you do have an illness, screenings can catch the disease early, and you can get appropriate treatment.

What you should do: Talk to your doctor about age-appropriate health screenings, schedule the tests, and make sure you understand the results.

Screening Tests You Need
Do you know what kind of medical exams you need and when you should have them? Check the chart on the following page.

General Screening Guidelines for Middle Age Women

Screening Tests	30s	40s	50s
General Health			
Full check-up	Yearly, or discuss with health care provider	Yearly, or discuss with health care provider	Yearly, or discuss with health care provider
Thyroid test	Every 5 years	Every 5 years	Every 5 years
Bone Health			
Bone mineral density test	Discuss with health care provider	Discuss with health care provider	Discuss with health care provider
Breast Health			
Clinical breast exam	Monthly self-breast exam; yearly by provider	Monthly self-breast exam; yearly by provider	Monthly self-breast exam; yearly by provider
Mammogram	Every 1-2 years	Every 1-2 years	Yearly
Colorectal Health			
Barium Enema (DCBE)			Every 5-10 years
Colonoscopy			Every 10 years
Fecal occult blood test		Yearly	Yearly
Flexible Sigmoidoscopy		Every 5 years	Every 5 years
Rectal Exam		Discuss with health care provider	Discuss with health care provider

Screening Tests	30s	40s	50s
Diabetes			
Blood sugar test		Starting at age 45. Every 3 years	Every 3 years
Eye and Ear Health			
Vision exam & Hearing test	Once initially, then as needed	Every 2-4 years	Every 2-4 years
Heart Health			
Blood pressure	Every year	Every year	Every year
Cholesterol test	Every 5 years	Every 5 years	Every 5 years
Mental Health	Discuss with health care provider	Discuss with health care provider	Discuss with health care provider
Oral Health			
Dental exam	Once or twice yearly	Once or twice yearly	Once or twice yearly
Reproductive Health			
Pap test & Pelvic exam	1 to 3 years*	1 to 3 years*	1 to 3 years*
Sexually transmitted disease	If you have multiple sex partners	If you have multiple sex partners	If you have multiple sex partners
Skin Health			
Mole exam	Monthly self-exam Every 3 years by health care provider	Monthly self-exam Every 3 years by health care provider	Monthly self-exam Every 3 years by health care provider

*After 3 consecutive normal tests. Discuss with your health care provider.

Reward: Knowing your health status and establishing a permanent health-maintenance plan. Catching diseases early, when they are in their most treatable stage.

6. Get a Baseline for Sexual and Reproductive Health

Goal: To maintain your sexual and reproductive health.

What you should know: Black women have a higher risk of developing two of the three main middle life reproductive issues—fibroids, infertility, and menopause.

Fibroids

The incidence of fibroids—the most common non-cancerous uterine tumors in women of childbearing age—is higher in African Americans than in other racial groups (by our late forties more than eighty percent of us have developed fibroids), and our fibroids tend to be larger and more numerous when they are first discovered. Though researchers haven't been able to pinpoint exactly what causes fibroids, possible risk factors include age, ethnicity, starting menstruation at an early age, delaying or avoiding giving birth, inactivity, and obesity. Heredity may also play a role. If your mother or sister has had fibroids, chances are you're also at increased risk of developing them.

Fibroids: Know Your Options

Bev, a 41-year-old mother of a daughter, started bleeding one day, and it wouldn't stop. "It was different from my period blood," she says. "It was bright red, and it wasn't time for my period. I bled for a year. I'd get up on a good day and the blood wouldn't be there, then a gush would start. So I wore pads twenty-four-seven for a year because I never knew when it was going to happen." Then one day she woke up in terrible pain and raced to the emergency room. There, she was told that she was "full of fibroids" and needed to see her gynecologist.

"I'd seen her. But she kept telling me I had to have a hysterectomy, and I didn't want one," Bev says.

Three months, two D&C procedures, and a pack of birth control pills later, Bev was still bleeding. "I was anemic. I was sick all the time. I was exhausted and cranky. My face was full of pimples. I was big as a house because all I wanted to do was eat and sleep," she says.

A move to Atlanta saved her sanity. Bev's doctor in her new city referred her to a group of specialists who told her she didn't have to have a hysterectomy. They said they could do a myomectomy, a less invasive surgical procedure that would get rid of the fibroids and preserve her ability to have children. It was the first time anyone had told Bev about a treatment option that didn't involve the removal of her uterus.

The emergency room doctor hadn't lied when he told Bev she was full of fibroids. After the myomectomy, Bev says the specialist told her: "'You had a lot; you had clusters like grapes, several big ones.' And she still saved my uterus. I'm pretty sure I don't want another child, but it's my uterus. I fought for it."

Infertility

Black women, so the theory goes, are supposed to be more fertile than the crescent of land that made up the biblical Mesopotamia. The truth is, however, we are just as likely to be infertile as other women. Roughly 10 percent of us experience difficulty conceiving (about the same rate as white women). Experts point to a number of reasons Black women experience infertility. Chief among them are age, sexually transmitted infections (STIs), fibroids, endometriosis, and obesity.

Debra didn't meet Glenn, the man who became her husband, until her late thirties. When they got married two years later, they found themselves on an accelerated path to starting a family. "Ideally, I wanted two years of just us," the 43-year-old said. "But that wasn't an option. We started trying on our honeymoon." Even then, however, the couple wasn't panicked. Debra knew other women with similar backgrounds to hers who had no trouble conceiving, and the news was filled with celebrities getting pregnant and giving birth in their forties. But their stories didn't become Debra's story. "I was the quintessential career woman, and I'm paying for it now."

One in five women has her first child after age thirty-five. To put it bluntly, that's ancient in medical terms. Your chances of conceiving decrease by as much as five percent a year after age thirty, and two-thirds of women age forty or older won't be able to get pregnant at all without a lot of help.

Untreated STIs are believed to be the leading cause of infertility in Black women. Chlamydia, gonorrhea, and pelvic inflammatory disease (PID) are more common in us. We also have higher rates of fibroids and endometriosis, both of which can hinder conception. And being overweight interferes with the hormones that cause ovulation.

Menopause

Recent studies have shown that the experience of menopause differs among racial groups. African Americans tend to have more estrogen-related symptoms (hot flashes, night sweats, urine leakage, and vaginal dryness). We are less likely to have somatic symptoms (headaches, difficulty sleeping, joint soreness, racing heart, and stiffness) than other ethnic groups.

For years, scientists prescribed HRT to combat heart disease. But in 2002 the National Institutes of Health halted a study when it was discovered that HRT caused more diseases—breast cancer, blood clots, heart attacks, strokes—than it prevented—colon cancer, osteoporosis. A second study was also ended early because, in that one, HRT appeared to increase the risk of strokes. HRT is no longer recommended for heart disease, and the Food and Drug Administration suggests that women who do take HRT to treat other menopausal symptoms should take the lowest dose possible for very short time periods.

What you should do:

Fibroids: Treatment for fibroids depends on where the tumors are located, their size, and the severity of your symptoms. If you're not having symptoms, your doctor will probably remain in a "wait and see" mode. He or she will check the fibroids at your annual gynecological exam and take action only if symptoms develop. If you develop symptoms, explore your treatment options—drug therapy, uterine fibroid embolization, surgery—so you and your physician can make better informed decisions.

Infertility:

- Lose weight.
- Don't smoke.
- Protect yourself from STIs.
- Know when you ovulate.
- Make sure you don't have an underlying medical condition.

Menopause:

- Have your hormone levels checked to establish your baseline, and discuss HRT alternatives with your physician.
- Talk to a nutritionist about how dietary changes —such as eliminating caffeine—and vitamin and mineral supplements can alleviate some menopausal symptoms.

Reward: Though none of the three reproductive issues we've just discussed are life threatening, they can affect your quality of life. By being aware of the issues and getting routine gynecological exams, you can ensure your sexual and reproductive health.

7. Know Your HIV Status and Practice Safer Sex

Goal: To learn your HIV status and practice safer sex so you don't become infected or infect others.

What you should know: Black women are now the fastest-growing group of people infected with HIV, the virus that causes AIDS—long thought of as a disease of gay white men and intravenous drug users. According to the Centers for Disease Control, in 2003 the rate of new AIDS cases for Black women was eighteen times higher than that of white women. We accounted for 69 percent of all new HIV diagnoses between 2000 and 2003. The disease has now become one of the top three causes of death for Black women ages thirty-five to forty-four, even as cases are leveling off or dropping among other populations in this country. And one in ten women diagnosed with HIV is older than fifty. Though the medical treatments that gained prominence during the 1990s have extended life for some people infected with HIV, there is still no cure for the disease. The good news is that HIV is 100 percent preventable.

What you should do: Talk openly and honestly with your sexual partner about sexual risks and sexual history, insist on using condoms, make sure you and your partner are regularly tested for HIV. If you test positive, talk to your doctor about your treatment options.

Reward: Knowing your HIV status and understanding the risks can protect your health and save your life.

8. Stop Smoking

Goal: Put out the cigarettes for good.

What you should know: You already know that cigarettes cause lung cancer, the number one killer of Black women in middle life. The most recent Surgeon General's report on smoking, however, also links the habit to leukemia; cataracts; gum disease; hip fractures; complications from diabetes; osteoporosis; post-surgery infections; a wide range of reproductive problems, including infertility; pneumonia; and cancers of the cervix, kidney, pancreas, and stomach. A University of Michigan study found that smoking rates among Black women increase with age, leading to higher mortality from tobacco-related diseases.

It is also important to note that though people tend to believe smokers weigh less than non-smokers—in fact, a common belief among smokers is that they'll gain weight if they quit—a U.S. Surgeon General's report found that heavy smokers (twenty or more cigarettes a day) weigh more than moderate smokers (ten to twenty cigarettes a day). Paradoxically, moderate smokers weigh less than light smokers (fewer than ten cigarettes a day). This relationship was particularly pronounced in Black women. Other studies have suggested a higher waist-to-hip ratio—two percent higher in Black women—among women who smoke than in women who don't.

On the positive side, Black women smoke less than all other women, and 74 percent of Black women who smoke reported that they want to quit, according to a 2002 Gallop poll. But, unfortunately, we have a much more difficult time sticking to a smoking cessation program than white women.

Special Insight

Linda Bradley, MD

Cleveland Clinic Obstetrics/Gynecology Foundation

The most pressing reproductive issues for African American women ages thirty-five to forty-five are uterine fibroids, increased risk of breast cancer, infertility, obesity—which ties in a little bit with infertility—and abnormal uterine bleeding. We share roughly the same risk as white women of getting ovarian cancer. The risk of getting uterine cancer in our population is a little bit higher because Black women are diagnosed at later or more advanced stages.

On Uterine Fibroids

No one knows why Black women are more likely to get fibroids than other groups of women. We do know that fibroids tend to be genetic. Obesity may be another tie in to one's risk of developing them. We also know that fibroids affect a woman's quality of life. Fibroids create a growth that can push on other organs. As a result, women with fibroids may need to urinate frequently. They may also have problems with constipation, anemia, tiredness, and lethargy. All of these problems can compromise our health status.

On Infertility

The biggest risk for infertility is the age at which women try to have children. Any woman who waits until she's thirty-five to forty is going to have greater difficulty getting pregnant. Also, women who are overweight have more problems with their periods, and that makes it more difficult to conceive. If a woman has had gonorrhea or chlamydia, she'll be at greater risk for infertility. Women with kidney failure, diabetes, or obesity also have a higher risk of infertility—it's as if the body knows that bringing a pregnancy to a woman who is already compromised will put her at greater risk. In addition, high stress levels can create an irregular menstrual cycle.

On Menopause and Hormone Replacement Therapy
We used to say that hormone therapy would decrease the risk of cardiovascular disease and stroke, but that wasn't borne out in recent studies. The healthiest thing you can do for your heart is to walk thirty-five to forty minutes a day and to eat less.

Now, hormone therapy is approved for osteoporosis, vaginal dryness, and hot flashes and sweats. In general Black women experience hot flashes and sweats and develop osteoporosis less often than other groups of women. But you can't lump all Black women in one category. Osteoporosis is usually seen in women who are thin and fragile. Women over their ideal body weight are less likely to have osteoporosis. That doesn't mean they can't get it, but they are less likely to.

That said, Black women *are* at greater risk for having lupus and asthma, which require treatment with steroids. If a woman has been on steroids for years, she's going to have accelerated bone loss. Also, a high number of Black women smoke, and women who smoke are at a higher risk of developing osteoporosis.

On Obesity
So many of our health problems are self-induced. Obesity is an issue for Americans in general, but more so for Blacks and our children. People worried about breast cancer should also know that research shows that overweight women have a higher incidence of developing breast cancer. Our culture tends to accept obesity, but we've gotten ridiculous about its acceptance. Women are prematurely going to their graves. It's a life and death situation.

Doctors would be put out of business if people stopped smoking, drinking, and overeating, or if they wore seatbelts and exercised. And yes, some people who do everything right will still develop cancer. But most diseases that physicians deal with are self-inflicted.

You should also know that secondhand smoke affects the people around you, too. It can take as long as two weeks for the nicotine in tobacco smoke to clear from a room. In children, secondhand smoke contributes to increased risk of asthma (the number of Black children who have asthma is 25 percent higher than in white children who have this disease), other respiratory difficulties, and ear infections.

And, finally, according to the American Council on Science and Health, 500,000 deaths each year (that's one of every five deaths) are attributable to cigarette smoking.

What you should do:

1. Learn the top benefits of quitting:
   - You'll live longer. Women who die of smoking-related diseases lose roughly 14.5 years of life. The sooner you quit, the more likely you are to get those years back.
   - You'll reduce your risk of having a stroke. Heavy smokers (two packs or more a day) are twice as likely as light smokers (half a pack a day) to have a stroke. That means even reducing the number of cigarettes you smoke could save your life.
   - You'll be less likely to have a heart attack. Women who smoke are more than two times as likely as women who don't smoke to have a heart attack. Your risk of a heart attack increases with every cigarette you smoke. Within eight hours of quitting, your heart attack risk starts dropping; within a year, your risk is cut in half.
   - You'll be less likely to die from lung cancer. We've said it before, but it bears repeating: Lung cancer kills more Black women than any other cancer. And 90 percent of those deaths are directly linked to smoking. The sooner you stop smoking, the sooner you decrease those odds.
   - You'll save the lives of your significant other and your children. You won't be the only one to reap the benefits if you stop smoking; environmental tobacco smoke puts your spouse and kids at greater risk of developing heart disease and lung cancer, even if they never smoke themselves. If you smoke during pregnancy, you increase your risk of having a stillborn baby or a child who dies from sudden infant death syndrome. If you quit, you increase the amount of oxygen

your unborn baby receives and improve your baby's chances of being born healthy instead of prematurely and with a low birth weight.

- You'll have better emotional health. Research shows women who smoke are more likely to be depressed.
- You'll save money. Put aside the money you normally spend on cigarettes to reward yourself for quitting. Don't wait too long—a special treat every two weeks may help you maintain your willpower.

2. Learn your smoking triggers: Do you find yourself reaching for a cigarette after meals, at parties, while you're playing cards, or driving in your car? Or do you use smoking to help you alleviate stress or cope with a bad situation, like the breakup of a relationship? Make a list of the times when you are most likely to smoke, and then do something else instead. For instance, if you usually smoke while you're talking on the phone, put a pad and pencil beside the phone and try drawing or doodling. If you smoke while you're driving, put your cigarettes in the trunk and remove the lighter. Listen to music instead of smoking.

   As you go down your list of triggers, however, don't try to change everything at once. Change one trigger at a time. It won't be easy, but stick to it. Then move on to the next item on your list. Keep going until you have checked off all your smoking triggers. When you can stop smoking at your "favorite" times, you are on your way to stopping all the time.
3. Avoid smoking traps: Don't go to a cigar bar; go to a movie or a smoke-free restaurant instead.
4. Fight the addiction to nicotine: As you are trying to quit, for a short time you may need to use products that replace the nicotine in cigarettes. These products—gums, inhalers, lozenges, patches, and sprays—have smaller amounts of nicotine than cigarettes and can help your body get over its need for nicotine, little by little. A nicotine-free pill, Zyban, was approved for use in this country in 1997. Similar products are in the works. Talk to your pharmacist or doctor about which product is best for you.

Reward: Reduced risk of developing smoking-related illnesses and improved general health.

9. Lose Weight

Goal: Lose twenty pounds.

What you should know: Obesity affects more than half of all adult African American women. It carries with it an increased risk of heart disease, diabetes, high blood pressure, respiratory disorders, arthritis, and some cancers. Losing just twenty pounds, however, can lower your risk and improve your health outcome. Keep in mind, however, that you and a friend can have similar diets and similar workout plans, but your metabolisms probably differ. That means you might not lose weight at the same rate—or even as much as—your friend does. So you need to do your health homework to find out what lifestyle changes and nutrition plan works for you. Visit www.mypyramid.gov to get a plan tailor-made just for you.

What you should do: Don't try to do it all at once. Even if you ate nothing at all for three days, you wouldn't drop twenty pounds. So break down your twenty-pound goal into smaller components. The most sensible approach is to try to lose a pound a week. But you'll still need to come up with a plan to lose that weekly pound.

- Buy a full-length mirror and look at yourself naked in it. During middle life, you have to get in touch with your body and your body image. When you're young, you look in the mirror frequently because you want to look good! In middle life, you may stop looking in the mirror because you don't want to face the truth, which is that gravity has set in. By looking in the mirror at your naked body at least once a month, you might be inspired to start making some changes.
- Decide on your behavior changes. To reach the pound-a-week goal, you'll need to stay between 1,200 and 1,400 calories a day. This may mean reducing your daily caloric intake by 400 calories and walking for thirty minutes three times a week.
- Set specific and measurable goals. You need to be able to measure your goal. If you say "I want to lose twenty pounds by Christmas," that's measurable; "I want to get into better shape" isn't. As you progress, you might find that your goal changes—from dropping twenty pounds to being able to jog

a flight of steps without getting winded—and this is fine.

- Be ready to start. If exercising is the goal, do you have any idea how you want to exercise, or do you have a vague plan to start when you find some time? The vague plan is a plan for failure. You need to be action oriented. Do you want to join a gym with a friend? Do you have a treadmill in your basement? Are you going to walk a mile at lunch each day? No matter which of these methods you choose, they all require taking action. This also applies to eating a healthier diet. Make healthier food choices at the grocery store (it's difficult to eat a bad late-night snack if there's nothing bad in your kitchen). Bring fruit to put in your desk drawer at work instead of cookies or candy bars.
- Set realistic expectations. The more unrealistic your goal, the less likely you are to meet it. Saying you're going to exercise an hour and a half each day when you haven't so much as walked a block in more than five years is unrealistic. Saying you'll walk with your co-workers during lunch is realistic.
- Give yourself time. Determine specific time frames to meet your long-term (twenty pounds) and short-term (one pound each week) goals. Examples of this: Losing two pounds in the next two weeks, six pounds in the next six weeks, and twenty pounds by the end of the year. Celebrate your accomplishments with a non-food reward. Try a massage or a new pair of walking sneakers.

Though this may sound like the slow track to weight loss, it's all about long-term success.

Reward: A healthier, more fit you!

10. Maintain Your Emotional Well-Being

Goal: To set aside depression, stress, and anxiety and to reclaim your joy.

What you should know: Until recently, there was very little information about emotional well-being and the effect of mental health disorders—depression, anxiety, and stress—in Black women. The data were limited to what women receiving treatment provided, and many of us don't receive treatment. What is known is that women are twice as likely as men to suffer depression and anxiety, and the two disorders together cost eighty-five billion dollars each year in treatment costs and lost productivity at work. The most recent research estimates that 17 percent of Black women have been diagnosed with a mental health disorder. Professionals believe that estimate is low, because so many of us don't seek help. When enough stressful events are clustered together at one time—economic insecurity, heavy caregiver responsibilities, violence, lack of social support, traumatic life experiences, racism —African Americans can become increasingly vulnerable to emotional distress and disease. Because the links between the mind, emotions, and body are complex, chronic states of stress and anxiety can have dangerous, even fatal, consequences.

Despite the emotional and physical problems caused by mental health issues, we often refuse to seek help. Some estimates say only 7 percent of Black women suffering from depression receive treatment. This is because 63 percent of us believe that depression is a personal weakness. In addition, only 31 percent of us consider depression a health problem, and close to 30 percent believe we can handle an extended bout of the blues better on our own. The stigma of being labeled "mentally ill" is not the only reason we avoid treatment. Other reasons include:

- Mistrust of health professionals, based partly on higher-than-average institutionalization in the past of Blacks with mental health problems. When we do seek treatment, we tend to go to the emergency room instead of to a mental health professional.
- Cultural barriers between doctors and patients; only about 2 percent of psychologists in this country are Black.
- Heavy reliance on family and religious community— rather than on mental health professionals— to help us cope during times of emotional distress.
- More discussions of physical problems than of mental health issues.
- Masking symptoms with substance abuse.
- Minimizing the serious nature of the problem.

Depression

A national study by the Black Women's Health Imperative found that 60 percent of us have symptoms of depression. Yet most of the time, we're depressed, and we don't even know it. Part of the problem is we don't recognize the symptoms. A National Mental Health Association survey concluded that only twenty-five percent of African Americans recognize that changes in eating habits and sleeping patterns are signs of depression. Depression often manifests itself differently in Black women; instead of the classic mood changes, we often display symptoms such as fatigue (in Black women this is frequently the only sign of depression, and it's usually not picked up by primary care physicians), backache, hypertension, overeating, or anger.

Anxiety and Panic Attacks

Two to three million women frequently experience panic attacks, the abrupt onset of an episode of unprovoked intense fear or discomfort. Women are twice as likely as men to have panic disorder. When a woman suffers severe and unexpected panic attacks, she feels like she is having a heart attack, going crazy, or losing control for no apparent reason.

For the past several months, Karen, forty-nine, has been having a recurrent nightmare about being in a serious car accident. "I'm always trapped in the car, which has flipped several times and is resting upside down. I always lose a limb and know that I'm about to die. I wake up just before that happens, and I'm covered in sweat. A few times my heart has been beating so hard I could see the movement above my bedclothes," she said. The dream is bad enough. But lately, Karen has found herself breaking out into a sweat whenever she gets behind the wheel of her car. "There have been days when I'm shaking too badly to drive, so I've had to call in sick at work."

What you should do:

Depression. Learn to recognize the symptoms of depression. You might be depressed—and should seek help from a mental health professional—if you've had any of the following symptoms every day for at least two weeks:

- Loss of interest in daily activities.
- A feeling of hopelessness or helplessness.
- Sleep disturbance

- Inability to think or concentrate.
- Significant weight loss or gain.
- Restlessness, agitation, irritability.
- Extreme fatigue.
- Low self-esteem.
- Less interest in sex.
- Thoughts of death or suicide.

You might also experience a number of physical problems, including itching, blurred vision, excessive sweating, dry mouth, headache, backache, and gastrointestinal complaints (constipation, diarrhea, indigestion).

Learn how to help yourself:

- Set realistic goals.
- Break large tasks into smaller ones.
- Be with other people as much as possible.
- Participate in activities that make you feel better.
- Exercise.
- Understand that you'll feel better gradually, not immediately.
- Delay making important decisions until the depression has lifted.
- Let your family and friends help you.

Anxiety. Learn the signs of an anxiety attack:

- Constantly worrying.
- Fearing the worst.
- Being very aware of your heart beating.
- Tension and muscle pains.
- Inability to relax.
- Sweating.
- Dizziness.
- Hyperventilating.
- Feeling faint.

Reward: An Increased sense of self-control and self-confidence.

Prescriptions for Psychological Wellness

It's important to have hope that things can get better and to maintain a positive attitude. Dwelling on the negative does not help us emerge from difficult circumstances. Surrounding ourselves with people who are supportive and caring does. Seek out sisters to dialogue and share experiences with as well as to confide in. And try the suggestions below. They've contributed to our resilience as a people. Perhaps, they'll help you too:

- Take care of your body. Find opportunities for movement. You don't have to spend a lot of money on a fancy gym. Walking works just fine. If you're concerned about the safety of walking in your neighborhood, do an aerobic activity inside your home or office.
- Get plenty of rest. This is key because in our zeal to do what others expect of us, we often don't get enough sleep. Being sleep deprived can have a significant impact on your psychological state and your ability to function.
- Nourish yourself with a healthy diet including generous proportions of fruits and vegetables. Take a multivitamin for good measure. Many people who do not eat nutritiously are at a disadvantage with respect to psychological health
- Nourish your spirit—either through formal religious observance or by sensing your connection to other people—and recognize your value.
- See yourself as important and worthy of care and support. Program yourself to have a positive view of yourself as a Black woman and act accordingly.
- Find and keep your joy. Celebrate yourself and indulge in the things you like to do—learning, creating, dancing, singing. These are not necessarily material things, which can be perishable or go out of style. If you invest in developing your mind and spirit, you'll get a much better return on your investment.
- Realize that you are OK, even if you don't do all of these things to perfection. Most things are not "all or none." There is a middle ground of balance for your life—strive for it.

SPECIAL INSIGHT

ANNELLE PRIMM, MD

Director of Minority and National Affairs for the American Psychiatric Association
Associate Professor of Psychiatry, Johns Hopkins School of Medicine

A psychologically well woman is balanced physically, emotionally, and spiritually. It's probably curious to include a physical aspect, but in actuality, physical health is an ingredient in psychological health. The whole point is that our minds, our brains, are not separate from our bodies; they're not separate from our spirit. There's a unity in those three things.

A woman who is psychologically well is able to meet her responsibilities in whatever her roles—parent, spouse, worker, student—and to cope with whatever stress she may encounter. She is also able to maintain a sense of self-esteem, regardless of whatever adverse circumstances she encounters. We all undergo hardship and stress at times, but the healthiest among us will be able to manage those difficult times to maximize a positive outcome—or at least minimize a negative outcome, without engaging in self-destructive behaviors.

The emotional well-being of some Black women is on the mark, and some of us have a ways to go. But it's important for us not to blame the victim. Studies show that the rates of psychological stress are higher among African American women compared to the general population. This is due to a number of factors. First, the environments in which we live. Being a woman in this country increases our risk of living in poverty, which can be a huge underpinning of psychological distress. Violence is another problem for some of us. We are often victims of violence, or we may witness others being victimized by violence.

From a social standpoint, women—across the board, but particularly African Americans—are expected to be caregivers. This often leads us to overindulge in self-sacrifice, meeting others' needs before our own. Many African Americans view this self-sacrifice as socially acceptable and expected. But being too selfless can become a trap if we strain ourselves to the limit. We really have no comfortable way of setting limits about what we're responsible for and what we're not. And while our motivation for being selfless is often benevolent, it can be self-destructive if we say "yes" too often and take on others' responsibilities.

This is where extended family comes in because when you're over responsible for the immediate family and your neighbors and your friends and your coworkers. This can sometimes tip the balance and lead to self-neglect. We have to be realistic about what we can take on and be mindful of protecting our health. Helping others, if taken to the extreme, can be destructive to us. We have to learn to set limits on how much we can do to preserve ourselves. Do, but don't overdo. And if you need to say "no," learn to say it without guilt.

People in our community are sicker and die sooner. There's a lot of loss and grief—whether it's loss of life or loss of health and functioning—that we as women are sort of left holding the bag. That adds to the burden that we have to bear.

Because of these burdens, Black women cope in different ways. Some get depressed and sad, some are self-destructive—either by abusing substances or overeating. Some withdraw. We have a particularly heavy burden to bear, so it's not surprising that we have high rates of psychological distress. But we must do whatever we can to maintain psychological, emotional, and social fitness so we can be resilient in the face of these assaults.

The Myth of the Angry Black Woman

Anger is not our only coping style, but it is certainly common among many African Americans—that sort of evil Black woman cultural stereotype. We need to realize, however, that a person's attitude problem may be masking bad feelings. Rather than purposely being difficult, such a person may, in fact, need help. Sometimes the anger is turned inward. It may be an expression of depression. Sometimes that anger is dealt with through substance use. Black women don't turn to substance abuse any more than any other group, but when we do, it can set us up for other problems, including health problems such as sexually transmitted infections.

Another reason for anger in Black women is that our dual roles —as women and Black people—are often devalued. This societal response to our ethnicity and gender can cause us to get very angry. It may cause us to work harder to prove our value, to tolerate discrimination, and to confront many limitations. These are tough challenges.

But if Black women seem angrier than other women, it could be because they've experienced greater emotional, physical, or sexual abuse. In fact, Black women have experienced sexual abuse at extremely high rates, and one way of responding to mistreatment is to distrust people and to be defensive. In some ways, anger could be seen as a healthy response to being exploited and taken advantage of. It's a way of externalizing feeling under attack.

Feeling angry all the time, however, can have a negative impact on our psychological health. But the psychologically fit Black woman will find a way— "making a way out of no way" as our forebears did—to channel her anger into action, to transcend and overcome the visible and invisible barriers and obstacles. Learning to manage our anger—to channel it into productive activity—is important. Joining support groups and getting counseling or therapy are ways that African American women who've been wounded or traumatized can begin to heal and to experience a sense of well-being.

11. Get Comfortable with Your Sexuality

Goal: Enjoy a healthy and satisfying sex life well into your later years.

What you should know: Surveys show one in three sexually active women is dissatisfied with some aspect of her sex life. One reason for this may be that women today often find ourselves pulled in fifteen directions—children, work, your partner's needs, parents with health issues. All of these can impact your sex life. And the reality is that after fifteen or more years with one person, sexual relationships often lose their bloom.

If your sex life is wilting, you could be suffering from fatigue. Women in their late thirties and forties might be experiencing perimenopause, the ten-year period before menopause that can affect everything from how well you sleep at night to your interest in sex. Fluctuating estrogen levels interrupt sleep, cause night sweats, and affect bladder control.

Fluctuating estrogen levels can also cause vaginal dryness, leading to painful intercourse. Perimenopause also affects testosterone, which a number of studies link to libido. But by age forty, it's estimated that a woman's testosterone has dipped by half.

What you should do: First, make sure there is no underlying medical condition—physical problems account for about 90 percent of sexual problems. If your physical health is good, then the next step is up to you. Counter bedroom boredom—both in and out of bed. Shake things up. Have a conversation with your partner about ways to liven things up. Experiment, be creative, and, most of all, have fun.

Claim yourself as a sexual being. Black women tend to be reluctant about openly discussing their sexuality, and the reasons for this reluctance are understandable. We have been objectified and sexually abused since slavery. Today, our own people sometimes demean us as sexual objects in rap lyrics and videos. But it is important to keep in mind that we were created as sexual beings, and it is our right to have healthy sexual lives.

Reward: A fulfilling sex life.

SPECIAL INSIGHT

Hilda Hutcherson, MD,

Obstetrics/Gynecology
Co-Director, New York Center for Women's Sex and Health
New-York Presbyterian Hospital

We are uncomfortable talking about sex. That's something that's been going on for generations. A lot of it is rooted in the church and our upbringing in the church. It's passed down from mother to daughter. I think that's the root of it. And I think people like author Zane are kind of changing it a little bit. By putting the issue out there. By normalizing sexual pleasure for Black women.

In order to have healthy sexual relationships as we move into middle life, it's important to acknowledge that bodily changes occur in all women as we get older, because of the changes in our hormones. Most of those changes are normal. There's a decrease in estrogen and testosterone, which affects our desire for sex. Decreasing estrogen affects our enjoyment of sex. Our arousal isn't the same. We have changes in our shapes. I heard someone say recently we go from a pear to an apple, with middle fat deposits, which make most women feel less than sexy. Who wants to climb out of her girdle before she has sex? It affects our self-esteem, because we tend to put on a lot more weight as we age than white women.

Also, many of us lack partners, as we get older. Black men have a shorter lifespan than we do. They get killed, they're in jail or they're looking for somebody younger. Many Black women in my practice are over forty and single. These women often don't feel comfortable with masturbation or solo sex. Some of us don't feel comfortable being with another woman. So if you don't have a partner, what do you do? We don't see an acceptable outlet for sexual tension.

Women with partners, however, can find ways to improve a lagging sex life. Right now, although we don't have an FDA approved source of testosterone—the hormone that drives desire in women—many gynecologists will prescribe an herb or a supplement that boosts libido and increases desire.

And I talk a lot to my patients about trying something new, different, and exciting, which seems to be more difficult for older women. Young women are much more likely to go out and buy a leather bustier and thigh-high stockings and stiletto heels, than a woman who is forty, forty-five, or fifty. I encourage women to bring that fantasy into their sex lives. Doing so could spark your interest in sex. I also suggest reading erotica. It might pique your curiosity and provide a roadmap to new pleasures for you and your partner to explore.

12. Don't Ignore the Warning Signals

Goal: Learn to listen to your body and take responsibility for what it tells you.

What you should know: If you want to live, don't ignore signs that your health—and maybe your life—is in danger. You know better than anyone else when something doesn't feel quite right with your body. Perhaps you've had a headache for several weeks or you've had trouble sleeping for several months or the vision in your right eye is suddenly blurry. These are all signs from your body that something has gone wrong. Being sick is no picnic and the prospect that you could be seriously ill is frightening, but suffering in silence, hoping a problem will go away on its own isn't very smart. If you are sick, the sooner you receive treatment for an illness, the better your outcome.

What you should do: Learn the signs (below) that something is going wrong with your health. Talk them over with a family member or friend, and seek help in getting medical attention to deal with them.

- Uncontrolled risk factors for heart disease, such as high blood pressure, high cholesterol, diabetes, and obesity.
- Shortness of breath.
- Wounds that don't heal.
- Blood in the stool.
- Fatigue that keeps you from doing normal activities.
- Recurring pain.
- Discomfort, pressure, heaviness, or pain in the chest, arm, or below the breastbone.
- Changes in the appearance of moles.
- Lasting numbness and weakness.
- Changes in appetite.
- Drastic changes in sleep patterns.
- Loss of vision.
- Unexplained changes in weight.
- Unexplained lumps or other abnormalities in your breasts.

Reward: Catching potential health problems early by instituting self-care and taking charge of your health is liberating—and it just might save your life.

After reading this section, you know the path to a "welltheir" you comes through the conscious choices you make. You've learned how to embrace the lifestyle that is so crucial to living well. You understand the importance of claiming wellness as a core value. You've started to set your wellness goals and you're beginning to invest in yourself. You understand the health risks of obesity and stress, how they impact Black women in particular, and what to do to reduce those risks. You know that in order to carry the health benefits that Black women have in middle life into later life, you have to *do the work*. Now it's up to you. And remember: The payoff for wellness is living longer and better every day of your life.

Life Satisfaction

SAYING YES TO YOUR LIFE

BY IYANLA VANZANT

Life satisfaction for women today is no longer intrinsically connected to what we can do, should do, or must do for others.

In September of 2002, Gemmia, my thirty-one-year-old daughter, was diagnosed with a rare, hereditary form of colon cancer. For the next fifteen months, we engaged every way imaginable to extend her life. As an advocate of and a believer in the body's natural ability to heal itself, she changed her diet. Understanding that live foods support the body's natural immunity, she began eating primarily live foods and juices. We made every attempt to eliminate stress by providing financial and emotional support. Following the African tradition, which advances the belief that a person who is ill must never be left alone, family members and friends surrounded her to provide nurturing and care. Throughout the process, Gemmia continued to plan for the future. She had a vision and refused to allow cancer to blind her to the possibilities for herself or her life.

Eventually Gemmia chose to augment her natural approach to healing with chemotherapy, believing that all forms of healing complement one another. Throughout the process, I watched her choose her vision of life over a pretty dismal diagnosis. In fact, there were many times we fought about the next step. She held tenaciously to her right to make life-affirming, self-supportive choices, rebuking my motherly fears at every turn. She firmly believed that she had to trust her own heart, making decisions and choices based on what was right for her, not for me. In fact, when I think about it, I realize that she had lived most of her life this way. She often told me, "I cannot think with your brain. Mine is working and it will let me know what to do." Often, I didn't agree with her choices, but since she seemed satisfied, I had some level of tummy comfort.

On Christmas Day 2003, Gemmia's physical life ended. As her mother I was devastated. As a woman, I was proud. Gemmia left this life having done most of what she always wanted to do. She traveled. She gave her best to people. She created a legacy for her daughter. She left this world surrounded by love, with few regrets. It was at her memorial service that I realized how much she had done in her short life and how gracefully she had left it. Gemmia had discovered the secret of life satisfaction. In a few short months, she made herself the single most important priority in her life.

Many of us over the age of fifty have not had the instructive privilege of watching the women in our lives age or leave life gracefully. Our mothers and grandmothers aged under pressure. Our aunties and godmothers aged under stress. The women we loved most often aged with worry over what happened, what did not happen, what might happen if they did not keep juggling the many balls in their lives. For many of the women we looked up to and leaned on, the balls became indistinguishable. It was difficult for them, and for those of us watching, to distinguish whose life these women were living. They lived for their children or grandchildren, hoping they would avoid familiar mistakes. They lived for the church and all of the lost souls encountered there, believing that serving God and others would give them all they felt was missing. They lived for their husbands, knitting together the threads of broken and dysfunctional relationships in search of satisfaction, fulfillment, and a sense of well-being. They lived in fear of making wrong choices, the pain of their past mistakes, and the grief that often accompanies regret.

Many of us over the age of fifty have not had the instructive privilege of watching the women in our lives age or leave life gracefully.

These hardworking, people-loving, self-sacrificing women had little instruction or inspiration that would lead to life satisfaction. Many of them had no clue it was possible. They were the backbone for so many, while their own sense of self, the heart and soul of their being remained malnourished, unaffirmed, and often denied. Their greatest satisfaction in life came not from self-actualization or self-realization but from making life better for others. Fortunately today, those of us who may have been the benefactors of Granny's efforts realize this is simply not enough.

Like Gemmia, women moving into midlife in the new millennium know they must have a deeper connection to self. While we have inherited certain ancestral memories and cellular programming from our foremothers, we recognize the importance of affirming and nurturing self, the mind, body, and spirit. We also understand that the true path to self and life satisfaction is a function of choice. Women today know that we must choose to take care of ourselves if we are to live longer, healthier lives. We must choose to honor our own needs, if we are to receive the fruits of our efforts and labor.

Life satisfaction for women today is no longer intrinsically connected to what we can do, should do, or must do for others. Instead, it is a function of understanding our behavior patterns and choosing new ones that are life giving and life affirming. While we may know each of these statements to be true, the challenge becomes doing what we know is required, doing what will lead us to a longer, more satisfying life experience. It is a function of choosing *me* over *we*, with the understanding that I cannot give you what I do not give myself. It is the choice of *I* over *you*, with the recognition that the better I am, the more I can offer you.

Life satisfaction for a woman is a function of being "self-full." We must be full of self-knowledge, self-trust, self-acceptance, self-value, self-worth, and self-love in order to give the best of who we are to the world.

As difficult as it may be to believe, women are not genetically predisposed to take care of others. We are, however, conditioned to believe that doing so is the path to satisfaction. As the first caregiver, teacher, and source of inspiration, women are not made aware that *affirming self does not equate to selfishness.* The fully realized and honored self of every woman gives those around her permission to be their best selves.

Life satisfaction for a woman is a function of being *"self-full."* We must be full of self-knowledge, self-trust, self-acceptance, self-value, self-worth, and self-love in order to give the best of who we are to the world. We must choose to reprioritize our lives, learning to give from the overflow of our time, energy, and resources, keeping what's in the cup for ourselves. In order to live and age gracefully, we must re-train ourselves in midlife. We must rediscover the sources of our joy and peace. We must also identify the sources of stress and feeling overwhelmed, making every effort to eliminate them.

In order to realize the fullness of self and life satisfaction, we must acquire the tools and develop the skills to keep our heads and hearts clear. In some cases this may be as simple as learning to say no without guilt. Or taking a day off without pay. In extreme cases, it may require that we let go of beliefs, situations, and sometimes people. It may also mean that we run the risk of upsetting people we have always put first. When you put yourself first, somebody else may get upset. Trust yourself to know what is right for you. Also trust they will get over it.

For months after Gemmia's transition, I beat myself raw wondering what I could have done differently. I wondered if there was anything I could have done to save her life. I had many, what I call, "Mommy Moments," moments of guilt and remorse. I also realized that I knew. I knew the day she had her surgery that she would not be with me. I knew but I could not accept this. Most of us know exactly what it is that we do that does not affirm, sustain, or advance our lives, fulfillment, and personal satisfaction. We know but we are not sure what to do about it, or how to do it differently.

It's been a little over a year since I released my precious gem. Now I can admit that we spent many months trying to save her life, and in that time she wasn't living. Gemmia came to that understanding long before I did. She understood that every one of life's moments is precious. It must be filled with joy and peace. Every moment is an opportunity to make a statement to ourselves and the world that we are grateful to be alive, awake, and aware. In our aliveness, we must seek and find satisfaction. In our awakeness, we must pay attention to ourselves first and take others as they come. In our awareness, we must make moment-by-moment shifts and changes to be better, feel better, and live fully. One of Gemmia's therapists made a very astute observation. He told her, "If you do not enjoy your life, cancer will." She took that to heart. May I offer that the very same is true of being stressed, overworked, overwhelmed, and taking care of others? It is up to each of us to choose who or what will enjoy our lives.

The world knows **Iyanla Vanzant** as an author who has written five *New York Times* bestsellers; an orator who delivers more than 250 keynote addresses annually; a soul-saving spiritual counselor who offers a common-sense process for discovering your spiritual identity and its inherent power; and a spoken-word artist.

Vanzant is also the CEO of Inner Visions Network Worldwide, Inc., in Silver Spring, Maryland, which offers workshops, classes, and a certification program in spiritual counseling and life coaching, based on the principles presented in her books.

Chapter 8

IN SEARCH OF LIFE SATISFACTION

Imagine for a moment that the life you most want is the life you are actually living. What would it feel like to live a life that is satisfying in every way? A life that reflects your deepest values, greatest passions, and most cherished goals. What steps would you have to take to get there in the coming months and years? If you are an African American woman in middle life willing to contemplate questions like these, tomorrow truly does begin today—as we begin to explore the concept of *"life satisfaction."*

In NCNW's survey on "quality of life" issues, life satisfaction for African American women encompassed three key dimensions: Your relationship to *self*, others, and spiritual life. In this section, you will learn how to develop practical strategies for enhancing each of these essential relationships. In doing so, you will discover a new path of possibilities that can dramatically increase the quality of your life.

When asked about life satisfaction, many of the college-educated Black women in NCNW's focus groups, between the ages of 35–59 with an annual income of at least $35,000, laughed heartily and responded, "You must be joking!" Their lives are so full of responsibility and trying to stay afloat that the idea of life satisfaction feels, at times, intangible.

African American women frequently say they do not have the "luxury" to consider life satisfaction. Often, they do not see themselves in the same way as other women, and many admit that they spend far too much of their lives in "survival mode."

Black women's lives have been long characterized by the "habit of surviving." Today's Black female "baby boomers" are the first wave of African American women who have had access to a level of education, financial resources, and experiences that gives them freedom and time to actively ponder life satisfaction. It often takes having your basic needs met to dedicate the time and energy to discover what satisfies you. When your most pressing priority is safety, shelter or food, for example, there is little time to be concerned about life satisfaction.

At the core of this balancing act of life satisfaction is a dynamic interplay between *connecting with self* in personal satisfaction, *connecting with others* in social satisfaction, and *connecting to God* in spiritual satisfaction.

Personal satisfaction is derived from creating and achieving the personal life mission and vision that has the most meaning to you. It rests, of course, on your ability to identify what you need and what you want—not what others need and want for and from you. It is about doing the things that help you realize your dreams and bring you joy.

Ultimately, what African American women must realize is that achieving life satisfaction is about personal decision-making and conscious action. It means understanding why you do what you do, what you value, and how to make choices that support your total well-being.

Why is this kind of conscious decision-making so essential for us? Because today, too many African American women in middle life are "living by accident," making haphazard or default choices in their daily lives that create unnecessary and dangerous consequences for their futures. When you do not pay attention to what you do and why you do it on a daily basis, you end up living by accident.

Your challenge is to embrace the concept of life satisfaction by learning to live on purpose--identifying what is most important to you and paying close attention to how you spend your time and energy.

How do Black women spend their time and energy? For many, the responsibility of taking care of others is so overwhelming that there seems to be little—if any—time to ponder personal satisfaction. The needs of children, spouse, elderly parents, or job demands are so pressing that they outweigh the needs of *self*. It is critical, of course, to care for those who depend on us. However, in order to be your best *self* and give your best to those you care about, you must learn to make your own needs a priority.

For many women, this kind of thinking feels somehow selfish. "How can I be thinking about myself when my children need me?" "My mother can hardly walk without my help, so I don't have time to think about what I want." And other Black women point to the time spent on the drama and negativity they encounter at work and with the people in their lives. At times, they find themselves playing the demanding roles of fixer, enforcer, cheerleader, and mediator. It is the high drama, which accompanies such roles, that drains vital energy. "I just try to keep the negativity out of my life," said one focus group participant while lamenting the phone calls she receives from drama-prone girlfriends. Others chimed in with similar stories.

Many of us can identify with Black women who grow addicted to drama, become its casualties, and suddenly find that their lives are no longer their own. As you deepen your connection to your *self,* create healthy relationships with others, and cultivate your spiritual connection, you will no longer allow drama, negativity, or an unquestioned sense of obligation, guilt, fear, or habit to rule your decisions.

Real life satisfaction means being true to yourself and living a life that is meaningful and joyful from the inside out.

Social Satisfaction

The majority of NCNW's focus group participants defined life satisfaction in terms of "social satisfaction." When asked, "What makes you feel good about yourself?" they consistently pointed to their children as the source of major accomplishment in their lives. More than 83 percent of focus group members took great pride in what they were able to do for their children. Historically, Black women have found a great deal of meaning and purpose in family and church life. There is perhaps no institution in which the dependability and strength of Black women is more obvious than in the family. For many Black families, women have served as heads of households who have held the family together and guaranteed its survival. As a result, many of us equate our sense of life satisfaction with our roles as mothers, wives, aunts, grandmothers, sisters, and mentors to extended family and friends.

Social satisfaction is the level of fulfillment you experience in your relationships with other people–family, friends, church, work, and community. Black women describe their families, especially their children and their involvement in church-based relationships, as their most important and sustaining social relationships. Those who have unsatisfying relationships, few or no loving relationships, or are disconnected from their families or communities, tend to place a lower value on themselves.

Those who give all of their attention to others without consideration for themselves, must ask, "How satisfied am I *really*?" This is not a recipe for selfishness. It is rather a prescription for cultivating self-awareness—the healthy balance between nurturing your relationship with others while also honoring your relationship with your *self*. These two relationships are not "either/or" propositions. Both are important.

Spiritual Satisfaction

Alongside our high value for family relationships, there is another aspect of African American women's identity that is decidedly stronger than for women of other racial groups—our spirituality. Attend any predominantly Black church in the United States and you will find that in nearly every congregation, African American women make up the majority of the parishioners. In NCNW's analysis of national research on Black women, 91 percent report a religious group affiliation.

Many researchers and scholars have identified Black women's strong roots in the church as an adaptive coping mechanism that has helped them face the stress and pain of race and gender prejudice. Let us be clear that the spiritual roots of Black women run far deeper than any mere coping strategy. At least 93 percent of the focus group participants indicated that spirituality informs their beliefs and determines their behavioral choices.

African American women's spiritual lives offer a profound source of self-meaning. Faith has served as the bedrock on which many Black women have built their lives. African American women rely on their faith as both a source of inspiration and strength.

NCNW's findings from its analysis of national data confirm that 81 percent of Black women ages 35-59 pray daily. Many of these women attribute their sense of life satisfaction to the spiritual growth they have experienced because of their belief in God. Prayer is another strong indicator of spirituality and life satisfaction. More than 60 percent of African American women believe their lives have meaning and purpose and that the future holds hope.

To Thine Own Self Be True

While spiritual growth and social relationships are important indicators of life satisfaction, *it is* the first dimension—relationship to *self*—that has proven to be most elusive for African American women. Most focus group participants did not identify *self* as a priority in their lives. Yet, a healthy sense of *self* is critical for making the daily decisions that will ensure successful aging.

Personal satisfaction means understanding and embracing who you really are, being honest with yourself, and creating a life you love because you believe in your self-worth. Your personal relationship with *self* is a primary relationship that must be nurtured and cultivated. Just as you must spend time with your family members in order to bond and connect in meaningful ways, you must also see yourself as worthy of your attention. Without genuine personal satisfaction, your social satisfaction will be impaired.

Your time, like your money, is one of the most valuable forms of life currency. How you "spend" your time will determine your future. In fact, some would argue that time is even more valuable than money. Time is the one resource that everyone receives in equal amounts.

The *Invest in Yourself* financial plan encourages you to dedicate one-tenth of your monthly income to building your financial future. By using this same kind of strategy for achieving life satisfaction, you can invest your time and energy to produce the rich dividends that African American women seek in middle life. Making the decision to dedicate one-tenth of your waking hours to cultivating your relationship with your *self* can change the course of your life forever.

Does satisfaction or dissatisfaction define your life?

As a life coach, I have worked with people from a wide range of backgrounds, income levels, and circumstances. Most come with some level of dissatisfaction in their lives and are ready to make a change. Here are some of the most common factors that lead to life dissatisfaction:

- You do not know your purpose.
- You do work you do not enjoy.
- Your marriage is unsatisfying.
- You would like a romantic relationship but do not have a satisfying one.
- You are under financial stress.
- You don't have fun.
- You have goals you want to reach, but they seem elusive.
- Life does not feel meaningful.
- You want more formal education, but have not completed it or taken steps toward completing it.
- You do what others want you to do, even when it is not what you want to do.
- Your relationships or friendships are in turmoil.
- You do not have hope for moving up in your career.
- Your home life is unsatisfying.
- Your spiritual life is lacking.
- You do not feel connected to your community.
- You do not feel good about how you look.
- Your health is suffering as a result of poor choices.

Ten years into her career, Kimberly reached a standstill. She was stuck. She dreaded getting up in the mornings. She had spent years working in an organization that, truthfully, she wasn't particularly excited about. She often daydreamed of what it would be like to leave her stable work with a federal employer, but never seriously entertained the idea of leaving. She wanted to pursue a new path—sales. It would offer her the opportunity to work in a more dynamic environment, give her more control over increasing her income, and allow her to do something she loves–interact with people every day. Although she didn't have the experience, a friend offered her an opportunity with a reputable corporation nearby, but she turned it down. Her family would not support her move. It was the same safe and secure career path they had all followed. Besides, you can't just change careers, she thought. "I started down this road, and it would be risky for me to job-hop now," she reasoned. "What if I'm not good enough? What if I fail?" "What if" scared her out of pursuing a more satisfying career. But as Kimberly pondered life five, ten or twenty years down the road stuck in the same place, she cringed.

Kimberly's tale echoes the stories of many Black women. She is dissatisfied with her life, yet she hesitates to change. Controlled by what others will think, she allows pressure from family and friends to define her life. While "safe and secure" may be values that helped her family members define satisfaction for themselves, "freedom and opportunity" may be the values that are more dear to Kimberly's heart.

One of the most important keys to life satisfaction is defining what satisfaction means to you. If you don't define it for yourself, someone else will. Or perhaps, like Kimberly, one day (hopefully!), you will get so frustrated with your level of dissatisfaction that you will make the change that satisfies your soul.

True life satisfaction comes when you live a life that is meaningful and rewarding to you in every area of your life.

The key to that definition is in the two words "to you." What is meaningful and rewarding to someone else may be a pointless burden to you. For example, I am most fulfilled when I am able to inspire others to live fulfilling lives. It pains me to see people suppressing their dreams, not believing in themselves, or living beneath their potential. I believe and know that everyone has a purpose. One of my goals is to help more people identify and live their unique purpose. I am passionate about it. I make a living at it. It satisfies my soul. However, if I suggested that you do the same thing, it might not have meaning for you.

Likewise, if you offered me a career as a corporate executive, I wouldn't be interested. Women who enjoy life satisfaction love what they do. They are able to express their values and passion in their lives. They are able to sustain themselves financially, and feel physically and spiritually fit. Even if all of these factors do not hold true simultaneously, life satisfaction finds those who know they have the power within to attain such goals—those who have hope.

Indeed, hope is also a key to satisfaction. As I coach Black women, I have discovered that those who are consistently pessimistic in their outlook on life—believing there aren't enough good men or that racism and sexism keep them from reaching their dreams—tend to be dissatisfied. Life satisfaction is anchored in the belief that something more is possible for your life. Hope is drained by pessimism. When you are consistently focused on what might go wrong and who might try to interrupt your plans, you have no room for hope in your life. This is not to suggest that you should ignore difficult issues, but you cannot allow them to keep you from your destiny.

If you do not feel hopeful about enhancing and enriching your life, how can you change? Hope can be found when we are inspired by the lives of people who are enjoying the success we may have believed was beyond our reach. By asking, "How did she do that?" you can begin to expose yourself to new possibilities.

Exposure alone won't lead to a more satisfying life. In fact, exposure without a road map can lead to frustration. What is the point of knowing something is possible without having the knowledge required to make it happen? Exposure to new possibilities must be balanced with a workable plan for bringing these possibilities to life.

Let's explore the specifics of what you can do today to ensure that the life you live tomorrow is the one you really want. People who make the journey from dissatisfaction to satisfaction begin by recognizing their disconnection from their own needs. This leads to the type of dissatisfaction that causes many women to reach their breaking point.

As they seek to fill the emptiness inside, they become more outwardly focused and inwardly disconnected. Angela mirrors the "lost self" experienced by countless African American women.

Angela's Story

Angela, a 39-year-old wife and mother of two, runs a successful business, is active in her church, and is the primary breadwinner for her family. Against her better judgment, she supported her husband Walter's decision to leave his job and join her business.

Angela's willingness to forego her own needs to satisfy the needs of others is a classic example of dissatisfaction. She did not believe that it was a good idea for her husband to leave his job and depend solely on her business to support the family, yet she could not stand up for her feelings on the matter.

Even though Angela works full time, she spends long hours running her business, maintaining her marriage, and supervising extracurricular activities for her children. Angela's daily pattern of living in fourth gear is a one-way ticket to burnout. As her stress level has skyrocketed, so has her weight. Her doctor cautioned her about her family history of diabetes. However, Angela is so stressed that sometimes food seems like her only friend, the only thing that does not want something from her.

Recently, weight-related health problems have begun to take their toll. When Angela was asked what would allow her to put herself back on her to-do list on a daily basis, she couldn't answer. "I feel so disconnected from myself that I don't know where to start. I guess I'm overwhelmed and dissatisfied with my life. My job seems to be to take care of everyone else, but who's there to take care of me? I'm not sure I can hold on for the ride."

As nurturers, women routinely minimize their wants and needs, and elevate the wants and needs of their loved ones and friends. Becoming blind to your own needs and priorities can be very dangerous. Dissatisfaction leads to frustration, stress, and resentment, which often seethe just beneath the surface and result in mad outbursts of legendary Black woman anger and toxic bad attitudes. When these same emotions are turned inward and frustration remains unexpressed, it can also result in undiagnosed depression, which we commonly see manifested in Black women's excessive weight gains and other stress-related illnesses.

The cumulative pressure of always being on call for family 24/7, and the non-stop cycle of doing everything continuously without support or a break, robs a woman of her sense of *self* and any hope of life satisfaction. Moving from dissatisfaction to satisfaction means that you must learn how to "honor yourself."

Honor Yourself

We have learned, as a financial principle, that you must "pay yourself first." But this is a principle that is not only true of money, but as a way of approaching life. Black women, as a group, have not put themselves first. Such an approach has often seemed like a selfish luxury. As a result, countless Black women are burned out, frustrated, stressed, and unable to fully realize their potential. If you—like so many African American women—are a head of household, the primary caregiver in the family, and a full-time worker, you may be the last person to receive your own attention.

Think of the instructions a flight attendant gives before take off. "In the event of an emergency, an oxygen mask will be released from above your seat. If you are traveling with small children or someone who needs assistance, place the mask over your mouth and nose first. Then help the person who needs your assistance."

It may seem counterintuitive to take care of yourself before helping your child or someone who is elderly or disabled, but all airlines dispense this advice before a flight takes off. Why? Because they know that if you do not get oxygen for yourself, not only will you be in trouble, those who depend on you will be in trouble too.

When your life is hectic—a nonstop whirlwind of taking care of everyone and everything that needs your attention—taking a break to reflect and prioritize yourself can seem impossible. To some, it may even feel irresponsible. However, self-care is key to honoring yourself. Many African American women will insist that they honor themselves every day. But their actions are not aligned with this priority. From food choices to relationship choices, honoring oneself means making self-care a top priority. Self-care is the oxygen mask on the plane. If you don't have it in the turbulent moments, you risk your life and the well-being of those who need you most.

When your needs are met, you are nicer to be around. You have more to give. You don't feel resentful of the things you do for others and you're happier. Many women resent their spouses and family responsibilities because they haven't taken time to nourish their own minds, bodies, and spirits. They don't even know what they need. Their mode of operation is simply to try to keep up. Attempting to meet everyone else's needs without regard for one's own is a recipe for anger, resentment, and a negative attitude toward life in general.

The stereotype of the angry Black woman with an attitude may reflect this reality. One of the underlying issues here is self-neglect as well as neglect by others. It results in self-protective behaviors that can create a self-sabotaging cycle. "I don't need a man," "I don't need anyone," is a common reaction to this dilemma. Self-neglect and neglect from others at a time when Black women need support, nurturing, and love create a downward spiral.

The decision to dedicate one-tenth of your waking hours to cultivating your relationship with your* self *can change the course of your life forever.

WHAT DO YOU NEED MOST?

Honoring your *self* and reversing the cycle of self-neglect and neglect by others means identifying what you need and then setting up your life so that your needs can be met.

What do you need in your life to be satisfied? It is within your control to make choices and establish boundaries that ensure your needs are met. As you strive for balance, you will begin to make choices that are good for you in order to get what you need. You may reject relationships that are unhealthy, end unhealthy lifestyle habits and no longer compromise your values. These decisions create the circumstances for achieving life satisfaction and model the concept of "honoring yourself" for your children and the people around you. When you learn how to honor yourself, you can set your sights on a new destination–happiness.

THE FORBIDDEN QUESTION: WHAT TRULY MAKES YOU HAPPY?

Dissatisfaction and disconnection from self can have serious consequences. At a recent women's conference, I asked participants to

Happiness

Are you happy? When was the last time you felt genuinely happy? Are you happy in your present relationship, with your job, about the place where you live? Do you know what makes you happy? Was there ever a time when you felt you were happy—you know—sitting on top of the world? Some-times we are afraid to ask these questions, and we are equally afraid of the answers.

Seek happiness. It is one of those supreme feelings. We make our own happiness, and we all deserve to have it in quantity. Make it a priority to participate in activities that will lift your spirits, and be around people who have positive attitudes. Let yourself have fun. It really is all right, and it is necessary for wellness. If you can't make yourself happy, who do you think can? It starts first on the inside and flows outward. Happiness is a precious gift. It belongs to you.

Adapted from *An Altar of Words*
by Byllye Avery

identify "What truly makes you happy?" Black women who work on this exercise often feel frustrated and hesitant; some even admit that they can no longer remember what makes them happy. Because their lives are so wrapped up in and dominated by the needs of others, it is almost as if they had been felled by self-induced amnesia. It had been far too long since they dared to connect with themselves.

After the conference, one woman approached me–still uneasy with the question. "I'm really bothered by what you said," Jeanie began. "It's so simple, but I can't answer it. You made me realize how disconnected I am."

At 40 years old, Jeanie, who is single and successful in her career but dancing to the tune of others, is certainly not alone. If you are walking in this sister's shoes, it may be time to push the pause button, sit down, and get up close and personal with your life satisfaction.

Life Satisfaction Inventory

The inventory below will help you measure your life satisfaction quotient. The more "yes" answers you are able to check, the more life satisfaction you are likely to experience on a daily basis. There is no score sheet for this exercise, because you alone can identify all that is needed to fulfill your life. However, these statements can show you which of your three primary relationships is most in need of your attention.

Over time, your work is to transform every checked "no" into a "yes" by learning to free yourself from old unquestioned habits and self-defeating patterns.

Life Satisfaction Inventory
How Satisfied Are You?

	Yes	No
Self		
I know my purpose.	❑	❑
My vision for my life excites me.	❑	❑
I welcome the opportunities that my later years will bring.	❑	❑
I am optimistic about aging.	❑	❑
I feel in control of my life.	❑	❑
I consistently take care of my body – eating healthy foods regularly.	❑	❑
I exercise three or more times each week.	❑	❑
I have a financial plan, and I am on the road to financial security.	❑	❑
I set personal goals and take steps daily towards my mission.	❑	❑
I love my work.	❑	❑
I take time off to do things I enjoy without feeling guilty.	❑	❑
I like who I am at this point in my life.	❑	❑
My life has meaning.	❑	❑
Others		
I have loving relationships with my mate and family.	❑	❑
I have trusted friends in whom I can confide.	❑	❑
I am satisfied with my love life.	❑	❑
I get along well with my co-workers.	❑	❑
I feel connected in a meaningful way to my community.	❑	❑
I am making a positive difference in the lives of others.	❑	❑

I can say "no" to others when necessary or appropriate.	❑	❑
I set and honor boundaries around my time and priorities.	❑	❑
I avoid relationships that drain my energy.	❑	❑
Overall, my relationships are healthy.	❑	❑

Spiritual Life		
I feel spiritually connected	❑	❑
I pray daily.	❑	❑
I trust my intuition.	❑	❑
My faith is stronger now than ever before.	❑	❑
I have relationships with people who encourage my spiritual journey.	❑	❑
I count my blessings on a regular basis.	❑	❑
My love for God is reflected in my love for others.	❑	❑
I learn spiritual lessons from my failures and mistakes.	❑	❑
I hold no grudges; I forgive all who have wronged me.	❑	❑

Now that you've completed the "Life Satisfaction Inventory," ask yourself, "How satisfied am I really?" In the chapters that follow you will learn more about who you are and what you really need in middle life. Remember, achieving life satisfaction is a process.

Chapter 9

THE FIRST COMMANDMENT— LOVE THYSELF, KNOW THYSELF, HONOR THYSELF

For so many African American women—perhaps you included —life moves at such a hectic pace that taking time for *self* seems nearly impossible. Yet, taking time for "you" is the first commandment of life satisfaction. When you are too busy to spend a few moments everyday "checking in" with *self*, you will inevitably become disconnected from the things that truly matter. The focus of your life will become completely external—meeting the needs and demands of everything and everyone but you. When this happens, the disconnection process will continue to escalate until one day you realize that your life no longer belongs to you and it no longer reflects who you are. You may start to ask yourself—*who am I, and what happened?*

I challenge you to pause today and dig deep for the answers that will help you invest in yourself. These answers will help you create the most satisfying life possible today and in the years to come. For if you want to know what your future will look like, look at the seeds you are planting today.

Self-connection is the most important tool you can use to create a fulfilling and satisfying life. In this chapter, we will discuss specific ways to cultivate a relationship with *self* by learning how to identify the values, passion, purpose, vision, and goals that will make up your "Invest in Yourself Plan" for life satisfaction.

SELF-WORTH AND SELF-LOVE

During my college years in California, I worked for a modeling agency that represented a lot of children. On this particular Saturday, I worked with two energetic and adorable six-year-old Black girls—Tammy and Nicole. These delightful little beauties were learning the ropes in a business that can be harsh on one's self-esteem. I noticed that Tammy was withdrawn and on the verge of tears as we practiced walking down the runway. When I took her to a nearby powder room and asked what was wrong, Tammy sat quietly. "Nicole said I'm not pretty like she is. She said I'm too dark to be a model and my hair is too nappy."

I grabbed a tissue and dabbed the hot tears streaming down her cheeks. She had been enjoying herself up until this point, and she was deeply hurt that her new friend—the only other Black child in the group—had said something so cruel.

"Tammy, you are absolutely beautiful!" I said emphatically. Turning her to face the mirror in front of us, I knelt beside her. "You are smart and kind and sweet—and that's what makes you really beautiful. Look at your lovely face and your beautiful dark skin—it's as soft and as pretty as velvet. And your smile lights up the whole room," I said lovingly smiling at her reflection in the mirror. Tammy's face brightened with a glimmer of hope in her eyes. After a hug, she began to regain her previous confidence.

Even today, I can still remember Tammy's look of dejection. The interaction between these two little girls is reminiscent of Dr. Kenneth B. Clark's "Doll Study," cited in the landmark 1954 *Brown v. Board of Education* Supreme Court case, in which Black girls preferred white dolls over Black dolls, when given a choice. Recent replications of this research by Powell-Hopson and Hopson in 1988 and Riley in 1995 have created similar results. This is a painful illustration of how long-standing and deep-rooted the issues of self-concept, value, and self-esteem are for African American women. Our devaluation starts from the moment we are able to understand words and absorb media images. Living in a society that elevates European features—skin tones, mannerisms, and personality traits impacts Black girls beginning in early childhood and the disenfranchisement continues throughout our lives. Such experiences influence how we feel about ourselves and each other, how we interact and compete with one another, and how we relate to the rest of society.

While insecurities affect people regardless of race or gender, African American women have consistently battled factors that threaten our identity and self-concept. Media images, societal expectations, and sometimes even people within the African American community do not hold Black women in high esteem unless they represent the qualities of non-Black women. While the negative impact on the psyche of African American women cannot be quantified, the impact is undeniable.

Most African American women are so used to the pressure of being "other" that it does not penetrate their conscious awareness on a daily basis. This "otherness" results in, more often than not, a lost sense of self. Motivated by a desire to meet unattainable conventional beauty standards and receive the approval of others, Black women often make decisions that negatively impact their emotional and physical well-being. These decisions often are not based on fulfilling themselves, but rather on masking frustration and filling a void.

In a society in which many African American women feel that they must constantly prove their worth—and confirm that they are good enough, we feel increased pressure to conform and make choices based upon what others think and need, rather than on what we want for and of ourselves. In order to disprove the pervasive stereotypes, images, and myths, we often mask our frustration and attempt to assimilate.

As recent market-research studies show, African American women disproportionately spend money on brand-name items, luxury cars, beauty products, and high-end material goods that are external symbols of success. Some overspend because of peer pressure, but much of this excessive consumerism is driven by low self-esteem. We internalize the messages and overcompensate for our hair and skin color. It's often difficult to break this pattern because it is so deeply hidden. The best antidote for low self-worth is free—it's called self-love.

Self-Love

Think of one person in this world you love dearly. Close your eyes and imagine yourself with him or her. Think about the things you do together and the ways in which you have been there for each other. If I were to observe your relationship with your loved one, how would I know that you love this person? To answer this question, I would most likely consider your treatment of this individual, your attentiveness, the level of respect you demonstrate, the kinds of things you do for him or her, and your concern for this person's well-being. If you profess your love for someone, yet treat that person terribly, I would question your sincerity. For me to believe that you love this individual, your actions need to mirror your profession of love.

Interestingly, most people readily apply this "actions speak louder than words" concept to their relationships with others, but not to their relationship to themselves. Yet loving yourself builds your confidence, self-esteem, and courage to make choices that lead to success. It is not about being self-absorbed and caring only about yourself. It is about acknowledging and meeting your need to be valued simply for being who you are.

- Each time you stand up for yourself in some way you are loving yourself.
- When you take time to treat yourself to a much-needed break, you are loving yourself.
- When you refuse to beat yourself up for past mistakes, you are loving yourself.
- When you consciously create a beautiful environment in which to live, you are loving yourself.
- When you choose to eat healthfully so that your body can function at its optimal level, you are loving yourself.

Consider the following statements in order to gauge whether yours is an attitude of self-love or self-neglect. Place a check mark beside the statements that are true for you.

- ❑ **I put everyone else's desires ahead of my own.**
- ❑ **I am uncomfortable saying no when I don't want to do something.**
- ❑ **I consider myself too busy to pamper or nourish myself daily.**
- ❑ **If I am not feeling well, I am unlikely to rest or take the day off from work.**
- ❑ **I put up with rude or inappropriate behavior from others.**
- ❑ **I skip meals because of my busy schedule.**

- ❑ **I am very hard on myself when I make a mistake, to the point of calling myself names. ("I'm so stupid for doing that" or "How could I be such and idiot?")**
- ❑ **I would feel guilty about treating myself to something special, even as a reward for reaching a goal.**

If you checked any of these statements you have some work to do! That's okay, though, because at least you know where you're starting from. If most of these statements do not apply to you, you are already in a self-loving place, and it will be easier for you to make a genuine connection to yourself on all levels.

Self-love cultivates your connection with your *self.* Self-knowledge is another essential part of self-love. Remember, you want to move from an attitude of self-neglect to self-love. In doing so, you will experience more peace, joy, and calm, along with less chaos, stress, and aggravation. You will begin to find the "you" that you were meant to be. Nurturing your mind, body, and spirit means you have more of yourself to give to those you love and to what matters most to you.

Adapted from *Listen to Your Life*

Finding Your Signature Strengths

No matter what inner vulnerabilities we may face, African American women have a history of being resourceful. For decades, Black women have loved and nurtured their families and made the most out of limited resources. By focusing more on what they did have rather than on what they didn't have, our foremothers persevered—leaving a powerful legacy from which we can draw inspiration today.

Perseverance. Dedication. Resilience. These are just a few of the "signature" character traits that are frequently used to describe African American women, based upon our collective experience. It is important to remember these collective strengths as you move toward your vision of a satisfied and fulfilling future. Most people overlook their greatest strengths. But in order to fulfill your greatest potential, it is essential that you acknowledge and use these strengths consciously.

Professor Chris Peterson, a psychologist at the University of Michigan, developed the Values in Action (VIA) strengths test to measure an individual's five signature strengths. In a January 2004 article in *Psychology Today*, Peterson reported that early indications in an online study of 110,000 subjects showed that "people whose top five strengths are curiosity, zest, gratitude, hope, and the capacity to love and be loved, score higher on surveys of life satisfaction than the rest of us." However, the most-often identified strengths in this online study were curiosity, fairness, love, judgment (open-mindedness), and appreciation of beauty.

Think of a time when you reached an important accomplishment that may have seemed unattainable or at least very challenging for you. What strengths did it take for you to achieve that goal? What character traits did you embody in the process? Make a list of them. These are the signature strengths that define you. You have what it takes to achieve personal life satisfaction. And it is important that you continually remind yourself that you do. So often, it is tempting to minimize your own strengths and forget all that you have done in the past to get to where you are now.

Self-investment begins with identifying your assets. One way to do this is to identify your signature strengths. I suggest that you start by researching your hidden strengths or untapped resources by taking the VIA strengths test and becoming acquainted with the twenty-four character strengths online at www.AuthenticHappiness.com.

Finding your signature strengths does not mean simply patting yourself on the back. Instead it can reveal hidden resources that allow you to harness the best that you have to give.

List your signature strengths below. If you are uncertain, ask someone you trust to give you feedback.

Your Signature Strengths

____

______________________ ______________________

______________________ ______________________

Invest in Yourself 101

One proven method for launching in-depth self-exploration is through journal writing. However, to produce the desired results you must make a firm commitment to "going fishin'."

Taking time for "you"
is the first commandment of life satisfaction.

Schedule a Weekly Life Satisfaction Appointment

Change your channel. We schedule appointments and make time for everyone and everything. Today is the day to book your own undivided attention. Block out at least one hour of uninterrupted time for yourself each week.

Begin your life satisfaction appointment by unplugging from the normal demands of your day. Take a long walk in nature, or let your mind expand by absorbing beautiful images in an art or photography book, or listen to your favorite instrumental music. Whatever respite you decide on, it should offer the time and space required to shift from doing and thinking to *being!*

Create your "Invest in Yourself" life satisfaction journal. Keeping a journal is an effective way to discover what's most important to you. Don't worry about writing perfectly or writing a certain number of words. Simply write. Put down the first thought that comes to mind and continue until you feel led to stop.

Your Life, Your Story: Life Review by Decades

In middle life, if you take time to reflect on the lessons life has offered, you realize that you know more about yourself than ever before. Experience truly is the best teacher. However, if you've never taken the time to review and embrace the experiences that have made you who you are, now is the time to begin.

Take this opportunity to reflect on your life by decades in your "Invest in Yourself" life satisfaction journal. Plan to devote 4–6 weeks to this process and schedule a review of one decade each week. Re-imagine the experiences of each stage, highlighting the most important life lessons you have gained. Whether you are thirty-five or fifty-five, it is always a revelation to perform this kind of self-examination.

Childhood. Think back to your childhood from birth to age nine. What are your most significant memories? What relationships do you remember as if they were yesterday? What activities consumed you? How did you feel about school? Who were the adults in your life? What worried you most? What made you happy? What important life lessons did you gain?

Adolescence. Now move forward to the next decade of your life. Ages ten to nineteen represent the journey from childhood to young adulthood. Reflect on your life as a pre-teen and a teenager. What were your greatest joys? Your deepest heartaches? Who did you love, and who loved you? What music did you dance to? What made you stand out? How did you feel about your family, your classmates, your church? What were your greatest accomplishments? Your greatest failures? What important life lessons did you gain?

Twenties. The twenty-something decade is filled with lots of experiments and self-discovery. You may have tasted the sweet thrill of life beyond the bounds of parental authority or crashed when you discovered that being responsible for yourself wasn't as easy as it seemed. What relationships and experiences in this decade forced you to grow? What are your greatest achievements? Your deepest regrets? How would you characterize your spiritual life during this period? What important life lessons did you gain?

Thirties. Once you cross the bridge over thirty, you are faced with major life decisions. Societal pressure and peer pressure demand that you become a so-called grown-up. What were the biggest decisions and the greatest challenges that you faced in your thirties? What did these challenges teach you about yourself, your strengths, and your weaknesses? (Or if you are presently in your thirties, what have you learned thus far?) What have been the most important lessons of this decade?

Forties. African American women in their forties experience many different stages of life. Some are seeing children off to college or helping them launch their own independent lives. Some are marrying and having babies for the first time. Some are divorcing and establishing new lives and new dreams. Some have chosen to remain single, with or without children. And still others are in the prime of their careers and experiencing the fruits of their labor. Contrast your life in your forties with your life in your thirties. What have been the most important lessons in this decade?

Fifties. African American women in their fifties are part of the new era. Today the fifth decade marks the launch into second adulthood or "living on your own terms." Or as one focus group member put it: *"Doing what I want, when I want to because I can!"*

The possibilities of this stage of life are incredibly exciting. Many fifty-somethings are inspired to explore new visions. Women in their fifties report feeling a new vitality and that their lives are getting better and better. Relationships undergo major transformations because old hesitations and once-upon-a-time fears have been tempered by the new reality that declares—"If not now…when?" Words like *purpose* and *destiny* take on new meaning. Second careers are launched, and once contemplated retirements may be postponed.

What lessons have you learned or are you learning during your fifth decade? What are you holding on to, and what are you leaving behind? What is most important to you now? What wisdom have you gained that you could have never imagined in the previous four decades of your life?

Now that you have reflected on some of the most important lessons from each decade of your life, you can connect the dots and see some of your life's recurring themes. Perhaps as you reflect on your past choices, there may be some things that you would like to change. However, all the lessons that you have learned can now claim a place in your wisdom box. Let this hard-earned wisdom help you make positive choices for your future. Remember, mistakes and failures are the blocks for building a better life—not reasons to beat yourself up. In middle life you can see how the choices you make today will create your tomorrow.

Ellen's Life Review By Decade

Childhood. I grew up in the segregated south in a traditional Black family. My parents encouraged me in every way. As a young child, I enjoyed playing and having fun, and going to church. I loved everything about school—reading, writing, and spelling bees thrilled me. I had wonderful teachers. My biggest dream was to be old enough to wear the safety patrol guard belt. I wanted to be a leader even then. My extended family was at the center of my life—grandmothers, great-grandmothers, church folks, and lots of aunts, uncles, cousins and friends. My life was more exciting than any television show.

Looking back, I realize that I learned two important lessons during my childhood. The power of unconditional love—having a family that supported and believed in me no matter what—made all the difference in who I was then and who I am now. My second lesson was that you don't have to have money to be happy. By today's standards, my family was very poor, but later in life I found out just how rich we were in love and caring.

Adolescence. I became the safety patrol captain. Smoked my first cigarette, lost my first boyfriend, and learned to play the flute in the school band. I always stood out because I was a very independent thinker with strong opinions and a big mouth, which my daddy predicted would get me into a lot of trouble. He was right. My teachers channeled all of my energy into the drama club, and I became a top orator.

I graduated from high school at sixteen. To declare myself an adult, I cut off my hair, displaying my newfound independence only to later regret it. But my biggest achievement was winning a scholarship to college, which made my parents incredibly proud. My greatest loss? Getting dumped by my first love before my senior prom because I wasn't willing to "go all the way." Greatest lessons? That if you set a goal—like winning a college scholarship—and work really hard, you could achieve it. That virtue had a high price, one that I was willing to pay to maintain my self-respect and dignity.

Twenties. I graduated from college and got married. I gave up great sex for security and respectability. I learned that there is no security —"things change." I tried hard to live up to everybody's expectations.

I could never figure out my career, but I knew that I could not be a teacher. Yet, I continued to try. There were a lot of highs during this period. I was proud of finishing my degrees and enjoyed the "idea" of being married. But my twenties also set the stage for my first big failure.

Thirties. In my twenties I thought I was grown, but in my thirties I found out what being grown really meant. I became a mother and shortly thereafter my marriage fell completely apart. I finally became respectable to myself. I had always been a responsible individual, but being a divorced single mom really grew me up fast and forced me into lots of new and unexpected experiences. I learned how to juggle hot coals to make ends meet, how to live with disappointment, and that I didn't have to give myself away to be a good mother.

I discovered my real passion—my big mouth needed an outlet—and I found it in public television. The door of opportunity was propped open and I ran inside. I became an assistant to a producer and I never looked back. Over the years I got passed over for promotions, watched higher-ups get credit for my ideas, but I refused to go down.

In my thirties, I learned one of my life's biggest lessons. *"Nobody else's dream or truth can save you, or make you happy."* Life is an inside-out job! No meaning can ever really come from outside of yourself. By the end of my thirties, I realized that I had given up way too much to support other people's dreams.

Forties. In my forties, I discovered I could keep my dreams alive and still be a great producer, mother, lover, friend and daughter! My friends and family struggled with me as I struggled with myself to shed old roles. They all wondered what was wrong with me because I was no longer following the "good long suffering Black woman" script. It was hard, but I stopped playing those roles. I became very self-possessed for a time. You can't go back to what was, you've gotta stay with what is. In my forties I started journaling, something I would have dismissed in the past. It taught me how to go inside.

In my forties, I got real serious about setting goals and achieving them. It was just like cooking a good meal. First you have to decide what it is you want to eat. Then you have to figure out the ingredients and let it cook according to the prescribed time. Not your prescribed time. I became more willing to take on my inner struggles and to take on corporate America. It was an exhilarating ride.

Fifties. In my fifties, I have gained a new sense of freedom. My children are grown up and gone. This is a time of both joy and sorrow. I found love again and lost both of my beloved parents in a very short time. My sisters wanted to award me the matriarch role. I declined to play another one. I said, "I may be the oldest sister, but remember I ain't your mama."

Corporate America has lost its appeal—the thrill is gone. Yet I stay in the game because family emergencies have depleted my retirement fund. I'm still a work in progress—I wish I had known about "retirement crisis." The lesson learned has been that I am responsible for me, and I should have never compromised my future to rescue others.

These excerpts from Ellen's life review by decade demonstrate the power of telling your story to yourself and connecting the dots. We can see Ellen's obvious strengths and some of her weaknesses and how her values evolved over the course of her life. This journal work allowed her to start reflecting on what was important to her, where she has been, and where she wants to go. It sets the stage for Ellen's work ahead in the *six self-discoveries*, the stepping stones for creating a unique path for middle life and beyond.

It's All About Choices

Catherine's view of aging was based on the experiences of her grandmother, "Big Mama." As an adult, she feared getting older because in her mind, aging was synonymous with strokes, diabetes, and financial struggle. While Big Mama was an incredible example of maternal love, Catherine could not see that Big Mama's lifestyle choices were a major contributor to the challenges she faced in her old age.

Big Mama's level of social satisfaction—interaction with family and her church community—was very high. However, her personal satisfaction—as a result of continual health and financial struggles—was low. She was a great cook, but everything on Big Mama's menu was heavy on fat, sugar, and salt. She ate something fried nearly every day of her life. She never exercised. She raised five children on meager earnings that were just enough to get by after her husband died.

Yet, Big Mama had always encouraged Catherine to follow her dreams. "You can do whatever you want," she insisted. "There are so many opportunities for a young woman in today's world. Make me proud, and take advantage of them." Catherine knew her grandmother might have had dreams of her own once upon a time but never had the satisfaction of realizing them. Her grandmother grew up in a different era, with fewer opportunities and more societal and personal stress than Catherine will ever face. In Catherine's mind, struggle and suffering are simply the inevitable burden that most African American women carry as they grow older. However, in reality, Catherine has the opportunity to dramatically affect the quality of her life as she ages by making choices that can create long-term life satisfaction.

Think of someone you know who has retired, and consider how their lifestyle choices at a younger age have shaped their present life. How did they end up in their current circumstances? What did their daily life and choices look like at thirty-five, forty-five, or fifty-five?

Consider this person, not out of judgment, but as someone you can learn from. Often you will discover that their choices and habits were made without a clear understanding of cause and effect. For some, bad outcomes were the result of hard and dangerous living. For others, it was the lack of knowledge about how to live a better life. Today, African American women ages 35-59 have greater access to information than ever before—information that can help us overcome the negative statistics that plague us. You can reverse the expectation that aging automatically means a poor quality of life. As you move forward, you must be deliberate in the choices you make. As I mentioned earlier, too many African American women are "living by accident," failing to recognize that *"no choice" is still a choice.*

My challenge to you today is to keep your life's choices at the forefront of your mind on a daily basis. Ensure that the decisions that you make contribute to a better future for you and those you care about. When you have to make a major decision in your career, relationships, finances, or health, ask, "Will this contribute to the fulfillment of my life's purpose? Will this choice help me reach the goals I have set?"

Middle life marks a critical shift in your personal evolution. You must now choose to be deliberate about your identity, your sense of self, and how you spend your time and energy.

THE SIX SELF-DISCOVERIES

Now that you have contemplated your life by decade and identified some of your most important lessons, let's begin to explore the six essential self-discoveries. These discoveries—your *values, passion, purpose and mission, vision, goals,* and *plans*—are central to successful living. As you fit together the pieces offered by this investigation, you will be empowered to make critical decisions about your life.

Who am I? Answering this question in middle life is the gateway to new self-discoveries. It will help you get to know what and who you value, your purpose and vision, your goals and plans. In turn, it will impact your relationships, health, finance, work, and spiritual life. The first step to life satisfaction is looking at yourself beyond role limitations with new eyes.

The six self-discoveries are central to who you are. In fact, many African American women have never had the time to examine who they are and what they stand for in this way. These explorations will add energy and enthusiasm to your life and allow you to affirm your authentic *self.* They can also help you clarify the direction and path that will bring you the most fulfillment.

Self-Discovery #1: Identify Your Values

Values are the principles or ideals that are most important to you. They represent who you are and the ideals that you are compelled to express through the actions you take every day. They are as essential to your inherent well-being as the air you breathe, the water you drink, or the food you eat. What do you really value?

Earlier, as you pondered the most significant experiences and lessons you learned in each decade of your life, you began to see what you value most. Freedom, excellence, education, adventure, beauty, achievement, health, humor—these are just a few of the values that may have meaning to you.

A woman whose values are "creativity" and "freedom," for example, may find herself extremely dissatisfied in a 9-to-5 job in which new ideas are unwelcome. Once she discovers her key values, it becomes much easier for her to make decisions about her career, relationships and everyday lifestyle preferences. Her desire for flexibility in her work schedule takes on a deeper meaning in her quest for life satisfaction as she discovers the importance of freedom and creativity in her daily life.

Some values develop as a result of life experiences, while others are simply a part of your essence. Review the following list of values adapted from my book, *Listen to Your Life*, and circle six values that spark excitement, meaning and connection within you. Don't circle any values you think you *should* have or that *others* think you should have. Circle only the values that best represent the qualities that convey your essential *self*—the parts of your being that you cannot live without. Identify from the list below the values you would like to express daily in your relationships, work, and general life.

Values List		
Excellence	Professionalism	Holiness
Adventure	Sincerity	Affection
Community	Compassion	Perfection
Freedom	Ministry	Truth
Beauty	Patience	Change
Humor	Control	Transformation
Accomplishment	Courage	Abundance
Empowerment	Risk	Spontaneity
Growth	Fun	Victory
Creativity	Security	Support
Achievement	Preparation	Energy
Education	Strategic Thinking	Curiosity
Service	Wealth	Communication
Partnership	Independence	Love
Joy	Charity	Family
Sensitivity	Purpose	Health
Integrity	Fairness	Fitness
Commitment	Righteousness	Political Consciousness

Now list your values below.

_______________________ _______________________

_______________________ _______________________

_______________________ _______________________

Self- Discovery #2: Uncover Your Passion

Passion is an intense enjoyment, excitement, or love for a particular activity, cause, or thing. Passion is exhilarating because it nourishes your soul. It is possible to be very good at something and yet not be passionate about it. You may possess some extraordinary gifts that you do not want to use on a daily basis. You may have some talents that come easily, but do not engage the core of your being.

The words "passion" and "purpose" are frequently used together. This is because your purpose is connected to the things that you are most passionate about. Your passion is something that comes naturally to you—perhaps even so naturally that you do not recognize it as a unique gift. You might assume everyone feels the same way about your passion that you do.

In my second book, *Listen to Your Life,* I describe purpose as "the point at which your values meet your passion." What is it that makes your heart sing? Is there something that, when you do it, causes time to fly? For example, when I was a child, I would ask my mother to drop me off at the library while she ran errands. I could stay in the library for three hours and it felt like fifteen minutes. I couldn't get enough of books. I didn't read them, I inhaled them. I loved the new worlds they opened to me and the way they brought my imagination to life. I loved what I learned from books and the discoveries I made. As an adult, I still love books. I love them so much, I write them! You could drop me off at my favorite bookstore any day, leave me there for three hours, and it would still feel to me like fifteen minutes. Why? Because I am passionate about the written word.

Pursue things that you are passionate because life will bring storms, test your perseverance and drain your energy. But if you have passion, your zest for life will empower you to persevere.

Unfortunately, countless women never tap into their true passion. And because their passion lies dormant, they are never truly satisfied. Some women may have accomplishments they are proud of; they may be very competent at several things and make a difference in the lives of others—but until they discover and create a sustained connection with their passion, they will never fulfill their true potential. In middle life, it's time to prioritize your passion—and dare to enjoy the special satisfaction it delivers.

Gifts vs. Talents. Your passion is often connected with a unique gift or talent that you possess. Knowing and acknowledging your natural gifts and talents is key to identifying your passion. Some women's gifts come easily and flow so effortlessly through their lives that they have a difficult time recognizing them. Because these gifts come easily, they assume that everyone possesses them. You often hear the terms, "gifts and talents," discussed interchangeably, but they're not the same.

A gift is a talent that is divinely given to you. You may not even be able to explain how you do it. A person who plays the piano by ear without ever taking lessons has been given a divine gift. They were born with it. If they are serious about developing it, they will learn more and enhance their skills, but the basics of it are innate. By contrast, a talent is a skill you have a natural propensity to develop. You work at it, develop it, and, if you are capable enough, you master it, even though it did not come naturally to you. You may enjoy a talent as much as a gift. You may have a passion for it, but you must work diligently to develop it.

Whether your gift or talent is bringing people together, teaching, serving, singing, writing, solving difficult problems, beautifying your environments, or bringing justice to unjust situations, it is important that you identify it.

Make a list of the natural gifts and talents you possess. There are things that you are good at but are not passionate about. These are talents that may support your purpose, but the fire at the core of your purpose is something for which you have an inextinguishable passion. This is an essential distinction because passion is what makes you leap out of bed in the morning excited about the day ahead. Passion keeps you moving forward and pressing toward a goal even when you are weary and all odds seem against you.

What Unique Experiences Ignite Your Passion? In addition to your gifts and talents, a third element of your passion is your experiences. Whether negative or positive, your experiences shape your character, desires, preferences, and personality. Some experiences touch you so deeply that they can change your life. Through the process of living through a particular experience, you may discover something that you must share with others. It becomes your passion. Experience may give you a "cause" to champion. For example, a woman who has endured and overcome abuse, may use that challenging experience as a platform to educate women about the warning signs of a potential abuser and how to keep themselves and their children safe from harm.

Look back to the earlier exercise in which you examined each ten-year cycle of your life and the lessons learned. What can you now recognize as some of your most essential life experiences? Write them down. Sometimes the experiences that we prefer to ignore because we see them as mistakes, failures, or shameful secrets are the ones most likely to empower us to make a difference in the lives of others.

Your Passions ________________________________

____

____

Your Gifts ________________________________

____

____

Your Talents ________________________________

____

____

Self- Discovery #3: Identify Your Purpose and Middle Life Mission

Your purpose in life explains why you are here. It reveals how you use your natural gifts, talents, and experiences to make a positive contribution to the world. Making a difference in others' lives is the central point of your purpose. If your purpose only impacts you, it isn't a purpose. It's simply a goal. When your purpose moves beyond yourself to touch the lives of those whose paths cross yours, then you find satisfaction within your soul.

My purpose in life is to use my gifts and talents for writing and speaking to inspire people—women in particular—to live fulfilling lives. The majority of opportunities that cross my path to fulfill my purpose are with women. While I do not shy away from inspiring men, I recognize that I have a calling to inspire women. It comes more naturally to me.

Your purpose may be even broader—encompassing everyone or it may be intentionally narrow. Perhaps your purpose deals specifically with people within your family, within your sphere of influence at home, work, and church, or within a specific segment of the population. You may have a gift for working with teenage girls, people with cancer, immigrants, children, or the elderly.

Who do you have the unique capacity to influence? Often you are able to reach people with whom you share a similar experience. Your ability to see the humanity and common ground that you share with others empowers you to fulfill your purpose in a variety of ways and to maximize the number of people for whom you can make a positive difference.

If you could sum up your purpose in one succinct sentence, what would it be?

____

____

____

This is one of the most important questions you can answer on the road to life satisfaction. Those who do not identify their purpose often have great difficulty establishing meaningful goals and making important life decisions. You will find the greatest satisfaction when you discover why you are here and how to live the life you were meant to live. Let's take one more look at the questions you have answered thus far:

- What do you value?
- What is your passion?
- What are your natural gifts and talents?
- What unique experiences have you had that will help you fulfill your purpose?

Mission Critical: Are You Living on Purpose?
Your personal mission statement is a precise and action-oriented description of your life's purpose. It explains who you are, what you love and value, and most importantly what action you will take to live what your life is about and what you stand for.

Personal mission statements are unique expressions. No two will look alike. This statement of your essence and purpose may take days, weeks, or months to complete. As your mission statement evolves, remember the process counts just as much as the product. Your middle life mission statement is another essential part of your self-discovery.

For African American women in middle life, writing your personal mission statement can be an extraordinary act of self-empowerment. Research has shown that individuals who put such statements in writing are much more likely to fulfill their missions. The written mission statement is like signing a contract that demonstrates your commitment to initiating the actions required to turn your dreams into reality. This vital expression of your purpose and values can become an important yardstick for your "Invest in Yourself Plan" for life satisfaction.

By following a few simple guidelines, you can create a personal mission statement of your own. Start with how you will accomplish your purpose through your everyday activities. Notice that I use the word "through." That is important to note because your mission should and can be accomplished through many different activities. It should be transferable from one job, project, responsibility, or activity to another. If you can only carry out your mission in one specific way, then it is not transferable. It does not allow you the flexibility to change course.

"My mission is to be promoted to vice president within the next three years" is not a transferable mission, and it does not explain how your mission will benefit anyone else. This statement is a wonderful goal, but it is inadequate as a mission. Take another look at my personal mission statement and discover how it is transferable to all areas of my life.

My purpose in life is to use my gifts and talents for writing and speaking to inspire people—women in particular—to live fulfilling lives.

Your personal mission statement should be short, to the point, action-oriented, and entirely your own. You cannot live out the mission someone else thinks you should have for yourself. It must be yours. Your mission will fit you like a glove. Living your mission gives you joy. In fact, at middle life you are probably living your mission to some degree even if you have never had the opportunity to put it into writing.

For example, being a nurse can be "what you do," but serving as a catalyst for healing may be the description that defines your mission. As a catalyst for healing, you can see how your purpose can be lived out in your personal and professional life. Your mission statement will be a comprehensive description of why you do what you do and explains how your life will impact the world around you.

Your personal mission statement addresses three fundamental questions: What is my life about? What do I stand for? What action am I taking to live my purpose? Here are a few examples:

- "My mission is to bring joy to others through the gift of music."
- "I wish to instill a thirst for knowledge in children."
- "I create beautiful environments in which to live, love, and learn."
- "My mission is to serve as a catalyst for positive change in stagnant situations."
- "My mission is to help people be healthy."

Notice that each of the mission statements above is not specific to a job or role. They could be applied to any of the five key areas of your life—relationships, work, money, health, and your spiritual life. For example, fitness expert Donna Richardson identifies her personal mission as "helping people be healthy." It is something she does through her work as an author, fitness expert, television personality, and speaker. But it could also describe how she encourages family and friends, crusades in churches across America inspiring women to "take care of their temples," gives of her resources, and cares for her own health.

Likewise, your mission statement should not describe a single role that you fill or a job that you have. Jobs and roles are temporary, but your mission can last a lifetime.

Your purpose explains why you do what you do. It explains why a certain career choice is right for you. If your mission is to help people be healthy, you could pursue any variety of career paths—doctor, nurse, fitness trainer, nutritionist, psychologist, counselor, yoga instructor, massage therapist, health instructor, scientist, pharmaceutical representative, and the list goes on.

If you were laid off from your job, and you understood your life's mission, you would not suddenly feel that your life was meaningless. You would understand that it was time to find a new role to help you continue living your purpose. If you observed family members putting themselves in danger of developing certain diseases or health problems, you would likely recognize your purpose in helping them improve their habits. If you were making a charitable contribution, you might be drawn to organizations that also fulfill your mission. Those who do not identify their purpose and their life's mission often have great difficulty establishing meaningful goals and making important life decisions.

THE MIDDLE LIFE MISSION STATEMENT WORKSHEET

Part I.
Name the purpose, philosophy, principle or cause that is most important to you. (What your life is about or what you stand for.) Feel free to add adjectives to clarify your statement.

Write the word (s) or phrase here:

____

Review the following list of action words. These verbs will help you express the action that you must take to fulfill your mission.

Circle any words that "grab" you.

Accomplish	Enrich	Practice
Affirm	Entertain	Praise
Appreciate	Establish	Promote
Build	Explore	Provide
Choose	Express	Pursue
Communicate	Facilitate	Receive
Compete	Finance	Renew
Complete	Generate	Research
Compliment	Give	Respect
Continue	Heal	Satisfy
Counsel	Identify	Save
Cultivate	Impact	Sell
Create	Implement	Serve
Defend	Improve	Share
Deliver	Inspire	Speak
Demonstrate	Invest	Support
Design	Lead	Sustain
Discover	Live	Touch
Discuss	Love	Travel
Educate	Measure	Understand
Effect	Mold	Use
Empower	Motivate	Value
Encourage	Nurture	Volunteer
Enhance	Open	Win
Enjoy	Organize	Work
Enlighten	Perform	Write

Part II:
Now identify the three verbs that describe the action(s) you will take or what you will do to fulfill your purpose.

____

____

Part III. Identify the individual(s), group(s) or cause(s) that you will serve or affect in a positive way.

____

____

____

Part IV. Now that you have drafted all three parts of your mission statement, let's put them all together.

My mission is:

____

____

____

Self-Discovery #4: Affirm your vision

Now that you have completed your personal mission statement, you are well-equipped to create a vision for your future. Your vision presents a vivid picture of what you want your ideal life to look like in the future. Unlike your personal mission statement, your vision, can be as long and descriptive as you would like. Your vision is like a feature-length film of your future life satisfaction unfolding over the next year, five years, ten years, twenty years, or more.

Alice's vision statement. "I am a retired school administrator, loving wife, and mother of two well-adjusted and successful adult children. I collect a full pension from the board of education and earn $30,000 per year in retirement income investments. I walk a brisk mile every weekday morning, and I commune with God and pray while I walk. I am active in church activities and am a soloist in our church choir.

My husband and I have a strong, healthy relationship and travel regularly to beautiful vacation getaways where we stroll along our favorite beaches glad to be alive and still in love."

Alice's vision is vivid and expressed in the present tense so that she can imagine herself living it right now. Being able to see yourself living your vision is the key to achieving it. Begin to explore a detailed vision statement for your life—including your work, health, finances, relationships, and spiritual life by making time to write in your "Invest in Yourself" life satisfaction journal.

Whenever your life veers off track, look to your vision statement for direction. Remind yourself of your vision often. Display it where you will see it frequently. As you visualize yourself in a new and better place, your mind will begin to create course corrections to get you to where you want to go. This is a powerful, yet common occurrence when you *seek* positive changes.

Take the time now to identify the most important visions you hold for your life in the following areas:

Vision Statements

Relationship Vision: ______________________________

____

____

____

____

Health Vision: ________________________________

____

____

____

____

Work Vision: ____

____

____

____

____

Finance Vision: ____

____

____

____

____

Spiritual Vision: ____

____

____

____

____

Self-Discovery # 5: Set Clear, Compelling Goals

Once you've established your vision, you're ready to set concrete goals. Your goals are the specific, tangible objectives you must achieve to bring your vision to life.

NCNW's focus group research indicates that African American women are far less likely to establish quantifiable personal goals than men and women of other racial groups. Why has goal setting proved to be so difficult for African American women? Preliminary evidence suggests that the inability to set personal goals is the result of Black women's inability to prioritize their own needs. This experience leaves them much more vulnerable to losing their vision.

When the *self* is poorly defined or consistently ignored, you end up fulfilling other people's goals, instead of establishing and satisfying your own. Your time and energy are focused on making certain that the priorities of your families, friends, employers, and colleagues are fulfilled at your personal expense.

However, goals are essential to your level of life satisfaction, achievement, and fulfillment. Every goal you set must contain five basic elements. When any single element is missing, you may find yourself floundering or ineffective in achieving what's most important to you.

Goals must be specific. Vague goals are ineffective. While you may reach your intended desire, the process is usually slower and sometimes more complicated when the initial goal is not specific. "I want to lose weight," is a vague goal. "I want to lose twenty-five pounds, trim six inches from my waist, and tone up my flabby arms so that they don't jiggle," is specific! Make sure your goals are detailed. The details will help you focus on the most important activities that will lead to the achievement of the goal.

Goals must be measurable. One of the reasons it is important to establish specific goals is that you want to be able to measure your progress. If you cannot measure your goal, it is not specific enough. You can measure your progress—and gain lots of encouragement in the process—when the stated goal is to lose twenty-five pounds, trim six inches from your waist, and tone your arms. When you've lost eight pounds, trimmed two inches from your waist, and started to see progress with the toning, you know you are more than 30 percent to your goal. You can practice the same goal-setting process in your relationship, finance, work, and spiritual lives. Always remember to define your goals so that you can measure your progress at every step along the way.

Goals must reflect your values, passion, purpose, mission, and vision. Remember that your goals are derived from your vision, which is built on your mission, which is built on your values, passion, talents, gifts, and experiences. Once you have gone through the process of self-discovery, identifying each of the elements discussed in this section, then your goals will increasingly reflect your authentic *self.* Re-examine any goal in your life that is no longer a reflection of your values, passion, purpose, mission, and vision. And don't be afraid to revise or discard your obsolete goals. As you learn more about who you are and define what life satisfaction means to you personally, it will be easier to see what goals need to be revised, updated or discarded.

At each stage of life, your vision will change, and therefore, your goals should change also. What was important to you at thirty may not be as relevant at forty or fifty. See your life as an on-going journey, and don't hang on to goals that no longer serve you.

Goals must have a deadline. A goal with no deadline is a dream. When you don't establish a concrete target date for reaching your goals, it is far more likely that you will never take action. Establish practical deadlines for your goals—then create realistic benchmarks that will indicate your progress along the way.

For example, if part of your vision is to be financially secure by age sixty-five (deadline) and your specific goal is to generate $4,000 per month in passive income, your timeline may indicate the milestones at which your investments generate $500 per month, $1,000 per month, $2,500 per month, $3,500 per month, and finally your desired goal of $4,000 per month. Your strategic plan begins with getting specific about the goal ($4,000 per month in passive income) and then setting a deadline (age sixty-five). You can practice this process with every goal you set.

Invest one-and-a-half hours every day to reviewing your personal goals. Using your personal mission statement as a compass to guide you in the right direction, identify the number # 1 goal you would like to achieve in each of the five key areas of your life within the next year:

 # 1 Personal Goals for the Next Year

Relationship Goal: ______________________________

____

____

____

____

Finance Goal: ______________________________

____

____

____

____

____

Health Goal: ______________________________

____

____

____

____

____

Career Goal: ______________________________

____

____

____

____

____

Spiritual Life Goal: ______________________________

____

____

____

____

Now identify the # 1 goal you would like to be able to accomplish in your lifetime in each of the five key areas:

 # 1 Personal Goals for Your Lifetime

Relationship Goal: ______________________________

____

____

____

____

____

____

Finance Goal: ______________________________

____

____

____

____

____

Health Goal: ______________________________

____

____

____

____

____

Career Goal: ____________________

____

____

____

____

____

Spiritual Life Goal: ____________________

____

____

____

____

____

Based upon the one year and lifetime goals you have set, you can identify what needs to happen in your life to accomplish your objectives.

Self-Discovery # 6: Create Your Life Satisfaction Action Plan
How do you bring your specific, measurable, purposeful goals to life by your stated deadline? You must take purposeful action!

Life satisfaction requires a daily personal investment. Is your investment producing the returns you want? Perhaps your returns are right on target in one area but not another. Before you can determine how to allot your daily personal investment of time and energy, you need to know what you are trying to achieve.

Earlier, I illustrated this concept by suggesting that you invest 10 percent of your waking hours in activities that build life satisfaction. How you spend your time will ultimately determine how you spend your life. To calculate how much time you should dedicate to building and maintaining life satisfaction, let's assume you sleep a full eight hours each night—a practice that can lead to more energy and a longer life. That leaves sixteen hours per day and 112 hours per week for work and other activities. For simplicity's sake, this means that you will dedicate one-and-a-half hours each day to creating a more satisfying life. You can transform your life when you live your plan every day. Unforeseen accidents, acts of God, and lottery windfalls notwithstanding, you will manifest what you focus on in your life. The choices you make every day create your circumstances—in your relationships, finances, health, work, and spiritual life.

This is why creating your action plan is so important. Taking the time to plan—and it doesn't always take a lot of time (although for some goals, it might)—allows you to consider your various available options.

To work your plan:

- Write down every action required to bring your plan to life.
- Identify the people you need to connect with.
- Outline the obstacles you will need to overcome.
- Detail the actions you will take to overcome them.

It's helpful to base your plan on the milestones you set when you established your original deadline. This way, you can match your action plan with your timeline. If this process gets overwhelming, ask for input from a trusted friend or adviser. You don't have to do it alone.

The Best Investment You'll Ever Make

Earlier, I challenged you to give 10 percent of your waking hours to cultivating and enhancing your level of life satisfaction.

Use a portion of this time to identify and implement the specific action plan that will lead you to the achievement of your goals. Incorporate goal setting and purposeful action into your daily routine. This type of conscious decision-making builds your level of confidence in your ability to take control of your destiny. Remember, it's all about living on purpose—establishing your personal mission based on your values and passion, setting compelling goals and executing your strategic action plan. These are the cornerstones of a satisfied life.

Working Your Plan

As you take action toward your goals, use these three guidelines to stay focused and on track:

Identify Your Priorities—Be Specific. Have you ever started your day with a plan for everything that needed to be accomplished and ended the day with the most important tasks still incomplete? Establishing your number one goal in each area of your life will keep your eye on the prize. Refuse to allow the things that matter most to you—your top priorities—to be sideswiped by less important activities.

Commit To Your Goals. To achieve your goals, you must make a commitment to them. Are there activities in your life that no longer suit you or take too much of your time? Drop those things from your schedule that do not support the creation of the personal and professional life that is meaningful and satisfying to you.

For example, you may choose to have lunch with a friend or relative once a week as a part of your goal to cultivate stronger relationships with your friends and family. You might choose to participate in an organized physical activity such as yoga, tennis, or aerobics to ensure you get your three workouts every week. In addition, you might choose to designate Friday nights for special family activities. And every Sunday evening, you might commit to spending 30 minutes reviewing how you will spend your time and money in the coming week.

Remember, commitment to your goals is measured by the consistent effort you make to achieve them. If you commit to spending ten hours per week to create your life satisfaction, and you make this commitment a daily and weekly priority, you can transform your life.

Hold Yourself Accountable. Your commitment to your priorities and your action plan should be something that you hold yourself accountable for. Write your action plan on paper and review it regularly. Many women find that their commitment is deepened when they share their goals with someone they trust—such as a coach, mentor, or friend—and ask that person to hold them accountable for what they say they'll do. Even if you need to re-negotiate your priorities and commitments, always be willing to hold yourself accountable for the choices you make.

Vanessa's Six Self-Discoveries

Vanessa used the six self-discoveries to get back on track with a dream deferred. The following excerpts from her "Invest in Yourself" journal demonstrate the power of putting your passion, your purpose, and your plan on paper.

Values

Service and Compassion. Offering my service and showing compassion to others is very important to me. When I was younger, we lived in the projects, and my father worked twenty-four hours a day to get us out. Even after he built our family a new home, he always took us back to the old neighborhood. He said he never wanted us to forget where we came from. He taught us that many people are unable to change their circumstances and that we'd been blessed to be able to change ours. His example taught us to always respect people and not to judge others harshly because we'd never walked in their shoes. This made me understand that we have a responsibility to help others, and there "but for the grace of God go I."

Humor. From early childhood on, I understood and enjoyed the power of humor. When my parents worried about money and how we would make it after my father lost his gas station, I made it my job to make my daddy laugh. If I could make him laugh when things were really hard, it was like making the sun come out from behind the clouds. Shifting perspective and lightening things up with insightful or even silly humor is my way of bringing light and fresh air back into a musty room. Today my humor helps everyone in my circle to stop taking ourselves so seriously. It reminds me of my favorite quote: "You don't stop laughing because you grow old. You grow old because you stop laughing."

Professionalism. Being a pro means making a commitment to doing quality work no matter what your job is. I learned early in life to always do my very best. When I graduated from college there were no jobs available in my field. So, I worked for a janitorial service. I carried the same work ethic into my cleaning assignments that I carry into my work today—doing my job well and doing it right. The quality of your work reflects your degree of integrity. Professionalism is both part of my essence and part of my experience.

Passion.
I have three passions: helping people, advocating for the welfare of children, and creativity. Stopping at age forty-four to identify my passions is really fascinating because I've never really thought about them before. What do I really love and what makes the time fly? I love helping people, especially children, and I love writing poetry—that's always been my creative outlet. No matter how far work and family responsibilities take me away, even an hour of writing poetry helps me make sense out of life and gives me enormous pleasure.

Purpose
Why am I here? To help those who can't help themselves.

Middle Life Mission Statement
To use my knowledge, skills, and creativity to advocate for children and enable them to reach their full potential.

Vision Statement
In my current job, I no longer work with young people. Now that I'm back in touch with my passions and my purpose, it's much easier to see my future. Here we go… In the next three-to-five years, my husband Roger and I will move to a beautiful island in the Caribbean and establish a Youth Development Center. There, we will enrich the lives of children by helping them seek and find new possibilities for their lives.

We will discover excellent funding sources to support our project and train an enthusiastic staff. Our efforts will help build the capacity of the community. Also, Roger and I will build a fabulous home on the beach, where we can enjoy each other every day of our lives. We will work hard and play hard. After work, I'll take time to write my poetry, and my husband will accompany me with his amazing original jazz compositions on the piano. Once a year we will sponsor a spoken word poetry festival to spotlight emerging talent in our new community. My husband and I will enjoy a beautiful retirement in our island paradise and always be young at heart.

Goals
- Research and identify international agencies that fund youth development work.
- Evaluate agencies, and see which ones share our values.

- Consider new stateside career opportunities that will increase my income.
- Explore investment opportunities that will make our money grow.
- Meet with a financial planner.
- Plan quarterly trips to the Caribbean over the next eighteen months to scout potential project locations.
- Identify three islands that would be hospitable to our efforts.
- Stay one month on a prospective island to test the viability of my vision.
- Have Roger work on his six self-discoveries.

Action Plan

As Vanessa used some of the suggested action plan review tips, she began to identify some of the potential obstacles surrounding her vision and goals. "Sometimes I can't see the real challenges involved in meeting my goals. In the past I'd move ahead on something I wanted to make happen, but as soon as a few obstacles appeared, I'd give up. This time, I want to do my homework in advance. By examining the obstacles closely early on, I'll figure out what works and what doesn't work. That will give me a much greater chance of fulfilling my goals."

Facing Obstacles

- Addressing unspoken fears
- Lack of finances
- Cultural differences
- Being an "outsider"
- Building trust with individuals in a foreign country
- Unpredictable weather, hurricane belt
- Leaving family stateside

As Vanessa looks at what's ahead, she'll concentrate on breaking her goals into manageable steps. She laughs and says, "Maybe our Youth Development Center will be located in Prince Georges County, Maryland, instead of St. Croix, but I plan to *live my mission* no matter where my dream finally unfolds."

"At the very least," Vanessa says, "we'll have some great vacations and develop a whole new network of friends. The great thing about having my personal mission statement written out is that I know I can fulfill my mission—of advocating for children—in many different ways."

SIX DECISION MAKING STRATEGIES

As you begin to make the choices that are right for you, refuse to accept excuses or to alter your course of action when obstacles get in the way. As challenges appear (and they definitely will!), consider these five decision-making strategies as you learn to value your true *self* and seek answers that are right for you.

Listen to Your Emotions

Emotions are real, and they may offer important messages, but they are not necessarily the truth. For this reason, it is not wise to make decisions based on your ever-changing emotions. Emotions are based in the moment, influenced by insecurities, and often illogical. Instead, use your emotions as a guide to teach you more about yourself.

If you are angry or irritated on a regular basis, explore the reasons why and ways that you can resolve the issue. If you are feeling overwhelmed, read that as a sign that you may be trying to do too much too fast or without enough support. Adjust accordingly. Anytime you feel a negative emotion, take time to acknowledge and ask, "What is this emotion trying to tell me?" Then allow yourself time to come down from your emotional "high" before acting on the emotion. The same strategy can be used for positive emotions. Excitement, for example, can cause you to make spur-of-the-moment decisions that spoil a well-thought-out plan. Allow yourself to feel excited but refuse to allow your choices to be ruled by your emotions.

Trust Your Intuition

This decision-making strategy is perhaps the most important. Your intuition is your spiritual intelligence. It is a divine inner voice that guides you in the right direction—even when logic would lead you elsewhere. However, in order to access your intuition, you must be connected with your *self*. You must be able to trust that you have access to the answers you need for your life. If you do not feel a sense of inner peace about a decision, do not feel compelled to move forward. Inner turmoil is often a divine message to be still or move in a different direction. Gather the information you need to make intelligent decisions about your life, but accept your intuition as an important decision-making tool. Women who trust themselves and listen to the whispers of their inner voices are more confident and certain about the direction of their lives.

Embrace Change and Seek Growth

We have all heard of the worker who was laid off and got hired for her dream job or started her own business—with great success. Or what about the woman whose spouse walked out, but in the end she found a better love the second time around? Then there are those who have a major health crisis that serves as a wake-up call and leads to a healthier and happier lifestyle. Problems offer you opportunities to upgrade your life. As you encounter unexpected changes along your path, make a decision to find the opportunity for growth or life enrichment in every situation. This approach to life allows you to always see life satisfaction as a real possibility. It empowers you to embrace change by refusing to be a victim of the inevitable curve balls that life throws in your direction.

Solve Your Problems Honestly

It can sometimes be easy to get caught in a trap of never-ending problems. Some women spend more time focusing on a problem than they ever spend trying to solve it. Make a decision to look at every problem or challenge as being solvable—or not. If it is a solvable problem, then focus your energy and time on the solution. If the problem isn't solvable, then let the problem go. This to-the-point decision-making strategy can help you focus more of your time and energy on the people and things that matter most to you. Rather than becoming seduced by drama and issues, take responsibility for solving problems and creating daily life satisfaction.

Reduce Risk

Many women never consider the possibility of life satisfaction because they are afraid. Fear stops them from moving forward because they don't want to take risks that will result in failure, rejection, or regret. The truth is that every choice has its share of risk. Whatever it is that you fear, ask yourself, "How can I reduce my anxiety or risk of failure in this situation?" Make a list. Brainstorm with others. Get the information you need. Open your mind to options you may not previously have considered. Stop asking, "What if I fail? What if I don't have what it takes?" and start asking, "What do I have to do to ensure my success?"

Face Your Fears

Whenever you get clear about who you are and what you want in life, fear usually steps in to challenge your resolve. Now that you have identified your values, passion, purpose, mission, vision, goals, and strategic action plan, don't be surprised if some unexpected twinges of fear emerge as you strive to move forward. Some apprehension is inevitable when you reach for new horizons. It's natural, and it doesn't necessarily mean that you should stop moving forward. Expect fear and move forward in spite of it! When you are willing to face your fear and refuse to let it keep you from living the most satisfying life possible, your fear will begin to subside.

Ask for Help

Because one of the most commonly-cited character traits for African American women is "being strong," we often mistake needing help as a sign of weakness. We identify with being invincible so much that we proudly proclaim: "I'll handle it, I don't need any help!" Nevertheless, being strong also means being honest enough to admit your own humanity. I have had women come into my seminars with stories of simultaneously working full time, going to college full time and raising children without their father. Others have managed multiple jobs while caring for aging parents or grandchildren.

While the resulting achievements are impressive, they often come at a price. Once Black women make the decision to move forward, many of us are willing to take on very heavy loads for the reward of transforming our life circumstances. This is undeniably admirable. It is evidence of one's commitment to achieving a better life. Our willingness to pay a hefty price for achievement can be an investment that pays off for the rest of our life and our family's lives.

However, there are no rewards for being Superwoman. In fact, as a friend once told me, "Being a Superwoman is a super myth." It is not possible to carry a heavy load indefinitely without heavy consequences. Establish limits for how much you can do alone. Honor your own humanity by admitting when you need help. Whether it is as simple as teaching your children to help with household chores or standing up for yourself and taking action when an estranged spouse owes child support, expect those around you who benefit from your efforts to also help lighten your load. Develop relationships with like-minded people. Exchange ideas and support one another. Honor yourself by admitting when you need a break, and then arrange for one.

Schedule a real vacation once a year and learn to lay your burden down. Ask for help and expect to receive it—from someone who can actually provide it.

Honoring yourself will require seeking and maintaining healthy relationships with others, the next step in creating your Invest in Yourself life satisfaction plan.

Chapter 10

BUILDING HEALTHY RELATIONSHIPS

When you look back over your life and think of your best memories, many of them will be connected to special moments shared with the people most important to you. While our lives can at times feel overburdened and overdriven, rushing from one task to the next, the truth is that no one lies on their death bed wishing they had checked off more items on their to-do list.

Unfortunately, too many of us look back and wish we had spent more time and energy creating meaningful relationships. The regret of holding a grudge too long, uttering a hurtful word, spending too much time trying to be right and too little time offering acceptance and forgiveness can linger for a lifetime. The richest lives are those that are filled with meaningful and satisfying relationships. Cultivating such treasures begins with knowing and being yourself—the concept we've discussed in Chapter nine.

Middle life is the time to revitalize your relationships. When you are not living a life that honors your true self, your relationships with family and friends suffer. When you operate from your authentic self you are clear about what you want in your relationships. You appreciate what you give and receive in your relationships. You do not devalue yourself based upon other people's opinions. You operate in truth and are committed to eliminating toxic patterns in relationships before they take root.

More importantly, you notice when your relationships need to be nurtured or healed. It is impossible to have mature and satisfying relationships when you must pretend to be someone else—acting as though you enjoy certain people and things, afraid to stand up for yourself and speak your mind, or pretending that someone else's unacceptable actions or words are okay with you.

When the fundamental values in your relationships are congruent, there's a solid foundation to build on. This is not to say that every aspect of your relationships must bow to the demands of your ego. Acceptance and adaptation are essential aspects of successful relationships. However, when your values oppose the values of those you interact with, ongoing issues will inevitably frustrate the formation of healthy relationships.

> *Friends are those who despite all the ways in which we could be jealous of each other, compare ourselves to each other, and despite all the opportunities we have had to betray each other's trust, lie on each other, steal from each other, and take advantage of each other's weaknesses—we have chosen not to go there in our relationship. We've certainly chosen not to stay there on those occasions when we have been less than perfect with each other. We've chosen to support each other, to celebrate each other, to stay true to each other, and to make ourselves available to each other in the good times and in the bad ones.*
>
> *Ask women how they define friendship, and they talk about such things as being known and accepted, understood to the core; feeling you can count on trust and loyalty, having someone on your side; having someone to share worries and secrets as well as the good stuff of life, someone who needs you in return.*
>
> *"Girl, I Know Just What You Mean"*
> *by Renita J. Weems, PhD*

A Mid-life Friendship Makeover

Janet was on the fast track with her new career. Although her new job was exciting, she was frustrated to find herself stuck in an energy-draining relationship with her former co-worker Sharon. Friends for years, Janet always offered Sharon a shoulder to lean on, but recently Sharon seemed to be stuck in the past doing the same things and talking about the same old problems. Sharon's negativity was beginning to wear on Janet.

As Janet moved forward in her life, she recognized that her friendship was moving in reverse. For the first time, she understood that she needed the same kind of cheerleading and support that Sharon counted on her to provide.

After a lot of soul searching, Janet decided to be honest with Sharon about the state of their relationship. Over a pleasant lunch, Janet explained that she no longer looked forward to their daily phone calls because they were dedicated to a litany of what was wrong in their lives instead of thanking God for what was right. She confessed that she didn't have everything all together—and that she needed encouragement and support too—especially on her new job.

To Janet's delight Sharon was eager to move their relationship to a new level. Sharon apologized for not being more supportive of her friend and admitted that her negativity stemmed from the fear that her lack of self confidence would lead her to a dead end in her life.

By identifying what was important in their relationship, Janet was able to ask her friend for what she needed. Inspired by Janet's example, eventually Sharon began taking steps toward a better life for herself.

Many women have never given any serious thought to what a mature and satisfying friendship looks like. However, in order to experience genuine life satisfaction, it is essential that you create balance in your relationships with those you live with, work with, and love.

Let's take a look at the relationships that can influence your life.

- Spouse or significant other
- Children
- Parents
- Siblings
- Extended family members (aunts, uncles, cousins, grandparents)
- Family friends
- Best friend
- Friends
- Co-workers (including bosses, staff, peers,etc.)
- Colleagues
- Acquaintances
- Neighbors
- Community
- Advisers and mentors
- Strangers and others who cross your path

"We must make the greatest effort to create loving spaces in our relationships where each partner can share his or her truest self as well as mess up and make up without being punished or losing the other's love."

From In The Spirit by Susan L. Taylor

Getting What You Need From Your Relationships

Life is relationships! And understanding who you are and what you need will help you get the most out of all your relationships.

Cheryl loved her work and the people she worked with, but her job did not provide the salary she deserved based on her performance review. She discussed her concerns with her boss, who twice in the last two years had given Cheryl small pay increases. However, the modest raises fell far below the salary scale for her experience and education, and failed to satisfy Cheryl's financial goals.

Once Cheryl recognized this stalemate, she realized she had a choice: Stay and accept the current reality, or move to a new company. Cheryl chose to move on and increased her salary by 30 percent. "I wish I'd done it sooner," she later admitted. "I was expecting my old company to fulfill a need that it couldn't meet. If I had been able to assess this business relationship minus my emotions, I would have made the decision to leave long ago."

Cynthia, age forty-five, is a wife and mother whose 12 year marriage was floundering. From the beginning, her husband Angelo was never committed to family life; he was unfaithful and unapologetic. Cynthia found herself filling the roles of breadwinner, primary parent, household handyman and more. After two separations and a recent unsuccessful reconciliation, Cynthia was finally ready to admit just how dissatisfied she was.

In a personal coaching session, I asked, "What do you need to get out of this relationship?"

"Nothing that I can actually get," she replied. "I am finally at the point where I just can't fake it anymore. This marriage is killing me inside. None of my needs are being met, and my dignity is in the pits." As Cynthia began to describe the kind of relationship she really wanted, she recognized that if she could not trust Angelo and they did not share similar values after twelve years, there was no hope left to build on. She was beginning to know herself and connect spiritually for the first time. As a result, Cynthia was finally able to value her basic relationship needs—such as trust, honesty, respect, mature love, and commitment.

Self fulfillment is not unusual among women who strive to know themselves and then chose to live authentically, figuring out what they need and asking for it. They gain clarity—as Cheryl did with her boss and Cynthia did with her husband—and learn that it is time to move on from a relationship. Or they reconnect in a more meaningful way in existing relationships, opening new doors that can be beneficial to both parties.

Now it's time to honestly review what you need and what's most important to you in your relationships.

Take out your *"Invest in Yourself"* journal and list the five most important relationships in your life. Then ask yourself, "What do I need from these relationships?" and then fill in your answers below.

Some common relationship needs include love, respect, stability, trust, adventure, fun, opportunity for growth, acceptance, support, and fair compensation. Be honest about your needs so that you can truly evaluate whether your relationships are meeting those needs.

Name	Relationship	Need

Next, for each person listed, ask yourself,

- What am I getting out of this relationship right now?
- What am I giving to this relationship?

Once you identify your needs, ask yourself, "Does this relationship satisfy my needs?" If your answer is no for a particular relationship, ask yourself, "Can this relationship ever meet my needs?" There are times when we want a person to fill a need that he or she simply cannot meet. This is important to know because it means that the relationship requires some changes. In some cases, it may require a permanent change and the acceptance that it is time to move on.

Do Your Relationships Need Work?

Here are a few signs that will help you determine when your relationships need work:

	Yes	No
Do you engage in bickering or arguments on a regular basis?	❑	❑
Do you have unresolved issues in any of your relationships?	❑	❑
Are you afraid to tell the truth for fear of offending others, even when you really need to speak the truth?	❑	❑
Do you feel you cannot be yourself or express yourself authentically in the presence of a friend or loved one?	❑	❑
Do you do certain things for the sole purpose of impressing people?	❑	❑
Do you feel unappreciated by the people you want to appreciate you?	❑	❑
Are there individuals in your life that you no longer speak to because of a disagreement of some sort?	❑	❑
Are there people in your life who regularly drain your energy?	❑	❑
Do people find it difficult to trust you?	❑	❑
Do you tolerate relationships with people who take advantage of you?	❑	❑
Do you hold grudges or refuse to forgive others?	❑	❑
Do you have relationships in which you need to offer an apology and ask forgiveness, but you have not done so?	❑	❑

	Yes	No
Are you comfortable telling people what your boundaries are?	❑	❑

If you answered "yes" to several of the above questions, your relationships with others will improve by considering the sections that follow.

Throughout the remainder of this chapter, we will look at simple strategies for building healthy relationships.

Seek and Maintain Healthy Relationships

As you consider how your relationships contribute to your life satisfaction focus on the quality of existing relationships rather than the quantity of relationships in your life.

Consider for a moment the legacy you would like to leave for the loved ones in your life. How can you create higher quality experiences with the people you care about most? Are there some things you've been meaning to do but haven't? What memories do you want them to have of you? Great satisfaction comes from knowing that the people in your life are better for having had you in their lives. As you travel along the path of your purpose, don't forget that your purpose encompasses every area of your life, especially your closest relationships.

People with healthy relationships tend to be happier and lead more fulfilling lives. You can always tell if a relationship is unhealthy by the symptoms it produces.

Healthy relationships begin with a healthy you. Healthy relationship—whether a personal or professional—are balanced and nourishing. They leave no room for bullying, selfishness, neglect, or ongoing negativity. Think about your relationship with your spouse or significant other, children, parents, family, friends, co-workers, and neighbors. How can you seek and enjoy healthier relationships?

At the core of many relationship problems is insecurity, selfishness, low self-esteem, fear, people pleasing, or other unresolved issues. In order to be the best in our relationships with others, we must first deal with ourselves. For example, do you always solve everybody else's problems and have no energy left to solve your own? Do you have unrealistic expectations of others and find yourself frequently feeling let down or disappointed? Are you unable to accept others for who they really are?

As you reflect on your relationship issues, don't be hard on yourself. Relationships offer us amazing opportunities for growth and lifelong satisfaction.

Relationship Issues that You Need to Resolve

Identify the relationship weaknesses or issues that you need to resolve.

____

____

Seek Relationship Role Models

Not everyone has witnessed healthy relationships firsthand.

That is why it is important to seek role models that you can learn from. Like a career mentor, a relationship mentor, can offer guidance, inspiration, and advice. Who are your healthy relationship role models?

Sarah's old supervisor, Gwen, was a powerful and unflappable problem solver. She skillfully and respectfully calmed the storms of office politics by always listening and showing respect for differences rather than allowing egos to triumph. Her positive philosophy—that "there's a solution for every problem"—turned anticipated crises into amazing win-wins. Gwen was an outstanding work relationship role model.

Sally and Joe had been married for thirty years. Their relationship was based on three principles—love, truthfulness, and friendship. Sally's secret? "Many a man can love you, but the trick is to find one who really likes you—just as you are." Although they may never agree on everything—Joe admires Sally's free spirit, enormous generosity, and her ability to always look at the glass half full. Sally and Joe are great relationship role models.

Relationship Role Models	Healthy Relationship Qualities
______________________	______________________________
______________________	______________________________
______________________	______________________________

While you identify what you need from the people in your life, find out what the people in your life need from you. *Learn to give people what they need—not what you think they need.* What you want to give may have no value to someone else if you are seeing the world through your eyes instead of theirs. Don't waste your time guessing or playing a mind reader. Ask this simple question whenever your relationships start to feel unnecessarily stressed: *"What do you need from me right now?"*

Give and take. It's important to maintain balance in relationships. If you are the person others continually rely on, make sure that your relationships are not lopsided. I am not suggesting that you keep score! I am suggesting, however, that a healthy relationship is one in which you both give and receive.

Be willing to end unhealthy relationships. Set boundaries in your relationships to protect yourself from unnecessary drama, disrespectful behavior, and potential dilemmas. When a person refuses to respect your boundaries, be willing to end—or at least, adjust—your relationship. Make room for healthy relationships by clearing out the unhealthy ones.

Speak the truth in all of your relationships. Communicate honestly and respectfully, and you can expect the same in return. Be willing to listen, even if you disagree with what you hear. Relationships based on truth are stronger and last longer. It is possible to speak the truth with a loving attitude. One of the best character traits you can develop is the ability to say what needs to be said, even when it is difficult to do so. Embrace the truth and you will lift the unnecessary burden that comes from "going along to get along."

Protect Yourself From Toxic Relationships.

Do you have any relationships that drain your energy? Some folks suck the life right out of everyone they come into contact with—

that is, everyone who leaves themselves open to having their energy siphoned. Perhaps the unbalanced relationship is not just draining your energy, but also your self-worth, money, or dreams for the future. Toxic relationships negatively affect your attitude, abilities, or disposition. They bring out the worst in you and consistently cause you stress, pain, harm, or damage in some way. No matter what it takes, you must stand firm and protect yourself when faced with toxic relationships. That means either eliminating the relationships from your life or changing your approach to the relationships in some significant way.

Are there any "toxic" relationships in your life?

Signs of a toxic relationship

- Unable to communicate honestly
- Lack of balance—one person consistently gives or takes more than the other
- Disrespectful interaction
- Manipulation or other deceptive behavior
- One person consistently has to work around the others' anger, fear, insecurities, and unresolved issues
- The relationship drains your energy

Toxic Relationships Checkup

If you find yourself trapped in toxic relationships, identify ways to eliminate them from your life as soon as possible. Here are a few questions to ask yourself to help you begin the process:

- What is it about this relationship that drains my energy or feels toxic?
- Am I willing to change the dynamic to create a healthier relationship?
- Is the other person willing to change?
- If the other person is not willing to change, am I willing (and is it appropriate) to end the relationship?
- If the other person is not willing to change, and I am unwilling to end the relationship, what can I do to protect myself from this unhealthy relationship?

Setting and Maintaining Clear Boundaries

In real estate, boundaries establish your domain. They dictate the territory you are responsible for maintaining. You may invite others to enter that territory or signal them to stay out. Boundaries give you a clear space for privacy, protection, and freedom. In your personal life, setting and maintaining boundaries accomplish a similar goal. Because boundaries are not always obvious, it is important to communicate all trespasses clearly and firmly. For example, "I find it disrespectful when you speak to me in that tone. Please don't do that again." It is a simple statement, yet it immediately establishes that someone has crossed a boundary that you will not permit them to cross in the future without consequences.

The problem for many Black women is that you know your boundaries but no one else does. When someone crosses a boundary and invades your space, failing to protect yourself through clear communication is like leaving the door to your home wide open, letting people trample in and out, and saying nothing about it. Most of us would call tolerating such behavior ridiculous. When you do not communicate your boundaries, this is precisely what happens.

Here are three guidelines for maintaining boundaries and reducing stress in your life:

1. Establish the basic boundaries at the beginning of new relationships when the stakes are low. Reinforce your boundaries often. Take special precautions whenever it appears that your boundaries have been crossed.
2. When a boundary is crossed, communicate your concerns clearly and firmly.
3. If your boundaries are not respected, take action and make the necessary changes to protect yourself.

Setting boundaries begins with learning to say "no," even to people you care about, especially when others' demands begin to infringe upon your personal needs. When you become comfortable saying

"The sooner you make a decision to set boundaries, the sooner your relationship stress will decrease."

"no" to requests that you are uninterested in or that will cause others to become dependent, you will increase your life satisfaction.

Diane comes from a large family where her siblings routinely borrow money without paying it back and rarely express appreciation for her generosity and support. Unfortunately, when Diane needed help—even when she was sick —no one in her family came to her aid. Diane started to feel resentful and "used up," until she identified her own poor boundaries as a major part of the problem. She loved her family members dearly and didn't want to feel guilty about setting boundaries. It wasn't until her lack of boundaries began to cause problems with her husband that she finally learned to say "no."

Many women find themselves in similar situations, especially when it comes to family members. The key is to remember that you are in control of the situation, and the sooner you make a decision to set boundaries, the sooner your relationship stress will decrease. Many African American women have allowed, and even unconsciously trained, family members to take advantage of their kindness. Not only does this hurt you, but it also hurts them. Being totally responsible for your family's problems lets them off the hook for finding their own solutions. They count on you to be their safety net, and never learn how to function independently.

Setting and maintaining your boundaries means making a shift in how you define "caring." Of course, you will be there for your family in times of crisis and you'll spend quality time with them, but you can no longer let anyone manipulate you into feeling guilty because you refuse to assume responsibility for their lives. You can remain kind and loving while being firm about the need to prioritize your time and resources.

Boundaries That Work

Make a list of your new boundaries or "rules" for dealing with relationships. Here are a few to get you started:

- I no longer allow anyone to preempt my weekly life satisfaction appointment.
- I no longer allow others to dictate how I spend my time.

- I no longer lend money to anyone based on feelings of guilt or obligation.
- When I lend money, I always set out the terms of the loan clearly in advance and in writing.
- I distinguish between family drama and genuine crises.
- I am no longer available for emotional manipulation or guilt trips.

Identify five important boundaries you would like to establish:

Relationship Boundaries

____

____

____

Practice the art of saying "no"

Part of setting boundaries is learning to operate from a place of truth in your relationships and having the courage to say "no" when you need to. Many Black women have taken on multiple responsibilities and are counted on in numerous ways in their families, communities, and at work. The idea of saying "no" seems almost sacrilegious. They have never had the option of saying "no" because often they were the only ones who could be counted on to get the job done.

Have you ever been asked to do something that you didn't want to do, but you said "yes" anyway? Many of us have done it. And for some, it is a consistent source of stress in their relationships with people at work, at home, and in their communities. Being able to say "no" is absolutely essential to enjoying life satisfaction. Think of it this way: Every time you say "yes" to something that does not help you serve your purpose, accomplish your top goals or enhance your level of life satisfaction, you are in essence saying "no" to those things that really matter to you.

There are simple, practical ways to begin saying "no" to the opportunities, responsibilities, people and events that do not serve your best interests.

It's easy to fill your life with commitments thrust on you by others, from projects you aren't excited about to making sacrifices that you don't want to. Being able to say "no" can be a very healthy response. If saying "no" makes you uncomfortable, here are five ideas to help you overcome your anxiety:

"N.O. Is My New Yes"

Don't succumb to the pressure to answer requests immediately. "Let me think about that" is an acceptable response when you're uncertain about saying "yes" to an invitation or making a firm commitment. Give yourself time to consider what's really being asked of you. If it is a particularly hard decision, pray about it. Then make a decision based on your legitimate needs and priorities.

Offer an alternative. Saying "no" doesn't mean being rude or inconsiderate of others' requests. It is possible to say "no" honestly without offending anyone. One way is to offer an alternative. "I won't be able to work on that project, but Mary might be interested." "Now is not a good time for me, but if you can check with me in another month, perhaps I can reconsider." "I'm not interested in having a big fiftieth birthday party, but I'd love to have a special celebration. Do you have any other ideas?"

Refuse to be manipulated. The "disease to please" is the main cause of saying "yes" too often. Don't allow others to make you feel guilty because you won't do what they want you to do. When you allow others to manipulate you, you begin to harbor resentment against them even though you allowed them to do it. Simply refuse to let guilt trips sway your decisions.

Make purposeful decisions. When you know your purpose and why you do the things you do, it becomes much easier to make decisions about what to say "no" to and what to say "yes" to. If you haven't already, get clear about your purpose. When you know your purpose, decisions about your work, relationships, finances and other issues become easier to make.

Tell the truth. Being upfront is the foundation for building strong relationships. You gain respect for yourself when you are not afraid to let others know where you stand. At this stage of your life, you do not have time for games. You are on a mission, committed to meaningful relationships built on a foundation of clear and honest communication. Be true to yourself and say "no" when you want to. Others will adjust and over time they will gain a better understanding of your boundaries.

Keep Making Progress, Even When Others Don't Support Your New Direction.

Millions of women, like you, reach middle life and feel compelled to make changes. They recognize that something more is available in life and are ready to reach for it. But as they begin moving forward, they are not always met with the support of those closest to them. Have you experienced this in your own life? It can be disheartening and frustrating when the naysayers are your own flesh and blood. However, pursuing a more satisfying life is a decision you can make despite a lack of support from others. Though not ideal, it is still important to recognize that your decisions do not have to be controlled by the needs or discouragement of others.

Often, such decisions are based on old relationship patterns. Many are in relationships that operate on the basis of who you were, not who you are. Some of you haven't shared the changes in our lives with friends and family. Your unexpected changes can inadvertently stir up their insecurities about your relationship dynamics.

However, this potential problem can actually offer you a new opportunity to connect in a meaningful way. Rather than focusing on their lack of support for your new life satisfaction goals, use this opportunity to open a conversation with your family member or friend about how you both have changed. Recognize that certain people in your life may not be capable of embracing your changes right now, but that is no excuse for you not pursuing your destiny.

Your determination to achieve life satisfaction is about *living your life.* Many people have pursued their passion and purpose without the benefit of cheerleading spouses, family, or even friends. It isn't ideal, but never let other people's limitations stop you from moving forward.

Remember Your Spirit

Again, it is essential that you connect first with yourself so that as you seek to build more fulfilling relationships in every area of your life, you are able to identify your needs, set your boundaries, and create healthy habits that nurture healthy relationships. But there is one more element of life satisfaction that ties it all together—your spiritual life. Are you ready to explore the role of spirituality on your journey to life satisfaction?

Chapter 11

Deepening Your Spiritual Connection

I can still hear the choir singing boldly and stomping their feet, creating a beat that stirs the soul deeper than any drum ever could. In that harmony of soulful voices, my young ears sensed the determination of Black folk from the rural South who had triumphed through Jim Crow and persistent inequality. My introduction to the Spirit happened one Sunday morning in the 1970s at Pine Grove Baptist Church in Iva, South Carolina. In the summertime, I'd go to the home church that had supported my grandmama since 1919. Although the worshippers had endured a kind of racism that I would never encounter, they were full of love and joy. As they sang an old Negro spiritual, the congregation stomped the wood floors in unison and clapped from the pews: "Jesus is a rock in a wearrrrrry lannnnd, a weary land, a wearrrrrry lannnnd! I know that He's a rock in a wearrrrrry lannnnd—a shelter in the time of storm!"

The strong tradition of spirituality within the African American community is undeniable—born of a need for survival in a world bent on pushing African Americans to their limits. African and African American slaves had a history of relying on God as their "rock in a weary land" and more than 140 years after the Emancipation Proclamation, their spiritual legacy can still be felt.

However, that legacy must be reaffirmed by each one of us. A relationship with the Divine cannot be passed down from generation to generation. Knowing God is something you must do for yourself. So the question is—are you satisfied with your spiritual life?

Strong and positive relationships with yourself and with others are essential to experiencing life satisfaction. Nevertheless, for an African American woman, there is one more relationship that serves as a foundation for it all—your relationship with God. You were created for a purpose by the Creator—and when you fulfill that purpose, you experience joy at its highest level. Being grounded spiritually gives you a broader and deeper perspective on life. It is a viewpoint that empowers you to understand and accept that life does not always go as you planned and that God always has a plan greater than the one we can see. A spiritually connected life challenges you to believe that all things are possible. It comforts you in times of stress or sorrow, brings peace in times of turmoil, encouragement in times of disappointment, and allows you to experience the truth of love and forgiveness.

African American women, perhaps more than any other group of American women, regard their relationship with God as being central to their lives. As numerous studies confirm, and the NCNW data confirm, African American women are more religious than African American men and all white Americans. Spirituality has been found to contribute to the life satisfaction of African American women regardless of age, income, or education.

For African American women, middle life is often the time when you be-come more conscious of your mortality and spirituality. As a teenager or twenty-something, you may have believed that life was promised forever. As you mature, however, experience teaches you how quickly life can change—or even end. This profound awareness of the preciousness of life and the value of our relationships can lead to a thirst for spiritual growth and meaning in life. As Gloria Wade Gayles states, "Only when Black women are spiritually connected can we realize our highest selves, and only then will we achieve spiritual health and empowerment."

"The Spirit, or spirituality, defies definition—a fact that speaks to its power as much as it reflects its mystery. Like the wind, it cannot be seen, and yet, like the wind, it is surely there, and we bear witness to its presence, its power. We cannot hold it in our hands and put it on a scale. But we feel the weight, the force, of its influence in our lives. We cannot hear it, but we hear ourselves speaking and singing and testifying because it moves, inspires and directs us to do so…

Focusing on Black women's spirituality raises the question: If we cannot define spirituality, how can we speak of spirituality distinctive to Black women. Not just to Blacks, but to Black women? Having acknowledged that we cannot see it, how can we suddenly ascribe to it such material qualities as race and gender? We cannot. But we can, and should, celebrate the way our connection to the Spirit bears the lineaments of our race, gender and culture. The Spirit speaks in the voice of, sings the songs of, dresses in the symbols of, wears the face of and moves in the rhythm of the people who receive it. For African American women, it produces spiritual songs, chants, rituals, movements, symbols, needs and energies that are distinctively Black and woman."

From *My Soul is a Witness: African-American Women's Spirituality*
Gloria Wade-Gayles

New spiritual awareness can often accompany reaching a crossroads in your life, when you begin to ask, "Is this all there is?" In your early adulthood, you may have set out to accomplish certain goals—career success, marriage, a family, or a home of your own. By middle life you may have accomplished some of these goals, and still felt that something was missing. Have you been there? Are you there right now?

In the following pages, you will learn some of the key steps for sustaining spiritual life satisfaction that can empower you to experience the transcendent joys available as you indeed grow older and wiser. For the purposes of our discussion, let's define your spiritual life as your relationship with God. It is important that we make the distinction that we are talking about a relationship, not a religion. Although spirituality and religion are often used as interchangeable terms, they are not one and the same. Religion is the practical expression of spirituality defined by membership in an organization and specific beliefs, practices, and rituals.

By contrast, spirituality speaks to people of all denominations and beliefs. The National Interfaith Council defines spiritual well-being as "the affirmation of life in relationship with God, self, community, and environment in a way that nurtures and celebrates wholeness."

The difference between being "religious" —following a set of rules, going to worship services every week—and having a strong spiritual life is also reflected in the NCNW research, which cited that while 40 percent of Black women in middle life attend weekly worship services, 81 percent pray daily. For African American women, spiritual life is an inextricable part of their identity and life satisfaction. Older Americans report that religion and spirituality help them cope with losses and difficulties. So it comes as no surprise that as Black women age, their spiritual roots grow even deeper and wider.

As you age, your longing for divine connection will likely also increase—even if that is not how you initially identify it. By seeking the lessons life has been teaching you, and moving forward based on what you've learned, you will begin to see the pattern of your life—and how everything has happened for a reason. You notice how many opportunities appear to have lined up perfectly—even miraculously—at the right time. Your faith is strengthened as you witness the hand of the Divine at work as you face life's most difficult challenges and obstacles. Such experiences often draw us to actively seek a deeper spiritual walk. Think about the goals you have set throughout this book—in the areas of health, finances, and life satisfaction. As I share the keys for building a strong spiritual foundation in your life, begin to reframe those goals through the lens of your spiritual journey.

Know that You Were Created for a Purpose

There is a scene in the movie, *The Color Purple,* in which Miss Celie (played by Whoopi Goldberg) decides to leave her abusive husband "Mister." Mister yells after her that she'll never make it because she's Black and ugly and nobody wants her. Defiantly and jubilantly, Miss Celie yells from the backseat of a yellow convertible with new-found freedom in her voice, "I might be Black! I might be ugly. But I'm still here! I'm still here!" She'd survived because she knew there was something more for her life.

If you're still here, there is a unique purpose for your life. In middle life you have a chance to reconnect with your purpose. Even on those days when your purpose may seem far away, being kind and loving, serving and helping others are the basics of serving God. While some of us were appointed for a special assignment, all of us were created to love and be loved. Whenever you get discouraged or the future appears cloudy, always remember you are here for a reason.

Understand that You Are a Vessel

One of the clearest ways to grow spiritually is to begin seeing yourself as a vessel through which the Divine Plan can work. As you go about your day, ask yourself, "How can I be a blessing? How can I help others experience love and compassion simply through their encounters with me?" Sometimes it is as simple as a smile to a stranger who needs her or his spirits lifted. At other times, it means being supportive and encouraging to others. And at still other times, it means doing what needs to be done because you are the only person available to do it.

Nurture Your Spiritual Life

Think of a relationship in your life that is fulfilling. How did you get to know that person? It is highly likely that you got to know her or him by spending quality time cultivating your connection. Through trials and triumphs, you began to know the person's character. The same is true of our spirituality. Through prayer and meditation, in particular, we are able to build a stronger relationship with God. Earlier in the book, I challenged you to dedicate one-tenth of your waking hours—or 1.5 hours per day—toward creating true life satisfaction. As a part of that dedication, you learned to schedule life satisfaction appointments. It's equally important to block out time on your daily schedule for your spiritual life. Devoting time to prayer and meditation or spiritual reading and reflection in the mornings will make a tremendous difference in your outlook on life. Spending those quiet moments to make your requests to God—requests for help, for peace, for grace—will help you feel more centered and balanced. Taking time to connect spiritually helps you affirm what is most important about life—loving yourself and others and making a meaningful difference in the world.

Pray for Guidance and Pay Attention to Your Intuition

Many people think of prayer as a ritual to engage in when something goes wrong. But as you seek to strengthen your spiritual life, I invite you to commit to making prayer a part of your daily life. However much time you can commit, make certain that you pray consistently. Prayer is an investment in your spiritual life, and like any other investment, it reaps greater rewards when you are consistent. There is no "right" way to pray. Instead, prayer is about heartfelt communication with God. It is reassuring and comforting to know that God hears our prayers and answers them. He may not always answer with the response we are seeking. Sometimes, the answer is "no." Sometimes, the answer is "wait." And at other times, the answer is "grow" into a new perspective. As you spend time in prayer, your mind begins to calm and God's presence can be felt. Through this presence, you often begin to sense the guidance and direction you need in key aspects of your life. Think back to a time in your life when you made an important decision based upon your intuition or an inner voice you felt leading you in a particular direction. That was a spiritual connection.

Intuition is divine intelligence—a sixth sense that God equips you with to help you make better decisions. With time, many women find that making that connection is critical to making decisions. I call it "allowing peace to guide your decisions." When you are spiritually connected, you rely on more than logic. You have faith, which includes the "evidence of things not seen." You have prayer, a practice that allows you to communicate with God. And you have the experience that allows you to look back over your life and see the times when life has worked out well when you followed your intuition.

Meditation—Practice the Art of Being Quiet

While prayer is primarily about *communicating with God, sharing your thoughts and needs, and asking for guidance or making requests,* meditation is about *quieting your mind and listening.* In today's fast-paced, high-tech world, silence is rare. But as we discussed earlier in this section on life satisfaction, taking time to listen to your inner desires is a critical element of connecting with yourself. Likewise, taking time simply to be quiet on a daily basis can do wonders for your level of life satisfaction. Meditation allows you to quiet your mind, listen for messages, intuition, and divine guidance. Many African American women in middle life cannot remember when they took time to be quiet and meditate. Indeed, doing nothing is an art that too few practice, but the benefits are tremendous: Less stress, connection with yourself and God, and time to relax.

Schedule time daily—even if only ten minutes—to do nothing. Sit comfortably in a spot where you can relax undistracted and focus on nothing but breathing. Feel your breath as you focus inwardly and inhale and exhale. You may want to choose a scripture or another spiritual reading or quotation to focus on. For example, "Everyday and in every way, my life is becoming more satisfying" or "With God, all things are possible." Repeat the affirmation or scripture in your mind as you deepen your breathing. Block out other thoughts by repeatedly focusing on your meditation. Do this as long as you need to until you feel refreshed and peaceful. Meditation empowers you to connect spiritually. It consistently elevates your thoughts to positive ones that will strengthen you. It can be easy to spend so much of the day engaging in thoughts or words that serve only to weaken you. Make a conscious choice to redirect your thoughts daily to higher ground through meditation.

Have Faith that More Is Possible

For most women in middle life, there may be one arena in which the success you've dreamed of remains elusive. In what life arena are you still waiting for your breakthrough? It could be in a relationship, finances, health, or career. By this point in your life, it may even seem that what you've always wanted may never happen. This is where you must practice faith. Faith is the "substance of things hoped for and the evidence of things not seen." It is a combination of assurance and anticipation. It means being sure that what you hope for can come to life. Without hope, you cannot have faith. What are you hoping for, yet doubting will actually happen? Faith also means anticipating the results you expect. When you anticipate something, you prepare for it. You act as though it will happen. You do what needs to be done so that when the opportunity arrives, you are ready! As you aim for and experience life satisfaction at this stage of your life, have faith that more is possible. It can be easy to get in a rut and believe that you've missed a window of opportunity along the way that will never open again. Perhaps it was a failed marriage or no marriage at all. Perhaps you always wanted to finish your degree, but haven't yet. Maybe you beat yourself up because you are not where you would like to be financially.

Without Hope, You Cannot Have Faith

I invite you to adopt a new attitude that embraces the fact that much more is possible for your life. Perhaps you didn't take the "traditional" route, but that doesn't mean that you must give up on the goals that are truly important to you. Give yourself permission to dream bigger dreams now. Throw away your preconceived notions about what's possible for a woman your age. Your life is a spiritual journey that offers lessons and opportunities along the way. With God, all things are possible. Practice your faith by stepping out to do the things that your heart yearns for. Make the commitment to cultivate your spirituality and refuse to settle for less than you deserve.

Trust God

As you've grown in years, you may have noticed in hindsight, that life usually works itself out. There is a saying that if you aren't currently in a storm, then you either just came out of one or you are headed into one. Life will always present us with challenges—some much more difficult to live with than others. Worrying about the storms of life certainly will not calm them. In fact, worrying seems only to make the experience of going through a storm feel more intense. The apostle Paul shares this calming advice: "Be anxious for nothing, but in all things by prayer and petition, with thanksgiving, make your request made known unto God. And the peace of God, which surpasses all understanding, will guard your hearts and minds." Make a decision to trust in every circumstance of life that if you are connected spiritually and connected to your true self, that you will be guided to do the right things at the right time—and that even when you don't, God will sustain you.

Trusting God is perhaps the best remedy available for stress, pain, fear, and a host of other negative experiences that stem from our desire to know the outcome of life at various stages. When your focus is spiritual growth, serving God and fulfilling your unique purpose, all things work together for good—even the things that may at first glance seem negative. It all begins with trusting in—the Divine.

The vision and goals you have may not come to pass in your timing, but be willing to persevere, believing that more is possible for your life and acknowledging that God is in control. Proverbs 3:5-6 perhaps illustrates this best with the scripture, "Trust in the Lord with all your heart and lean not on your own understanding. In all your ways acknowledge Him and He shall direct your paths."

You have reviewed your life by decade and identified the lessons learned and acknowledged the significant successes you have enjoyed along your journey. As you forge ahead with a new vision for the next stage of your life, remember to never stop learning and to continue looking for the lessons. A fulfilling spiritual life is one in which you are consistently growing and becoming more of who you were created to be. This process continues your entire life. For every living thing on Earth, the evidence of life is growth and movement. When any life form stops moving and growing, it is confirmation that it is no longer alive. Personal growth and a willingness to face new challenges with an open mind and heart are sure signs that your spiritual life is fully alive.

Be Thankful

True life satisfaction is steeped in a feeling of abundance—a knowing that there is more possible for your life. One of the most universal spiritual principles is gratitude. In a society that focuses so heavily on material possessions and superficial status symbols, remaining grounded in gratitude can sometimes be a challenge. However, as you may have learned over the years, there is always something to be thankful for. On a daily basis, identify the many things in your life for which to be thankful. Often we take for granted the things we should be most grateful for—the things that would actually devastate us most if we lost them. Consider your physical abilities—walking, talking, breathing, and your awareness of your surroundings. Not everyone who woke up this morning has those abilities. Consider the love in your life and people on whom you can rely—the people who look out for you, show you mercy, or bless you abundantly. Consider your material possessions. Perhaps you'd like to have more, but choose to grateful for what you have right now in your life.

As an African American woman, sometimes you can become so focused on what you lack you may fail to notice that you have more freedom, wealth, and opportunities than the majority of people around this world could ever imagine. On a day when you feel particularly blessed—a day like today—take out your life satisfaction journal and make a list of the things you are thankful for. Create a list of at least ten things. On those days when you are frustrated or need a larger perspective, pull out your list and review it.

Read it aloud and focus on what you do have and less on what you don't have. This shift in attitude can change your outlook on life. When you practice an attitude of gratitude, you honor the many satisfying aspects of your life. As you pursue higher levels of life satisfaction, it is powerful to acknowledge the abundance of good that already exists in your life.

I leave you with a proven strategy that will guarantee the spiritual life satisfaction that you seek and deserve. These seven keys to spiritual life satisfaction are straightforward strategies for cultivating your spirituality offered to us by St. Paul in his first letter to the Corinthians. Experiment with these seven spiritual keys, and watch your life transform.

Love Is Patient

People won't always do what you want when you want them to. Practice being patient—whether with your children, your significant other, or the grocery cashier who takes too long to ring up your order. Everything happens for a reason—and that includes the right timing of when things happen. Be patient and learn the lesson that comes in the process of enduring the wait.

Love Is Kind

Every single day, choose to be kind. Ask yourself each morning, "How can I be a blessing to someone today?" Whether it is a kind word, a loving gesture or helping someone in need, seek ways to be kind daily. Not only will it be a blessing to those you encounter, but it simply feels good to your soul.

Love Does Not Envy

There will always be someone who appears to have "more" or to be doing better. Make a decision not to be envious of others, but in every circumstance of life to find a reason to be thankful. Jealousy poisons your attitude, builds resentment, and can ruin relationships. Rather than envying those who have something you would like to have, learn from them. Be inspired by them. And simultaneously, choose to be content with what you have while you journey toward something better.

Love Does Not Boast and Is Not Proud

Resist the temptation to boast about yourself, your accomplishments, or your loved ones. It often only makes others feel "less than," which of course, is not an expression of love. Practice humility. Allow your accomplishments to speak for themselves. Others often notice your good work and deeds, even without you having to make a big deal of them. In fact, it is far more attractive to simply "be" great than to convince others of your greatness.

Love Is Not Rude or Easily Angered
We've all had our moments when our behavior has been less than considerate. But next time you feel the urge to be inconsiderate of others or to jump to conclusions, stop yourself. Take a deep breath and ask, "What would be a more loving response to this situation?" That doesn't mean that you allow others to walk all over you. You can speak the truth to people in a very calm manner, without being rude. Be considerate of others' feelings and be willing to give people the benefit of the doubt.

Love Keeps No Record of Wrongs
Have you ever known someone who remembered every mistake you ever made or everything you ever did wrong? Although you have grown and become a better person, all they can remember is the person you used to be. It is very frustrating and you may even find yourself ready to distance yourself from that person. Learn from the past behavior of others—and protect yourself accordingly, when necessary—but resist the temptation to continually bring up everything someone has done wrong. Love others by encouraging them toward a better future, not defining them by their past.

Love Rejoices in the Truth
So often, it seems we are afraid of the truth. When something is wrong, we pretend everything is OK. Often both parties will pretend even when both parties know what the problem is. One of the most important love skills you can learn is to be honest. Refuse to live lies or to accept lies as truth. Have truthful conversations with yourself and others. It allows you to get to the core of issues faster. It empowers others to trust you. It relieves the stress of tiptoeing around the real issues. Learn to speak the truth in a spirit of love and kindness, and your life will be richer. And simultaneously, choose to be content with what you have while you journey toward something better.

My hope is that you have been inspired. The opportunity to live a satisfying life lies at your fingertips. Taking advantage of that opportunity is within your control. It is all about the choices you make. I pray you will connect with yourself, others and spiritually to uncover the true answers for your life. As you make changes that will create an exciting future, expect to feel fear as you move beyond your comfort zone. It's natural. But don't allow that fear to keep you from the life you were meant to live. Rely on your character of strength, perseverance and passion to propel you towards success in every area of your life. If you do, life satisfaction will find its way into your path now and for years to come.

Afterword

By
Cheryl R. Cooper
Executive Director
The National Council of Negro Women

As we celebrate the 70th year of the National Council of Negro Women, we thank you for joining us on this extraordinary journey to empower African American women in the vital middle years of life.

When I took on the role of executive director of NCNW, I reflected on our founder, Mary McLeod Bethune, who dedicated her life to helping generations of African American women seek new opportunities, and on our President Emerita, Dr. Dorothy Height, who continues to empower Black women today. I was awed by their incredible legacies. What inspired me to come to NCNW is my unshakable faith that more is possible for the 18 million African American women in America. I could feel Dr. Bethune's words echoing in my heart, "Without faith, nothing is possible. With it, nothing is impossible. Faith in God is the greatest power, but great faith is faith in oneself."

This message of faith is what moved me to answer the call to guide NCNW in its first major initiative of the 21st Century. I knew then, as I know now, that African American women in middle life need no longer settle for less than they deserve. The time has come to set a new direction for ourselves and our futures.

As I've listened to the stories of our focus group participants, I have gained renewed respect for African American women's capacity, possibility, and power. I know that armed with a new vision, African American women will soar to new heights. *Tomorrow Begins Today* outlines this new vision that says: Now is the time.

Now is the time, because I saw an African American woman in New Orleans, who never had a savings account, take hold of this vision and use it as the foundation to buy her first home. Now is the time, because women in Los Angeles are walking off their obesity and stress, restoring their health and peace of mind. Now is the time, because I have witnessed the new vitality that lifted up a Sister in Chicago—the kind of resurrection that enabled her to identify her own needs and dare to fulfill them without guilt or fear. It is the countless daily victories of African American women throughout the country that inspired NCNW to do everything that we could to bring you the tools contained in this book. *Tomorrow Begins Today*, read as a whole, proclaims the overarching message that living longer and living better is within our grasp.

African American women are no longer powerless. We are no longer limited by how the world defines us—we now have the opportunity to define ourselves.

Tomorrow Begins Today tells us the good news: More African American women than ever before are financially stable and have begun to cultivate healthy lifestyles. We are enjoying the accomplishments of our children and the fruits of our efforts in our communities. But these desirable outcomes are not yet available to all African American women. And that is why, now is the timeæno matter which decade of your life you are currently in—to master the art of setting goals, taking action, and celebrating your life's achievements. This is the philosophy at the heart of NCNW's "Invest in Yourself Plan."

This will not always be an easy journey. It requires us to be brave enough to make conscious choices about our lives and to take concrete action based on a well-conceived plan for our future. And it will call upon each of us to ask ourselves challenging questions about how we manage our finances, how we look after our health, and whether we are living our most satisfying lives.

Today is the day to reflect on where we have been and where we want to go. Today is the day to understand that at middle life, we have choices. Today is the day to give meaning to our lives. This book's powerful themes of self-reflection, self-reliance, and self-responsibility are a message of hope for Black women. And today is the day to spread this message to your sisters, daughters, mothers, and friends.

Together, let us now begin to invest in ourselves, invest in each other, and lead the way. Please join us on this journey, and share your thoughts along the way, because tomorrow truly does begin today.

About the Authors and Editor

Sheryl Hilliard Tucker

Sheryl Hilliard Tucker is an executive editor of *MONEY* magazine, the nation's premier investing and personal finance publication and the former editor-in-chief and vice president of *Black Enterprise*, the nation's leading magazine on African-American business. As head of *MONEY*'s national editorial research projects, Tucker has continued to garner an outstanding reputation as a journalist, researcher, public speaker, and seminar leader discussing personal finance, entrepreneurship and career development.

Tucker has edited several books, including *Prime Time: The African American Woman's Complete Guide to Midlife Health and Wellness*, and has served on the board of the American Society of Magazine Editors.

Kendra Lee

An award-winning writer, Kendra Lee has been a professional journalist and editor specializing in health issues for nearly two decades. As the principal of K. Lee Editorial Consultants, she has served a wide range of editorial clients including, the National Medical Association, the Office of Minority Health, and the Health Resources Services Administration. Lee is a former staff editor at *YSB* and *Urbane* magazines and contributing editor to *Crisis, Heart & Soul*, and *Upscale* magazines. Her writing has appeared frequently in *Essence, Baltimore Magazine*, FT.com, and NiaOnline.com. Lee has been a contributing writer to three books: *Like a Natural Woman, Dr. Ro's Ten Secrets to Livin' Healthy*, and the fiction collection *One Hand in My Pocket.*

Valorie Burton

Valorie Burton is a sought-after life coach, speaker, and author of *What's Really Holding You Back?, Listen to Your Life* and *Rich Minds, Rich Rewards*. She is the former co-host of The Potter's Touch with T.D. Jakes. She founded and later sold her own public relations firm and was named one of the nation's thirty rising stars in public relations by PR Week Magazine in 2000. Today, through her writing and speaking, Burton lives her passion for helping women claim more fulfilling lives. She lectures and coaches entrepreneurs who have created multi-million-dollar businesses and professionals seeking a more purposeful path.

As a columnist for Tom Joyner's BlackAmericaWeb.com, Burton motivates the site's one million weekly visitors. She also serves as the "resident" life coach for Washington, D.C. 's WPGC-AM (HEAVEN 1580) radio station.

Cheryl Woodruff

A publishing pioneer, award-winning editor and former publishing executive, Cheryl Woodruff spent two decades at Ballantine Books, a division of Random House, Inc., where she edited countless titles across the hardcover, trade paperback, and mass-market lists.

In 1991, Woodruff became one of the highest-ranking African Americans in book publishing as the founding editor, vice-president, and associate publisher of Ballantine's One World imprint, the first multicultural imprint established at a mainstream publishing house. Under her guidance, One World received wide critical acclaim and published such national bestselling authors as Bebe Moore Campbell, Johnnie L. Cochran, Jr., Herb Boyd, Connie Briscoe, Cristina Garcia, Colin Channer, and Queen Afua. Woodruff was also responsible for the first hardcover edition of *The Autobiography of Malcolm X* published in more than twenty years. In 2001, she launched Cheryl Woodruff Communications, LLC, a publishing consulting firm.

Dr. Dorothy I. Height

Widely recognized and honored as one of the great civil rights and women's rights leaders of contemporary history, Dorothy Irene Height has spent decades providing inspiration and leadership to countless organizations in the struggle for equality and human rights for all people.

As president of the National Council of Negro Women for forty years, Dr. Height led an ongoing crusade for justice, opportunity, and dignity for women and Black families. In the 1960s, Height placed the NCNW on an action course of issue-oriented politics, leading the civil rights movement for voting rights and desegregated education. In the following decades, she labored tirelessly to provide hope to Black women and their families, and to increase the status of all women in our society.

Dr. Height has been the recipient of more than twenty honorary degrees and fifty awards honoring her decades of outstanding public service. In 1994, Dr. Height was awarded the Presidential Medal of Freedom, the nation's highest civilian honor. In 2004, to mark her ninety-second birthday, she received the Congressional Gold Medal.

Cheryl R. Cooper

Cheryl R. Cooper joined the National Council of Negro Women (NCNW) as executive director in June 2002. Prior to coming to NCNW, Cooper was chief of staff for AARP. Before joining AARP, she served as the administrator of the Congressional Black Caucus Foundation; she has also worked for the Coastal Corporation and PricewaterhouseCoopers.

A certified public accountant, Cooper's commitment to her community has allowed her to serve with distinction on numerous boards, including the Washington Convention Center Authority and the Ellington Fund (Duke Ellington School for the Arts), the advisory board of the National Foundation for Teaching Entrepreneurship, the Board of Governors of the D.C. Chapter of the Institute of Internal Auditors and as treasurer, board of directors, of the D.C. Institute for Mental Health.

ABOUT THE NATIONAL COUNCIL OF NEGRO WOMEN

The National Council of Negro Women (NCNW) is a council of national African American women's organizations and community-based sections. Founded in 1935, the NCNW mission is to lead, develop, and advocate for women of African descent as they support their families and communities. NCNW fulfills this purpose through research, advocacy, and national and community-based services and programs on issues of health, education, and economic empowerment in the United States and Africa. With its 39 national affiliates and more than 200 sections, NCNW is a 501(c) 3 organization with an outreach to nearly four million women.

Domestically, NCNW translates its philosophy of public education, community service and advocacy through a number of activities including:

- Disseminating information about issues affecting African American women and their families
- Promoting healthy lifestyles and behaviors through wellness projects
- Sponsoring events such as *The Black Family Reunion* to build on our strengths and traditional values
- Training and supporting women and youth in career development and community leadership
- Supporting economic development and entrepreneurship
- Providing mentoring and educational support to our young people

NCNW builds upon its expertise gained through its domestic programs to help improve the social and economic status of women internationally, particularly those in the rural areas of Africa. The International Division carries out its program goals by offering training and technical assistance for the long-term development that is compatible with local culture, needs, priorities, and resources, and that leads to self-sufficiency and local sustainability.

NCNW's national headquarters is located at 633 Pennsylvania Avenue NW in a historic building, now known as the Dorothy I. Height Building. The national office acts as a central source for program planning and seeks to fill the gaps that exist in our communities. For more information about NCNW, please call (202) 737-0120, or visit www.ncnw.org.